Richmond County North Carolina Court Minutes

COURT OF PLEAS AND
QUARTER SESSIONS

MINUTE BOOK 1
1779-1786

Lee G. Barrow

HERITAGE BOOKS
2007

HERITAGE BOOKS
AN IMPRINT OF HERITAGE BOOKS, INC.

Books, CDs, and more—Worldwide

For our listing of thousands of titles see our website
at
www.HeritageBooks.com

Published 2007 by
HERITAGE BOOKS, INC.
Publishing Division
65 East Main Street
Westminster, Maryland 21157-5026

Copyright © 2007 Lee G. Barrow

All rights reserved. No part of this book may be reproduced or transmitted in any form or by any means, electronic or mechanical, including photocopying, recording or by any information storage and retrieval system without written permission from the author, except for the inclusion of brief quotations in a review.

International Standard Book Number: 978-0-7884-4494-4

Foreword

This book is a transcription of the oldest minute book for the Court of Pleas and Quarter Sessions for Richmond County, North Carolina (which at the time also included present-day Scotland County). It was transcribed from a microfilm copy of the original minute book purchased from the North Carolina State Archives.

The author has attempted to copy these minutes in such a way to be as readable as possible while remaining faithful to what is found in the original book. Most misspellings and obvious errors have been entered as they appear in the original with the apparent mistake underlined; some words which are consistently misspelled, such as "registred," have been entered without indication. Some punctuation marks, such as commas between names, have been added to improve clarity. All surnames have been capitalized in order to assist the reader in locating them.

The following symbols are used:

?   A question mark indicates that the original was very difficult to read and the word entered represents the author's best guess.

[!]   An exclamation point indicates an incongruity such as a statement that is missing words or contradicts itself in some way.

\ /   Slashes enclose text which was clearly inserted in the original as an afterthought or a correction.

[ ]   Brackets enclose text added by the author, either as an assumption of missing text or as a comment.

)
)   Right parentheses over one another represent wavy vertical lines.

Richmond County Court of Pleas and Quarter Sessions Minute Book 1, 1779-1786

Fay? Thomas ANDERSON
command you to take the body of
____ to take the body of
Fay? Thomas ANDERSON

<u>December 1779</u>   *[Page 2 blank] Page 3*

State of North Carolina
Richmond County

At a court began and held for the County of Richmond, at the Presbyterian Meeting House, on the twenty seventh day of December one thousand seven hundred and seventy nine and in the fourth year of American independence.

Jurists
- John CRAWFORD)
- Charles MEDLOCK)
- H. Wm. HARRINGTON)
- Wm. LEGATE)
- John WALL)
- Wm. LOVE) Esqr.
- John DONALDSON)
- Robert WEBB)
- Richd. PEMBERTON)
- George JEFFERSON)
- John ROE)

On motion the court proceeded to chose the general officers for the county &c.

Ordered that Wm. LOVE Esqr. be appointed Clerk for the county aforesaid.

Ordered that John DONALDSON Esqr. be appointed to serve as Sheriff the coming year.

Ordered that Charles MEDLOCK Esqr. be appointed Register for the county aforesd.

December 1779 — Page 4

Ordered that James HICKS and George WALTERS be appointed coroners for the County of Richmond &c.

Ordered that Robert WEBB Esqr. be appointed Entry Taker for Claims of Land in the County of Richmond &c.

Ordered that John CRAWFORD Esqr. be appointed County Surveyor &c.

Ordered that William LEGATE Esqr. be appointed Ranger for Richmond County &c.

On motion the Last Will and Testament of Samuel HUNTER decd. was proved in open court by the oath of John COVINGTON Sr. and Henry COVINGTON two of the subscribing witnesses who saw the other witness subscribe his name thereto &c.

Court adjourned until tomorrow 10 o'clock.

Court met according to adjournment.
    Present   John CRAWFORD   )
                   Charles MEDLOCK   )
                   H. Wm. HARRINGTON   )
                   John WALL   ) Esqr.
                   Wm. LEGATE   )
                   John DONALSON?   )
                   Richd. PEMBERTON   )

Wm. LOVE Esqr. came into court and gave bond and security as Clerk agreeable to law.

On motion James HICKS Esqr. came into court and qualified as a Justice of the Peace &c.

Ordered that Tilloson OBRYAN be appointed to serve as Constable the ensuing year &c.

December 1779 — Page 5

Ordered that Edward ALMOND be appointed to serve as Constable the ensuing year &c.

Ordered that the Sheriff summons Henry Wm. HARRINGTON, Charles MEDLOCK and James HICKS Esqrs. to serve as Jurors at Salisbury Superior Court on the fifteenth day of March next &c.

On motion Edward ALMOND came into court and qualified as Constable for the ensuing year &c.

Robert WEBB Esqr. came into court and qualified as Entry Taker and gave bond agreeable to law &c.

Ordered that Benjamin SMITH be appointed to serve as Constable the ensuing year &c.

Court adjourned untill tomorrow 10 o'clock.

Met according to adjournment &c.
    Present   John CRAWFORD   )
                       Charles MEDLOCK   )
                       H. Wm. HARRINGTON) Esqrs.
                       John WALL   )

Ordered that John RAY have leave to build a water grist mill on the Great Juniper, about one mile and a half below Thomas JOHNSON's mill &c.

Ordered that Benjn. SMITH be exempted from serving as a Constable the ensuing year being objected to by a member of the court &c.

Ordered that a road be laid out, the nearest and best way, leading from the road that goes to Coles Bridge, beginning about two miles on this side of the Chalk Fork and from thence to the Under Mine Branch, thence to Murphy's Cowpens on Jordon's Creek, and that the following persons or any twelve of them be a jury to lay off the course (vizt) ...

<u>December 1779</u>   <u>Page 6</u>

...John MATHEWS, Isaac BRIGMAN, Philip JAMES, Wm. SMITH, Thos. GIBSON, Wm. BRIGMAN, Benjn. COVINGTON, George WEBB Sr., Jesse BOUNDS, Thos. CRAWFORD, Mark DEES, Wm. WEBB, Thomas TURNER, Moses TURNER, and Thomas JOHNSON and make report to the next court &c.

Ordered that a road be laid off out of the Under Mine Road the nearest and best way to Betty's Bridge on Drowning Creek and that any twelve of the following persons be a jury to lay off the same (vizt) Duncan BLUE, Silas OVERSTREET, Alexander WATSON, Mark DEES, James SMILEY, James IVY, Duncan McMILLAN, John BLUE, Moses JOHNSON, John RAY,

Alexander WATSON Jr., Samuel ROSE, Dugal BLUE, and make report to the next court &c.

Ordered that Henry Wm. HARRINGTON Esqr. be appointed overseer of the road from Haley's Ferry to where the new road comes in leading to the Cherraws and that his own hands work thereon &c.

Ordered that the ~~several~~ \following/ rates be allowed to the several ferries in this county (vizt)

    For every loaded waggon train & driver.................................. 5 dollars
    Ditto   empty Ditto .... $3^{1}/_{2}$ Do
    For every cart loaded, team & driver.. 3 Do
    Do   empty Ditto .... 2 Do
    For man and horse .... $^{5}/_{8}$ Do
    For afoot man or horse... $^{5}/_{16}$ Do
    For cattle sheep or hoggs each pr head .... $^{1}/_{16}$ Do

Toll, bridge keepers on Drown Creek

December 1779   *Page 7*

    For every loaded waggon train & driver.................................. $2^{1}/_{2}$ dollars
    Do   empty & Do .... $1^{5}/_{8}$ Do
    For every loaded cart, team & driver....................................... $1^{1}/_{2}$ Do
    Do   empty Do .... 1 Do
    For man and horse .... £ 0-2-6
    Cattle pr head 4
    Sheep or hoggs pr head.. 4

John CRAWFORD Esqr. came into court and qualified as surveyor of the County of Richmond and gave bond agreeable to law &c.

Ordered that the Sheriff summons the following persons to attend at the next court as juriors, (vizt) John COLE, Moses CHAMBERS, Hendley SNEED, Charles HINDS, Wm. TERRY, John JAMES Jr., John PARNEL, Daniel SNEED, Thoroughgood PATE, Zacharias MOREMAN, Timothy HURLEY, Henry ADCOCK, Daniel SMITH, John LONG? Jr.?, Daniel THOMAS, Edward WILLIAMS, Wm. JORNIGAN, Jehuele CROWSSON, James PATTERSON, Dudley MASK, James PHILLIPS, Owen SLAUGHTER, Wm. NEWBERY, James BOSTWICK, Wm. ADAMS, Darby HANAGAN, Absolum HINES, James PRICE, Thos. DOCKERY and Wm. ASHLEY and make return to the next court &c.

Charles MEDLOCK came into court and qualified as Register for Richmond County, and entered into bond agreeable to law &c.

Ordered that James DOWNING, Wm. WEBB, Elisha COTTENGAME, John WATKINS, Isaac YATES, David SNEED Jr. be appointed to serve as Constables the ensuing year &c.

Ordered that James HICKS Esqr. be appointed overseer of the road from the Province line to the fork of the road above Colo. MEDLOCKs and that all the hands contiguous work thereon &c.

December 1779   Page 8

Ordered that Isreal SNEED Jr. be appointed overseer of the road from the fork of the road at Colo. MEDLOCKs to Mrs. COLEs and that all the hands contiguous work thereon &c.

Ordered that John COLE be appointed overseer of the road from his own house to Terry's Path and that all the hands contiguous work thereon &c.

Ordered that James YATES be appointed overseer of the road from Terry's Path to Cole Bridge on Drowning Creek and that all the hands contiguous work thereon &c.

Ordered that Charles HINES be appointed overseer of the road from Munrows Bridge to Mountain Creek and that all the hands contiguous work thereon &c.

Ordered that James BOSTICK be appointed overseer of the road from Mountain Creek to Little River and that all the hands contiguous work thereon &c.

Ordered that John COLEMAN be appointed overseer of the road from Little River to the middle of Mountain Creek and that all the hands contiguous work thereon &c.

Ordered that Daniel SMITH be appointed overseer of the road from the middle of Mountain Creek to the Cattfish Road and that all the hands contiguous work thereon &c.

Ordered that William HUNTER be appointed overseer of the road from Cattfish Road to Mr. John COLEs, and that all the hands contiguous work thereon &c.

Ordered that Thomas CRAWFORD be appointed overseer of the road from George WEBB Sr. to Adcock Ferry & that all the hands contiguous work thereon &c.

Ordered that John COLE (Maryland) be appointed overseer of the road from the race path below Hitchcock up Crawford old road to the county line and that all the hands contiguous work thereon &c.

December 1779   Page 9

Ordered that James CAMPBLE be appointed overseer of the road from Wm. BLEWITT Ferry to Rockey Fork Bridge and that all the hands contiguous work thereon &c.

Ordered that Thos. ADAMS be appointed overseer of the road from the Rockey Fork Bridge to Drowning Creek and that all the hands contiguous work thereon &c.

Ordered that the be [!] adjourned until the last Monday in March to the same place &c.

    Test Wm. LOVE Clk.   John CRAWFORD   )
                                    Charles MEDLOCK   )
                                    Henry Wm. HARRINGTON) Esqr.
                                    John WALL   )

March 1780

At a County Court began and held for the County of Richmond at the Presbyterian Meeting House on the last Monday in the year of our Lord one thousand seven hundred and eighty and in the fourth year of American independence &c.

    Present   Charles MEDLOCK)
                          John WALL   ) Esqr.
                        Robert WEBB   )

The Last Will and Testament of George JEFFERSON Sr. was proved in open court by the oath of Susanna WILLIAMS, Winney WILLIAMS and Susanna WILLIAMS &c.

John DONALDSON Esqr. came into court and qualified as Sheriff and gave bond agreeable to law &c.

A deed from Solomon FISHER to Jehuile CROWSSON & proved by the oath of Philip JONES ordered to be registred.

March 1780   Page 10

A Grand Jury sworn, John COLE foreman &c. Moses CHAMBERS, Hendley SNEED, Wm. TERRY, John PARNAL, Thoroughgood PATE, Timothy HURLEY, Henry ADCOCK, John LONG, Daniel SMITH, Daniel

THOMAS, Edward WILLIAMS, Wm. JARNIGAN, Jeheule CROWSSON, Owen SLAUGHTER, James BOSTICK, Wm. NEWBERRY, Darby HANAGAN &c.

Ordered that James AULD Esqr. be appointed Attorney for the state this present term &c.

James HICKS Esqr. came into court and qualified as a Justice of the Peace &c.

Court adjourned until tomorrow 10 o'clock.

Court met according to adjournment.
Present John CRAWFORD)
    Charles MEDLOCK)
    John WALL   ) Esqr.
    Robert WEBB)

A deed from William HUNTER to John WILSON and proved in open court by the oath Wm. LOVE ordered to be registred.

A deed from John CRAWFORD Esqr. to John WILSON and proved in open court by the oath of Mark ROLLINS, ordered to be registred &c.

A deed from Thomas CRAWFORD to John WILSON and proved by the oath of John CRAWFORD ordered to be registred &c.

A deed from John CRAWFORD Esqr. to John WILSON and proved by the oath of Mark ROLLINS ordered to be registred.

March 1780   Page 11

A deed from John CRAWFORD Esqr. to John WILSON and proved by the oath of Mark ROLLINS ordered to be registred &c.

A deed from John CRAWFORD Esqr. to John WILSON and proved by the oath of Mark ROLLINS ordered to be registred &c. [*repetition of above sic*]

A deed from John CRAWFORD Esqr. to John WILSON and proved by the oath of Mark ROLLINS ordered to be registred &c. [*sic*]

A deed from John CRAWFORD Esqr. to John WILSON and proved by the oath of Mark ROLLINS ordered to be registred &c. [*sic*]

The Last Will and Testament of Francis BRICE deceased was proved in open court by the oath of Matthew TUCKER one of the subscribing witnesses thereto &c.

A deed from George WEBB to Henry ADCOCK proved in open court by the oath of Jesse BOUNDS, ordered to be registered &c.

On motion William HUNTER Sr. and Elisabeth HUNTER came into court and qualified as Executors of the Last Will and Testament of Samuel HUNTER deceased &c.

On motion Samuel GARLAND, John GARLAND and Edward WILLIAMS came into this court and qualified as Executors of the Last Will and Testament of George JEFFERSON deceased.

March 1780   *Page 12*

Ordered that the Executors to the Last Will and Testament of George JEFFERSON sell the perishable property belonging to the said estate &c.

A deed from John MATHEWS to Jehuele CROWSSON and proved in open court by the oath of John CROWSSON ordered to be registered &c.

Felix KENAN of Duplin County Executor of the Last Will and Testament of Francis BRICE late of this county deceased, came into this court and after the ~~last~~ \said/ will was exhibited and proved – was duly qualified as Executor thereto according to law &c.

Ordered that the Sheriff sell all the perishable estate of Francis BRICE deceased on Thursday next.

Court adjourned untill tomorrow 9 o'clock.

Court met according to adjournment &c.
    Present   John CRAWFORD)
                    Charles MEDLOCK) Esqr.
                    Robert WEBB   )

Ordered that Josiah LYONS be appointed overseer road from John CHILES ferry on Pee Dee to the Cherraw Road, and that LYONS hands Simon THOMAS, Daniel THOMAS, Wm. HALES, and JEFFERSONs hands work thereon &c.

Ordered that George CARTER be appointed overseer of the road (that leads to Overstreets Bridge on Drowning Creek) from the Cherraw Road to the bridge on the Rocky Fork of Hitchcock, and all the hands between Catfish Road and Mountain Creek work thereon.

March 1780   Page 13

Ordered that Laurance OBRYAN be appointed overseer of the road (that lead to Overstreets bridge on Drowning Creek) from the Rocky Fork Bridge, to James old cowpens, and that all the hands from said bridge down the Rocky Fork to the mouth, thence a direct line to John BOUNDS thence along the road to Drowning Creek, thence up said creek to Wm. ASHLEYs, thence to the head of the Rockey Fork thence down said fork to the bride work thereon &c.

Ordered that Mark DEES be appointed overseer of the road from James old cowpens to Overstreets bridge on Drowning Creek and that all the hands contiguous work thereon &c.

Ordered that Isaac BRIGMAN be appointed overseer of the road, that lead out of the Chalk Fork Road, about two miles from the said creek, to the Gum Swamp Bridge and that all the hands contiguous work thereon &c.

Ordered that Thomas CRAWFORD be appointed overseer of the road from the Gum Swamp Bridge to the Rocky Ford on Shew Heel, and that all the hands contiguous work thereon &c.

Ordered that the following rates be allowed to ordinary keeper for this county (vizt)
     Good West India rum 8 dollars pr half pint and so in proportion
     Norward? rum 7 dollars pr half pint

March 1780   Page 14

     Good peach brandy 5 dollars pr half pint and so in proportion &c
     Good whiskey 4 dollars pr half pint
     Dinner five dollars
     Breakfast and Supper 4 dollars each
     Two quarts of corn 1 1/2 dollars and so in proportion
     Lodging in a good feather bed and clean sheets one dollar
     Fodder pr bundle 1 dollar &c
     Pasturage for 24 hours 1 dollar &c

~~Ordered~~ A deed from George WEBB to Laurance EVERITT acknowledged in open court ordered to be registred.

Ordered that Robert Esqr. [sic] be appointed to take the examination of Margeratt WEBB relative to the right of dower, to a certain peace of land conveyed to Laurance EVERITT &c.

A deed from Thomas DOCKERY to Sarah COVINGTON proved in open court by the oath of Wm. LEGATE Esqr. ordered to be registred.

A deed from Thomas DOCKERY to Mary COVINGTON proved in open court by the oath of Wm. LEGATE Esqr. ordered to be registred.

A deed from Thomas DOCKERY to Hanah COVINGTON proved in open court by the oath of Wm. LEGATE Esqr. ordered to be registred.

Jehuele CROWSSON came into this court and qualified as administrator for the estate of John CROWSSON deceased and gave bond agreeable to law &c.

March 1780   Page 15

Ordered that the Sheriff sell all the perishable estate of John CROWSSON deceased, &c.

Ordered that the following persons be appointed to serve as juriors at the next court (vizt) Nathaniel HARRINGTON, James BOSTICK, George CARTER, Thos. ADAMS, Benjn. COVINGTON, Charles HINES, John COLE, James PHILLIPS Sr., Wm. COTTENGAME, John MATTHEWS, Wm. SPEED, John POWERS, Solomon SNEED, David SNEED Sr., Ishem HALEY, Wm. WATKINS, John JAMES Sr., Wm. HICKS, Wm. NEWBERY, Jesse BOUND, John THOMAS, Thos. SUMMERAL, Nathl. WILLIAMS, Savage LITTLETON, Wm. WOODLE, James MERIDITH, John COVINGTON Sr., Stephen TOUCHSTONE, Henry COVINGTON, and William HUNTER and that the summon and make return thereof &c.

Ordered that John TURNER be appointed to serve as Constable the ensuing year &c.

On motion Robert WEBB Esqr. returned two entrys of land bearing date fourth day of January 1780 the one containing three hundred acres the other seventy five.

Ordered that William GAINER be appointed overseer of the road from Masks Ferry to Matthew RAYFORDs and that John MASK Sr. John MASK Jr. and Benjamin DUMAS's hands work thereon &c.

March 1780   Page 16

Ordered that Wm. ADAMS be appointed overseer of the road from Davis's Path to the county line and that all the hands contiguous work thereon &c.

Ordered that John COLE (Maryland) be appointed overseer of the road from the race paths below Hitchcock Creek, to Davis's Path, and all the hands contiguous work thereon &c.

Ordered that William LEGATE Esqr. be appointed overseer of the road in room of Valentine MORRIS.

Ordered that Lawrance EVERITT be appointed overseer of the road in room of James CAMPBLE.

Ordered that the Sheriff bring to the next court, John, Francis, Joseph, and George BRICE orphans of the late Francis BRICE deceased to dealt [sic] with according to law &c.

Court adjourned untill court in course.
 at Mr. John COLEs barn. John CRAWFORD)
           Charles MEDLOCK)
 Test. Wm. LOVE Clk. Wm. LEGATE) Esqr.
           Robert WEBB)

June 1780   Page 17

At a County Court of Pleas and Quarter Sessions began and held for the County of Richmond on the last Monday in June one thousand seven hundred eighty at Mr. John COLEs.
 Present John CRAWFORD Esqr.

Ordered that the court adjourn untill court in course &c.
    John CRAWFORD Esqr. Test. Wm. LOVE Clk.

September 1780

At a County Court of Pleas and Quarter Sessions began and held for the County of Richmond on the last Monday in September in the year one thousand seven hundred eighty at Mr. John COLEs &c
 Present Charles MEDLOCK Esqr.

Ordered that the court adjourn untill court in course &c.
    Charles MEDLOCK Esqr. Test. Wm. LOVE Clk.

December 1780

At a County Court of Pleas and Quarter Sessions began and held for Richmond County on the last Monday in December in the year one thousand seven hundred eighty &c.

Prest. Charles MEDLOCK)
        Robert WEBB   ) Esqrs.
        Wm. LEGGETT   )

December 1780   **Page 18**

On motion James COLE and Edward WILLIAMS came into open court and qualified [*blot*] Justices of the Peace in County of Richmond.

Ordered that Thomas CRAWFORD be appointed as Clerk of the Court in said county.

On motion Elisabeth JEFFERSON relict and wife of George JEFFERSON deceased agreeable to the Last Will and Testament of the said George JEFFERSON came into open court and qualified as Executrix thereto agreeable to law &c.

Ordered that John STEELY and Thomas OLIVER be summoned to appear at court for converting? the property of Francis BRICE deceased &c.

Court adjourned until tomorrow 11 o'clock.

Court met according to adjournment.
        Present   Charles MEDLOCK   )
                  Edward WILLIAMS   ) Esqrs.
                  James COLE   )

A deed from Robert and John SAVAGE to Henry COVINGTON for fifty acres of land, ordered to be registred.

December 1780   **Page 19**

Felix KENAN Executor of the estate of Francis BRICE came into court, and settled to the satisfaction of the said court and there appears to be a ballance due from the said Felix KENAN to the widow and orphans of the said BRICEs estate to the amount of forty thousand nine hundred and fifty pounds thirteen shilling and ten pence half penny. Ordered that the said Felix KENAN pay the same to widow and guardiens of said orphans, and take their receipts and transmit the same, to this court, which will then settle his accounts in full &c.

Ordered that Charles MEDLOCK Esqr. be appointed Commissioner to receive a specific provision tax for the year one thousand seven hundred and eighty for the County of Richmond.

Ordered that Charles MEDLOCK Esqr. be appointed to purchase provisions for the use of the army in the Southern Department.

Richmond County NC Court Minutes, 1779-1786

Ordered that John HILYARD be appointed to serve as Constable in the uper ~~road~~ part of this county.

Ordered that Edward WILLIAMS be appointed overseer of the road from Mountain Creek to the Catfish Road and that hands that formerly worked thereon [blot] be under him &c.

December 1780   Page 20

Ordered that John GOWERS be appointed overseer of the road, from Mountain Creek to Little River, and the hands contiguous work thereon.

Ordered that Hendley SNEED be appointed overseer of the road from Coles Mill Creek to the fork of the road by Colo. MEDLOCKs and that all the hands between Solomon's Creek and Falling Creek work thereon &c.

Ordered that Benjamin MOREMAN be appointed overseer of the road from Haley's Ferry unto the road by the old school house and Thomas MOREMANs hands Robert WILSONs and Isreal SNEED work thereon &c.

Ordered that John SPEED Esqr. be appointed overseer of the road from Haley's Ferry to the forks of the road by Colo. MEDLOCKs &c and that all the HALEYs and ~~them? that worked on~~ Geo. HARRINGTON [blot] hands work thereon.

Ordered that Isreal MEDLOCK be appointed overseer of the road for Colo. MEDLOCK house to the province line and all the hands contiguous work thereon &c.

Ordered that Solomon JONES be appointed overseer of the road from the Grassy Island to Mountain Creek and all the hands contiguous work thereon.

Ordered that Edward SMITH Jr. be appointed overseer of the road from Mountain…

December 1780   Page 21

…Creek to Munrows Bridge to Drowning Creek and the hands contiguous work thereon.

Court adjourned untill 11 o'clock tomorrow.

Met according to adjournment.
    Present   Charles MEDLOCK)
                       Edward WILLIAMS) Esqrs.
                       James COLE   )

On motion Colo. John DONALDSON came into court and qualified as administrator on the estate of Nicholas STONE deceased and gave bond agreeable to law &c.

Ordered that James COLE Esqr. be appointed to take the inventorys from the Bladen line up to Cartledge Creek.

Ordered that Edward WILLIAMS be appointed to take the inventory from Cartledge Creek to the Montgomery line &c.

A list of jurors to attend at the next court (vizt) Nathaniel HARRINGTON, John BOSTICK, George CARTER, Thomas ADAMS, Benjn. COVINGTON, John COLE (Maryland), James PHILIPS Sr., William COTTENGAME, John MATTHEWS, James POSTON, John POWERS, Solomon SNEED, David SNEED Esqr., Isem HALEY, William WATKINS, Jehulle CROWSSON, William HICKS (turn over)...

December 1780   *Page 22*

...William NEWBERY, Jesse BOUNDS, John THOMAS, Thomas SUMMERAL, Nathaniel WILLIAMS, William WOODS, John COVINGTON Sr., Henry COVINGTON, John Batt BEARD, Savage LITTLETON, James MERIDITH Jr., Stephen TOUCHSTONE, George BOUNDS, William HUNTER Sr. &c.

Ordered that John MASK be appointed overseer of the road from Little River to Matthew RAYFORDs and the hands contiguous work thereon &c.

Ordered that John WALL Esqr. be appointed overseer of the road from Adcock's Ferry to the crossroad, by said ADCOCK's [*blot*] house and the hands contiguous work thereon &c.

Ordered that the administrators of Nicholas STONE deceased sell all the perish\able/ property at publick sale according to law &c.

The Last Will and Testament of John MASK deceased was proved in open court by the oath of Martha MASK.

Ordered that John WALL, John CRAWFORD, and Benjamin BEARD, be appointed assessors for the said county &c.

The names of those who are appointed to serve as Constables the ensuing year (viz) John LONG Jr., John JAMES Jr., Elisha COTTENGAME, John BLUE, Thomas GIBSON and George WALTERS &c.

December 1780

Ordered that John COLE (Maryland) be appointed overseer of the road from the race path to Crawfords old road beyond John JAMES, and the hands contiguous work thereon &c.

Ordered that Josiah LYON, Benjamin DUMAS, and Joseph HINES attend as a Venire at Salisbury Superior Court &c.

Court adjourned untill court in course.

Test. Thos. CRAWFORD Clk.   Charles MEDLOCK)
                                 James COLE   ) Esqrs.
                                 Edward WILLIAMS)

September 1781

At a County Court of Pleas and Quarter Sessions began and for the County of Richmond at the house of Mr. John COLE \on the last Monday in September/ in the year of our Lord one thousand seven hundred and eighty one an in the sixth year of American independence &c.

Present   Edward WILLIAMS)
           James COLE   ) Esqrs.
           Dudley MASK   )

Dudley MASK Esqr. came into court and qualified as a Justice of the Peace for said county &c.

John WALL, John CRAWFORD, and Benjamin Batt. BEARD assessors for the said [sic] for the year 1780 returned their assessment, and was allowed to Mr. John WALL and John CRAWFORD the sum of two thousand one hundred and sixty pounds each for their services &c.

September 1781

John MASK and Dudley MASK came into court and qualified as executors of the Last Will and Testament of of John MASK Sr. deceased.

Ordered that the perishable part the estate of John MASK deceased be sold at publick sale.

Ordered that John WALL Esqr. be appointed Commisioner for the County of Richmond.

Ordered that the wife of Isreal MEDLOCK deceas'd be call'd on for the papers of the Register's office, and to the Clerk of said county.

The court settled the depreciation of present currency at the rate of two hundred for one.

Ordered that Zacherias McDANIEL be appointed to serve as Coroner for Richmond County.

Ordered that Edward WILLIAMS be appointed to serve as Sheriff for the year one thousand seven hundred and eighty one &c.

Ordered that John JAMES be appointed to serve as Constable the ensuing year.

Ordered that Dudley MASK be appointed to take the inventory from the inhabitants of the uper district of Richmond County.

Ordered that [John?] SPEED Esqr. be appointed to take the inventory from the inhabitants of the lower end of Richmond County.

September 1781   *Page 25*

Court adjourned untill court in course.

	Edward WILLIAMS	)
Test. Thomas CRAWFORD Clk.	James COLE	) Esqrs.
	Dudley MASK	)

December 1781

At a County Court of Pleas and Quarter Sessions began and held for the County of Richmond on the last Monday in December in the year one thousand seven hundred and eighty one &c.

Present	Charles MEDLOCK	)
	Wm. LEGATE	)
	Robert WEBB	) Esqrs.
	Edward WILLIAMS	)
	James COLE	)

A deed from John WILSON to John WALL dated the nineteenth day of May one thousand seven hundred and eighty and proved in open court by the oath of Christopher REYNOLDS ordered to be registred.

John MASK Jr. executor of John MASK Sr. deceased came into court and exhibited the sale of the said estate [blot] to the amount of one hundred and eighty seven pounds twelve shilling specie &c. £187-12

A deed from Charles HARBERT to John DOWNING and proved in open court by the oath of Aquila? SHEPHERD, and ordered to be registred.

December 1781   Page 26

John SPEED Esqr. came into court and qualified as a Justice of the Peace for Richmond County.

On motion Thomas DOCKERY obtained leave to build a water grist mill on Cartledge Creek near to where he now lives and on his own land &c.

The Last Will and Testament of John COLE deceased was proved in open court agreeable to law by the oath of John JAMES, Robert WEBB, and John TUCKER &c.

Rachel COLE and John COLE executors to the Last Will and Testament of John COLE decd. late of this county came into this court and after the said will was exhibited and proved they were duly qualified as executors thereto agreeable to law &c.

Court adjourned untill tomorrow nine o'clock.

Court met agreeable to adjournment.
     Present   Charles MEDLOCK)
                        Robert WEBB   )
                        James COLE   ) Esqrs.
                        John SPEED   )

Edward WILLIAMS Esqr. came into court and qualified as Sheriff for the County of Richmond and gave bond and security agreeable to law &c.

Ordered that William HUNTER Sr. ~~and~~ executor of the Last Will and Testament of Samuel HUNTER dec'd. be empowered to sell...

December 1781   Page 27

...agreeable to the will a waggon and gear, one mare and a horse and make return to the next court &c.

Sarah CROWSSON wife of Jehuele CROWSSON deceased (late of this county) came into [*blot*] court and qualified as administratrix upon the estate of her husband Jehuele, and gave bond and security according to law and exhibited an ventory [*sic*] of the said estate upon oath containing all the perishable property thereto belonging.

Sarah HICKS late wife of John DONALDSON of said county deceased came into this court and delivered up all accounts belonging to the estate of Nicholas STONE deceased of the said county that came into her possession upon oath &c.

Ordered that John JAMES Sr. be appointed overseer of the road from John COLEs mill to the Catfish Road, and all the hands contiguous work thereon.

Ordered that Edward WILLIAMS be overseer of the road from Mountain Creek to Cattfish Road, and all the hands contiguous work thereon &c.

Ordered that William BAKER be overseer of the road from Mountain Creek to Little River and the hands contiguous work thereon.

December 1781   Page 28

Ordered that James YATES be overseer of the road from the fork of the roads to the Cumberlin line and to keep the bride in repair and the hands contiguous work thereon &c.

Ordered that Thomas GIBSON be appointed overseer of the road, from Falling Creek to the fork of the road, and the hands contiguous work thereon &c.

Ordered that Isreal SNEED be appointed overseer of the road, from Johnsons Creek to Falling Creek and the hands contiguous work thereon.

Ordered that Daniel HICKS be appointed overseer of the road from the Province line up to Solomon's Creek and the hands contiguous work thereon &c.

Ordered that John SPEED Esqr. be appointed overseer of the road Colo. MEDLOCKs to Haley's Ferry and from thence to the old school house and that all the Quakers below Hitchcock Creek and the Scotchmans on Solomon's Creek work thereon &c.

Ordered that the Sheriff summon the following persons to serve as juriors at the next court (vizt) John MASK, James MERIDETH, William MASK (Major), George WALTERS, John COLEMAN, William BAKER, Richd. PEMBERTON, Daniel SMITH, Daniel THOMAS, Thomas BLEWITT, Laurance EVERITT, Henry ADCOCK, Henry COVINGTON, John COVINGTON, William HUNTER...

December 1781   Page 29

...William JARNIGAN, John WALL, Daniel HICKS, Moses CHAMBERS, Hendley SNEED, Benjamin COVINGTON, John JAMES Sr., Thomas GIBSON, Joseph HINES, Jonathon NEWBERY, William HICKS, Silas HALEY, David SNEED Sr., John PARNEL, Darby HANAGAN, Thomas SUMMERAL, William MORRIS, Nathaniel ~~William~~ HARRINGTON,

Isreal SNEED Jr., Thomas CRAWFORD, Nicholas STONE, David SNEED [Jr.?] &c.

Ordered that William HUNTER be appointed overseer of the road, from opposite to John JAMES? to Crawfords Road, and up Crawford Road to Cartledge Creek and all the hands contiguous work thereon &c.

Ordered that Thomas WATKINS be appointed overseer of the road from the race path into the road opposite to John JAMES's and all the hands contiguous work thereon.

Ordered that John MASON be appointed overseer of the road from from the Catt-fish Road to the county line and all the hands contiguous work thereon. Court adjourned untill tomorrow 8 o'clock.

Met according to adjournment.
Present   Charles MEDLOCK)
                  Robert WEBB   )
                  James COLE   ) Esqrs.
                  John SPEED   )

December 1781   Page 30

Ordered that John WALL, John CRAWFORD, and Benjamin Esqr. [! Benjamin BEARD] be appointed assessors for in Richmond County for the year 1781.

Ordered that John SPEED Esqr. be appointed Collector of the Taxes for the year 1780 from Cartledges Creek, to Crawfords Road, thence with the road to the county line including all the inhabitants in the lower end of the county.

Ordered that Wm. WALL be appointed over Collector of the Taxes for the year 1780 from Cartledges Creek to Crawfords Road, thence with the road to the county line including all the inhabitants in the uper end of the county &c.

Ordered that the Sheriff sell all the perishable property belonging to Jeheule CROWSSON deceased make return to the next court.

The Last Will and Testament of John DONALDSON deceased late of this county was exhibatted in open court and proved by the oath of John JONES Esqr. who saw the other subscribing witness assign his name thereto &c.

Sarah HICKS late wife of John DONALDSON deceased of this county Executrix of the Last Will and Testament of the said John DONALDSON came into this court, and after the will was exhibatted & proved, in open court, was duly qualified [blot] as Executrix thereto agreeable to law &c. Ordered that Letters Testamentary issue to her.

December 1781   Page 31

Ordered that Sarah POSTON orphan child of Robert POSTON late of this county deceased be bound unto Edward WILLIAMS for six years and three months as an apprentice &c.

The petition of Simon THOMAS Jr. Executor of \the Last Will and Testament of/ Simon THOMAS Sr. late of this county deceased upon oath setting forth the loss of the deceased will by having his house robed, and on motion being made the said Simon THOMAS Jr. was admitted to produce witnesses to prove that the said Simon THOMAS Sr. [blot] made a will by the oath of Thomas DOCKERY and also proved by the oath of Daniel THOMAS the different articles mentioned to the several legatees therein nominated as pr. affidavit filed in this office.

Ordered that the Sheriff sell twenty? seven head of hogs formerly bought by John LONG belonging to the estate of Nicholas STONE deceased &c.

Ordered that the Sheriff bring the children of John RYE deceased to the next court &c.

Ordered that the Sheriff bring to the next court James HINES and a girl child now in the possession of Edward SMITH to be dealt with agreeable to law &c.

John SPEED Esqr. came into court and gave bond and security agreeable to law for his collections of the taxes for the year 1780.

William WALL came into court and gave bond and security agreeable to law for his collection of the taxes for the year 1780 in the uper district.

December 1781   Page 32

Ordered that the county tax for the year one thousand seven hundred and eighty be ten shilling on every hundred pounds of taxable property &c.

Ordered that the Sheriff summon John THOMAS, Benjamin DUMAS, and Daniel SNEED to attend as a venire at Salisbury Superior Court in March next, &c.

Ordered that Samuel PATE be appointed to serve as Constable the ensuing year &c.

Ordered that Joseph RYE be appointed to serve as Constable the ensuing year &c.

Ordered that John HILYARD be appointed to serve as Constable the ensuing year &c.

Court adjourned untill court in course.

Test Wm. LOVE Clk.
    Charles MEDLOCK)
    Robert WEBB   )
    James COLE   ) Esqrs.
    John SPEED   )

March 1782

At a County Court of Pleas and Quarter Sessions began and held for the County of Richmond at the Court House therein on the last Monday in March one thousand seven hundred and eighty two, &c.

Present Dudley MASK)
     Robert WEBB) Esqrs.

Court adjourned untill tomorrow, 10 o'clock.

March 1782   Page 33

Court met according to adjournment.
Present Charles MEDLOCK)
     Dudley MASK   )
     James COLE   ) Esqrs.
     Robert WEBB   )

A deed from John JAMES Sr. to William WEBB, and proved in open court by the oath of Edward ALMOND ordered to be registered &c.

A deed from Isaac DAVIS to Joseph LASETER and proved in open court by the oath of Isreal WATKINS ordered to be registered &c.

A deed from John WATKINS to Wm. WATKINS and proved in open court by the oath of Isreal WATKINS ordered to be registred.

A deed from James POSTON to Samuel CURTIS and proved in open court by the oath of Daniel HICKS ordered to be registered &c.

A list of the jury to the present term returned, (vizt.) John MASK, James MERIDETH, William BAKER, Daniel SMITH, Daniel THOMAS, Thos. BLEWITT, Lauranc EVERIT, Henry ADCOCK, Henry COVINGTON, John COVINGTON, Wm. JERNIGAN, John WALL, Daniel HICKS,

Moses CHAMBERS, Hendley SNEED, Benjn. COVINGTON, John JAMES Sr., Thos. GIBSON, Joseph HINES, Silas? HALEY, David SNEED Sr., John PARNEL, Nathaniel HARRINGTON, Isreal SNEED, Nicholas STONE, David SNEED Jr. &c.

March 1782 *Page 34*

The Last Will and Testament of Samuel DAVIS, late of this county deceased was exhibited in open court and proved by the oath of Benjamin MOSELY one of the subscribing witness who saw the other witness assign their names thereto &c.

And the Last Will and Testament of Samuel DAVIS late of this county decd. was exhibited in open court and proved, Mary Ann WILLIAMS DAVIS, wife of the said Samuel deceased came into this court and was qualified as Executrix thereto agreeable to law &c.

The Last Will and Testament of Richard THOMPSON late of this county deceased was exhibited in open court and proved by the oath of Wm. McDANIEL.

Thos. Plumber WILLIAMS came into court and qualified as Deputy Sheriff &c.

Ordered that Joseph SIMKINS be appointed Constable in the district of Dudley MASK Esqr.

Court adjourned untill tomorrow 10 o'clock.

Court met according to adjournment
    Present   Dudley MASK)
                     James COLE   ) Esqrs.
                     Robert WEBB)

Ordered that John CRAWFORD and Benjamin BEARD Esqr. be allowed the sum of six? thousand dollars each for their services as assessor for this county for the year 1781 at that John Esqr. [! *John WALL*] be allowed...

March 1782 *Page 35*

...the sum of one thousand dollars for his services for the said year 1781 &c.

Ordered that John CRAWFORD Esqr. be appointed Attorney for the state this present term, and that he be allowed the sum of twenty five pounds for his services &c.

Ordered that Dudley MASK be appointed Commission of the specific provision tax from Cartledge Creek to the uper end of this county, and that John SPEED Esqr. be appointed from the said creek to the lower end of the county &c.

John CRAWFORD came into court and exonerated himself from the security of John DONALDSON deceased, administrator of the estate of Nicholas STONE Sr. deceased.

Ordered that Joseph [!] be exempted from paying his county tax &c.

Court adjourned untill tomorrow 10 o'clock.

Met according to adjournment &c. Present

Ordered that the black smith tools now in the possession of Robert WEBB Esqr. formerly the property of Jehule CROWSSON decd. sold for the currency for the said estate at public vendue, and on motion made ordered that the said tools be sold again at publick sale for specie &c.

March 1782 Page 36

Edward WILLIAMS and John MASK presented by the grand jury for prophane swearing came into court, submitted and was fined agreeable to law.

John LONG and Zacherias MARTIN, presented by the grand jury for prophane swearing, came into court, submitted and was fined agreeable to law.

On motion Isaiah STEELY being of lawful age came into this court and took the oath of allegiance to this state.

A list of juriors to attend at the next court (vizt) Edward CROSLAND, Jesse BOUNDS, Wm. NEWBERY, Wm. WEBB, Barnaby SKIPPER, Wm. HICKS, Thomas CURTIS, John BOUNDS, Joseph RYE, Wm. MORE, Wm. MASK (Major), William McGUIRE, Richard PEMBERTON Sr., John LASENBY, John COLEMAN, Wm. WATKINS Jr., John SNEED, Thos. WATKINS, Wm. WATKINS Sr., John POWERS, Wm. TERRY, Nelson GIBSON, John DAWKINS, George FREEMAN, Thos. SUMMERAL, Jacob MANGRUM, Darby HANAGAN, James EASTERLING, George WALTERS, Joseph GADD Sr., John CHILES, John COLE Sr., Timothy HURLEY, Laurance OBRYAN, Simon THOMAS &c.

On motion John CHILES moved for a Did. Po. to take the examination of Thos. CHILES and Wm. ROBERTS before Mark ALLEN Esqr. of Montgomery County &c.

Zacherias MARTIN and Elisabeth MARTIN late wife of Wm. SPEED deceased came into this...

March 1782   Page 37

...court and qualified as administrators [*blot*] the estate of the said Wm. SPEED deceased and gave bond & security agreeable to law &c.

Ordered that the Sheriff sell all the perishable property belonging to the estate of [*blot*] Wm. SPEED deceased and make return to the next court.

Ordered that John CHILES be bound over to the next court and to be of good behaviour in the mean time in the sum of £100-0 John COLE and John PARNEL his securitys each in the sum of £50-0.

Ordered that Alexander WATSON be bound over to the next court, for his good behavior in the sum of £100-0 John COLE Sr. his security in the sum of £100-0.

Ordered that Edward McFERSHON be bound over to the next court for his good behaviour in the sum of £100-0 John COLE Sr. his security in the sum of £100-0.

Ordered that the Sheriff bring the orphan children of David CAUDLE to the next court to be dealt with according to law &c.

Ordered that the Sheriff bring the orphan children of Robert POSTON to the next court to be dealt with according to law &c.

March 1782   Page 38

Ordered that the county tax be five shilling in the hundred pound for the year 1781.

Ordered that the Clerk be allowed the sum of four thousand pounds for his exaficio service from the year 1779 to March term 1782 &c.

Ordered that Isreal SNEED and John ~~SNEED~~ DAVIS be appointed to serve as Constables the ensuing year &c.

Court adjourned untill court in course.

                                  Charles MEDLOCK)
                                  Robert WEBB   )
Tes Wm. LOVE Clk.   James COLE   ) Esqr.
                                  Dudley MASK   )
                                  John JONES   )

June 1782

At a County Court of Pleas and Quarter Sessions began and held for the County of Richmond on the last Monday in June in the year one thousand seven hundred and eighty two and in the sixth year of American independence &c.

Present   Charles MEDLOCK   )
                 Wm. LEGGATE   )
                 John JONES   ) Esqr.
                 John SPEED   )
                 James COLE   )

Ordered that Morgan BROWN Esqr. be appointed Attorney for the state this present term &c.

June 1782   Page 39

A deed from Anthony IVEY to River JORDON and proved in open court by the oath of Morgan BROWN Sr. ordered to be registred &c.

Grand Jury sworn &c. John COLE foreman, Jesse BOUNDS, William NEWBERY, William WEBB, Barnaby SKIPPER, William TERRY, Joseph RYE, John SNEED, William McGUIRE, Jacob MANGRUM, Derby HANAGAN, Simon THOMAS, William WATKINS and John POWERS &c.

John SPEED and Benjamin COVINGTON Esqr. came into court and qualified as Justices of the Peace &c.

Ordered that John CHILES have leave to build a water grist mill on Naked Creek, on his own land within a mile from the mouth &c.

John CHILES came into court and was discharged from his recognizances &c.

Alexander WATSON came into court and was discharged from his recognizance &c.

Edward McPHERSON came into court and was discharged from his recognizance &c.

Court adjourned untill tomorrow 10 o'clock.

Met according to adjournment.
       Present   Charles MEDLOCK   )
                        Jame [!] COLE   ) Esqr.
                        Benjamin COVINGTON)

A deed from William BAKER and wife to Charles ROBERTSON Jr. and proved in open court by the oath of Jacob COCKRAHAM ordered to be registred.

June 1782

A deed from William BAKER to Charles ROBERTSON Jr. and proved in open court by the oath of Jacob COCKRAHAM ordered to be registred &c.

Edward WILLIAMS Esqr. (Sheriff) came into court and protested against the insufficiency of the goal [*jail*] of said county.

Issable BURT wife of William BURT late of this county decd. came into this court and qualified as Administratrix upon the estate of the said William, and gave bond agreeable to law &c.

Ordered that the Sheriff sell all the perishable part of the estate of Wm. BURT deceased and make return to the next court &c.

On motion ordered that a judicial attachment issue, against the goods and chattels lands and tenements of John WATSON late of this county agreeable to the Sheriff return in the suit of Wm. LOVE against the said WATSON &c.

Elisabeth HUTCHEN wife of James HUTCHEN late of this county deceased, came into this court and qualified as Administratrix upon the estate of the said James HUTCHEN and gave bond agreeable to law &c.

Wm. MASK vs. Daniel McDANIEL on motion ordered that the Plaintiff have judgment by default.

On motion ordered that Wm. MASK obtain a Did. Po. to take in the…

June 1782

…examination of Margeratt McDANIEL and Issable McDANIEL, James McQUEEN and John McQUEEN before Thos. CHILES of Montgomery County returnable to the next court &c.

Ordered that Anthony POSTON be bound uno Edward WILLIAMS Esqr. untill he comes of age &c.

Edward WILLIAMS Esqr. Sheriff made a return of the sale of the estate of Jeheuele CROWSSON to the amount of six thousand, eight hundred and three pounds in paper currency and thirty pounds in specie &c.

Richmond County NC Court Minutes, 1779-1786

On motion the court ordered that Elisabeth HUTCHENS and William MASK be appointed gaurdens to Mary, Elisabeth, Anthony, Samuel, Jesse, and William HUTCHENS children of James HUTCHEN late of this county deceased and gave bond and security agreeable to law &c.

A deed from William COLEMAN to Owen SLAUGHTER and proved in open court by the oath of Jonathon NEWBERY ordered to be registred &c.

Benjn. BEARD Esqr. came into court and qualified as a Justice of the Peace &c.

The Sheriff made a return of the estate of William SPEED, to the amount of one hundred and ten pounds one shilling and eight pence specie &c. £110-1-8

June 1782   *Page 42*

Ordered that the collection of the specific tax in the uper end of this county discharge Charles ROBERTSON from his specific tax for the year 1781.

Dudley MASK and John BOUND Esqrs. came into court and qualified as Justices of the Peace for said county &c.

The Last Will and Testament of Benjamin MOREMAN deceased was exhibited in open court and was proved by the oath of Isem HALEY who saw the other subscribing witness assign his name thereto &c.

The Last Will and Testament of Thos. MOREMAN was exhibited in open court, and proved by the affirmation of Isem HALEY and the oath of Silas HALEY who saw the other subscribing witness ascribe his name thereto.

After the Last Will and Tesatament of Thomas MOREMAN late of this county decd. was exhibited in open court and proved agreeable to law Thomas MOREMAN Jr. came into this court and qualified as Executor thereto agreeable to law &c.

Isem HALEY Executor of the Last Will and Testament of Benjamin MOREMAN late of this county deceas came into this court and after the said will was exhibited and proved – was duly qualified as Executor thereto according to law &c.

June 1782   *Page 43*

Ordered, that Thomas CRAWFORD, Holden WADE and William WALL be appointed Commissioners for this county, to inquire into the confiscated property.

Daniel HICKS came into this court as garnishee and declares upon oath, that he had no property in his hands belonging to Jethro MORE at the time when Mr. Patrick BOGGAN levied his attachment in his hands and summoned him as garnishee &c.

Ordered that John BOUNDS Esqr. be appointed to take the inventorys of all the inhabitants from the lower end of this county up to Maskes? Creek, and from the head of said creek along the old road, to Drowning Creek Bridge &c.

Ordered that John SPEED Esqr. be appointed to take the inventorys of all the inhabitants from Maskes Creek to Hitchcock Creek, and from the head of said creek a direct course to the Cumberland line &c.

Ordered that James COLE Esqr. be apppointed to take all the inventorys of the inhabitants from Hitch-cock Creek to Bigg Mountain Creek.

Ordered that Dudley MASK Esqr. be appointed to take all the inventorys of the inhabitants from Bigg Mountain Creek to the uper end of the county &c.

Ordered that John CRAWFORD, Benjamin BEARD and John WALL Esqr. be appointed Assessors for the year one thousand seven hundred and eighty two &c.

June 1782   *Page 44*

William HUSBANDS came into court and was bound over to June court in the sum of £100-0 William WALL and William WEBB securitys each in the sum of £50-0.

A deed from William NEWBERY to John CHILES and proved in open court by the oath of Moses CHAMBERS and John SPEED ordered to be registred.

Ordered that John CHILES have leave to build a water grist mill on Mountain Creek it being on his own land &c.

Charles CARTER bound to appear at next June court in the sum of – £100-0-0. George CARTER his security in the sum of £50-0.

Ordered that John CHILES be allowed the priviledge to keep an ordinary at Richmond Court House upon giving bond & security.

Ordered that Daniel HICKS be exempted from paying a four fold tax for the year 1780.

Ordered that Allen McKASKILL be exempted from paying a four fold tax for the year 1780.

Ordered that Sampson WILLIAMS be appointed Constable for the ensuing year &c.

Ordered that John PEARCE be appointed Constable for the ensuing year &c.

Ordered that Burrell STRICKLIN be appointed to serve as Constable for the ensuing year.

Court adjourned untill tomorrow 9 o'clock.

June 1782

Court met according to adjournment.
  Present   Charles MEDLOCK)
            William LEGGATE)
            James COLE   ) Esqrs.
            John JONES   )
            John SPEED   )

Burrel STRICKLIN came into court and qualified as Constable for the ensuing year &c.

Ordered that James MERIDITH? be appointed overseer of the road from Little River, to the road that runs [blot] from Matthew RAYFORD to Coleson's Ferry and that Thomas PICKETT, John MASKS, Dudley MASKS, David CAUDLE, William MORE, Joseph GADD Jr., Wm. FRAZER, and William MASKS hands work thereon &c.

Ordered that John SPEED Esqr. be appointed overseer of the road from the fork of the road by Colo. MEDLOCKs, to the ferry, and from the ferry to the old road by the school house and his own hands, the HALEY's, Andrew MOREMAN, Benjn. MOREMAN, Wm. MOREMAN, Thos. & John MOREMAN work thereon &c.

Ordered that Isreal SNEED be appointed overseer of the road from Solomon Creek to Falling Creek, and the hands contiguous work thereon &c.

Ordered that Zacherias MARTIN be appointed to serve as Constable the ensuing year &c.

June 1782

Ordered that Benjamin POWEL be appointed to serve as Constable the ensuing year &c.

On motion Zacherias MARTIN came into court and qualified as Constable &c.

Ordered that the Sheriff the following persons to attend as juriors at Salisbury Superior Court on the fifteenth day of ~~March~~ \September/ next (vizt) John WALL, John COLEMAN, and William MASK.

Ordered that Edward WILLIAMS be appointed to serve as Sheriff the insuing year &c.

The Last Will and Testament of Richard ADAM Sr. was duly proved in open court by the oath of George CARTER one of the subscribing witnesses there to who saw the other witnesses subscribe their names thereto &c.

Richard ADAMS Jr. Executor to the Last Will and Testament of Richard ADAMS Sr. late of this county deceased, came into this court and after the said will was exhibited and proved was duly qualified as Executor thereto according to law &c.

Ordered that the Sheriff summon the following persons (viz) John MASK, James MERIDETH, William BAKER, Richard PEMBERTON...

June 1782   *Page 47*

...Daniel SMITH, Daniel THOMAS, Thomas BLEWITT, Laurance EVERITT, Henry ADCOCK, Henry COVINGTON, John COVINGTON Sr., William HUNTER Sr., William JERNIGAN, Daniel HICKS, Moses CHAMBER, Hendley SNEED, John JAMES Sr., Thomas GIBSON, William HICKS, Silas HALEY, David SNEED Sr., Solomon RYE, Isaac YATES, John TURNAGE, Robert WILSON, John PEMBERTON, John CROWSSON, Lott STRICKLIN, Thomas BROWN, Stephen COLE, Nicholas STONE, George CARTER, Richd. ADAMS, Thomas ADAMS, John SMITH and Thomas DOCKERY to attend at the next court and make return thereof &c.

Thomas BLEWITT came into this court as garnishee and upon oath says that he had no property of Abner WILLIAMS in hand at the time Colo. Thomas WADE's attachment was livied in his hands of the said WILLIAMS's.

William HUSBAND came into court and was discharged from his recognizance &c.

Ordered that the County Surveyor lay of the widow's third of Nicholas STONE Sr. ~~land~~ late of this county deceased &c.

Ordered that Isreal SNEED be appointed to serve as Constable the insuing year &c.

June 1782 — Page 48

Ordered that John SPEED Esqr. be appointed Collector in the lower district of this county for the year 1781.

Ordered that William WALL be appointed Collector in the uper district of this county for the year 1781.

Ordered that Mark DEES be appointed overseer of the road, from the Court House to the Polely? Bridge and from thence to Cornelious's Pond, and all the hands contiguous work thereon &c.

Ordered that the Sheriff be allowed the sum of three thousand pounds ex officio services for the year 1781.

Ordered that the county tax be eight shillings on every hundred pounds value of taxable property for the 1781.

Court adjourned untill court in course.

Test. Wm. LOVE Clk.

Charles MEDLOCK)
James COLE)
Wm. LEGGATE) Esqrs.
John SPEED)
John JONES)

September 1782 — Page 49

At a court began and held for the County of Richmond, at the Court House therein on the tenth day of September one thousand seven hundred and eighty two, for the express purpose of appointing a Commissioner in the said county agreeable to the act of the General Assembly of this state to collect and receive the specific provision tax for the year 1782 &c.

Present

Charles MEDLOCK)
Robert WEBB)
Dudley MASK)
John JONES) Esqrs.
John SPEED)
Benjn. COVINGTON)

Ordered that Charles MEDLOCK Esqr. be appointed County Commissioner of the specific provision tax for the year 1782 and gave bond and security agreeable to law &c.

The court adjourned &c.

	Charles MEDLOCK	)	
	Robert WEBB	)	
Test Wm. LOVE Clk.	Dudley MASK	)	
	John JONES	)	Esqrs.
	John SPEED	)	
	Benjn. COVINGTON	)	

<u>September 1782</u>   <u>Page 50</u>

At a County Court began and held for the County of Richmond at the Court House therein on the last Monday in September in the year one thousand seven hundred & eighty two and in the sixth year of American independence.
   Present   Charles MEDLOCK)
                   James COLE   ) Esqrs.
                   Robert WEBB   )

Edward WILLIAMS Esqr. came into court and qualified as Sheriff for the insuing year and gave bond and security agreeable to law &c.

A deed from David DUMAS to John DEGARNETT proved in open court by the oath of James MEREDITH, ordered to be registred.

A deed from David DUMAS to John DE GARNETT proved in open court by the oath of James MERIDITH, ordered to be registred. [*repeat sic*]

Ordered that Henry ADCOCK be excused from serving as a jurior the present term &c.

Ordered that Silas HALEY be excused from serving as a jurior the present term &c.

Ordered that James MERIDITH be excused from serving as a jurior the present term &c.

<u>September 1782</u>   <u>Page 51</u>

A grand jury sworn, John COVINGTON Sr. foreman, Wm. BAKER, Daniel SMITH, Daniel THOMAS, Thomas BLEWITT, Henry COVINGTON, Wm. HUNTER, William JORNIGAN, Moses CHAMBERS, Hendley SNEED, John JAMES, William HICKS, Thomas ADAMS, Richd. ADAMS, and Isaac YATES &c.

On motion Elisabeth HALES came into this court and qualified as Administratrix upon the estate of William HALE late of this county deceased and returned upon oath an inventory of the deceased estate, and gave bond agreeable to law &c.

Richmond County NC Court Minutes, 1779-1786

Ordered that the Sheriff sell all the perishable part of the estate of William HALES deceased and make return to the next court.

Thomas Plummer WILLIAMS came into open court and qualified as Deputy Sheriff the insuing year &c.

Isaiah STEELY came into court and entred into recognizance for his appearance during this term in the sum of £100-0. John CROWSSON security in the sum of £50-0.

Court adjourned untill tomorrow 9 o'clock.

Met according to adjournment.

September 1782   Page 52

Isum HALEY Executor of the Last Will and Testament of Benjamin MOREMAN deceased returned upon oath an inventory of the deceased estate.

On motion Elisabeth HUTCHEN Administratrix of the estate of James HUTCHENS deceased came into this court, and returned a true and perfect inventory of the deceased estate &c.

Ordered that the Sheriff sell all the perishable estate of Benjamin MOREMAN deceased and make return to the next court &c.

Ordered that the Sheriff sell all the perishable part of the estate of James HUTCHEN deceased and make return to the next court &c.

~~Ordered~~ Deed from George WALTER to Solomon GROSS and proved in court by the oath of Ezra BOSTICK ordered to be registred &c.

Ordered that the Clerk give up the administration bond of John DONOLDSON Administrator of the estate of Nicholas STONE deceased unto John CRAWFORD Esqr. in pursuance of a former order of this court to release the said John CRAWFORD from his securityship of the said John DONALDSON deceased, present on the bench Charles MEDLOCK, William LEGGATE, James COLE, and John JONES Esqrs.

September 1782   Page 53

Ordered that Zacherias JOHNSON be exempted from paying a four fold tax for the years 1780 & 1781.

William McGUIRE came into this court and qualified as administrator upon the estate of John McGUIRE deceased and gave bond & security agreeable to law &c.

Ordered that Alexander WATSON be exempted from paying a four fold tax for the year 1780.

Ordered that Dugal BLUE be exempted from paying a four fold tax for the year 1780.

Edward WILLIAMS Esqr. came into this court and protested against the insufficiency of the county goal [jail].

Charles MEDLOCK Esqr.)
    vs.)
John LEGGATE of Bladen County) Petition
Roger CRAIG in Randolph County)
John SLAWSON in Cumberland County) Upon which petition the court ordered a jury (vizt) John MASK, Solomon RYE, John TURNAGE, Robert WILSON, Lott STRICKLIN, Stephen COLE, Nicholas STONE, Randolph HALEY, John SMITH, Daniel SNEED, John SNEED, and Charles HUCKABY who being sworn upon their oaths do say they find damages for the plaintiff the sum of one hundred pounds specie and so they say all &c.

September 1782   Page 54

William MASK)
    vs.) Att't. Def. Inq.
Daniel McDANIEL) In which suit the following jury was sworn (vizt) John MASK, Solomon RYE, John TURNAGE, Robert WILSON, Lott STRICKLIN, Stephen COLE, Randolph HALEY, John SMITH, Daniel SNEED, John SNEED, Charles HUCKABY and Nicholas STONE who upon their oaths do say that they find damages for the plaintiff the sum of sixty pounds specie and so they say all &c.

A deed from Henry ADCOCK and Archelous MOREMON to John AULD Esqr. acknowledged in open court ordered to be registered &c.

Ordered that William LEGATE Esqr. take the aknowledgements of the femes Delilah ADCOCK and Ann MOREMAN as to their right of dower to the foregoing conveyances from Henry ADCOCK & Archelous MOREMON to John AULD Esqr.

Ordered that William McDANOLD have leave to build a water grist mill on Naked Creek &c.

On motion of Mary Ann WILLIAMS DAVIS, ordered that he have leave to obtain a Did. Po. to South Carolina to take the examination of Mary BARRENTINE in South Carolina. To be taken before George HICKS Esqr &c.

Ordered that Solomon GROSS be discharged from the citation of the commissioner of the confiscated property of this county in...

September 1782   Page 55

...pursuance of a discharge from Superior Court at Salisbury &c.

Ordered that Charles ROBERTSON be discharged from the citation of the commissioner of confiscated property in this county in pursuance of a discharge from Superior Court at Salisbury &c.

Ordered that the County Surveyor lay of the widow HALE's third in certains land lying in this county belonging to her deceased husband.

Ordered that William SEAMONS indemnify the parish from the maintenance of a bastard child begotten by him upon the body of Elisabeth SLAUGHTER and that Edward WILLIAMS be security for the same &c.

Joseph MARTIN   )
    vs.   ) Att't.
Abner WILLIAMS)   In which suit the following jury was sworn (vizt) John MASK, Solomon RYE, John TURNAGE, Robert WILSON, Lott STRICKLIN, Stephen COLE, Nicholas STONE, Randolph HALEY, John SMITH, Daniel SNEED, John SNEED and Charles HUCKABY who upon their oaths do say that they find damages for the plaintiff the sum of fifty three pound ten shilling and so they say all &c. £53-10.

September 1782   Page 56

Court adjourned untill tomorrow 9 o'clock.

Met according to adjournment &c.
    Present   James COLE   )
                    John JONES   ) Esqrs.
                    Benjn. BEARD   )

Ordered that the Sheriff sell all the perishable estate of John McGUIRE deceased and make return thereof to the next court &c.

On motion of Joseph MARTIN ordered that a Did. Po. issue to South Carolina to take the examination of John WILSON and William ALSTON in a certain suit John CHILES brough[t] against him.

John SPEED   )
   vs.   ) Att't.
Duncan BLUE   ) In which suit the following jury was sworn (vizt) John MASK, Solomon RYE, John TURNAGE, Robert WILSON, Lott STRICKLIN, Stephen COLE, Nicholas STONE, Randolph HALEY, Daniel SNEED, John SNEED, Charles HUCKABY and Joseph RYE who upon their oaths do find damages for the plaintiff the sum of seven pounds eight shilling specie & so they say all &c.

Edward WILLIAMS   )
   vs.   )
John LEGGATE, John SLAWSON   ) Petition
Ezedick? SLAWSON   )
Roger CRAIG, William BLACK   ) ~~In~~ Upon which...

<u>September 1782</u>   <u>Page 57</u>

...petition the court ordered a jury (vizt) John MASK, Solomon RYE, John TURNAGE, Robert WILSON, Lott STRICKLIN, Stephen COLE, Nicholas STONE, Randolph HALEY, Daniel SNEED, John SNEED, Charles HUCKABY and Joseph RYE who being sworn upon their oaths do say that they find damages for the plaintiff for the sum of one hundred and sixty pounds specie and so they say all &c.

Ordered that the Sheriff sell a bay horse the property of William CAMPBLE attached by John McCRAY (gentleman) and make return to the next court &c.

David JORNIGAN   )
   vs.   )
William BRIGMAN   ) Petition
Daniel McINNISE   )
Daniel McINNISE [!]) Upon which petition the court ordered a jury (vizt) John MASK, Solomon RYE, John TURNAGE, Robert WILSON, Lott STRICKLIN, Stephen COLE, Nicholas STONE, Randolph HALEY, Daniel SNEED, John SNEED, John CROWSSON and Joseph RYE who being sworn upon their oath do say that they assess damage for the plaintiff the sum of fourteen pounds nine shillings and ten pence specie and so they say all &c.

September 1782 Page 58

William WALSH came into this court and acknowledged himself indebted to this state in the sum of – £500-0 for his appearance. Arthur DEES and John FARLEY his securities each in the sum of – £250-0.

Ordered that Nicholas GREEN be exempted from paying a four fold tax for the year 1780.

Wm. LOVE)
    vs.   ) Judicial att't.
John WATSON) In which suit the following jury was sworn (viz) John MASK, Solomon RYE, John TURNAGE, Robert WILSON, John CROWSSON, Lott STRICKLIN, Stephen COLE, Nicholas STONE, Randolph HALEY, Daniel SNEED, John SNEED, and Joseph RYE upon their oaths do find for the plaintiff the sum of one hundred and sixty pounds specie and so they say all &c.

John CRAWFORD, Benjamin \BEARD/ Esqr. assessors for the year one thousand seven hundred and eighty two made a return of their assessment to the amount of fourty five thousand seven hundred and six pounds three <u>three</u> shilling and received by the court, ordered that they be allowed the sum of six pounds each specie for their services as assessors &c.

John BULL came into court and was over [!] for his appearance at the next court in the sum of – £250-0. Daniel CARMICAL and Daniel McKOY securities each in the sum of – £125-0. Forfeited.

September 1782 Page 59

Robert SPEED came into this court and was bound for his appearance to the next court in the sum of £100-0. John SPEED his security in the sum of £50-0.

Ann HILL, Elisabeth MARTIN and George HILL evidences in each the sum of £100-0.

Ordered that William THOMAS Jr. take the state oath in open court in ~~order~~ a renewal of his alegiance to this state.

Court adjourned untill tomorrow 9 o'clock.

Met according to adjournment &c.
    Present   Charles MEDLOCK)
                      James COLE   ) Esqrs.
                      John JONES   )

Leonard LOCK   )
    vs.   )
Neil McCARTER   ) Petition
Daniel McKETCHAM   )
Daniel McFERSHON   ) Upon which petition the court ordered a jury (vizt) John MASK, Solomon RYE, John TURNAGE, Robert WILSON, John CROWSSON, Lott STRICKLIN, Stephen COLE, Nicholas STONE, William TERRY, Randolph HALEY,...

September 1782   Page 60

...John COLE and Joseph RYE, who being sworn upon their oaths do say that they find for the plaintiff the sum of fifty one pounds eighteen shillings and nine pence with interest from May 1780 untill paid and so say they all &c.

John WALSH   )
    vs.   ) Petition &c.
David GADDON, Archabald CAMPBLE   )
Archabald SMITH, Duncan McMILLON   ) Upon which petition the court ordered a jury (vizt) John MASK, Solomon RYE, John TURNAGE, Robert WILSON, John CROWSSON, Lott STRICKLIN, Stephen COLE, Nicholas STONE, William TERRY, Randolph HALEY, John COLE and Joseph RYE, who being sworn upon their oaths do say that they find for the plaintiff the sum of one hundred and thirty six pounds five shilling agreeable to his accounts and so they say all &c.

Ordered that Edward ALMOND be allowed the sum of fifteen shilling for his services as Constable &c.

Agreeable to an of [!] this court formerly made directing the County Surveyor to lay off the widow's right of dower in the tract of land belonging to Nicholas STONE deceased containing six hundred and fourty acres the surveyor...

September 1782   Page 61

...made his return as follows Beginning at a state [stake?] in in the sixth and home lines of said track on the north west side of Cartledge Creek in the low grounds near to where the road crosses said creek and runs thence south sixty degrees east, across the said tract to where it intersects the fourt line, thence runing the reverse of the \said/ fourth line south twenty five degrees west, thirty six chains to a corner in said line, thence north sixty degrees west, reverse of the first course a the said tract to where it intersects the sixth line of said tract, then to the beginning Containing two hundred and thirteeen and one third acres &c.

Patrick TRAVERSE)
vs.)
Daniel SOUTHERLAND)
Archabald McCOY, Alexr. McCOY)
Robert GILLIS, Neil McARTER) Petition
Thos. BROWN, John HAMILTON)
Peter McKELLER, Peter McARTHUR)
James MUNROW and John McNEAR) Upon which petition the court ordered the aforegoing jury to be sworn who upon their oaths do say that they find for the plaintiff the sum of two hundred and fifty pounds specie and so they say all &c.

<u>September 1782</u>   <u>Page 62</u>

Ordered that a Did. Po. issue to South Carolina to take the examination of [*blank*] BLANE in So. Carolina before [*blank*] Esqr. and make return to the next court to be held for said county, upon the prayer of Charles HUCKABY against John CHILES &c.

Thomas WADE)
vs.) Att't.
Abner WILLIAMS) In which suit the foregoing was sworn and upon their oath do say that they find for the plaintiff the sum of twenty pounds and so they say all &c.

The Clerk bound over to the next court to give evidence against William WALSH in the sum of – – £50-0. Isreal WATKINS in the same – – £50-0.

Court adjourned untill tomorrow 9 o'clock.

Met according to adjournment.

John CHILES)
vs.) Att't.
Daniel McDANIEL) In which suit the following jury was sworn (vizt) John MASK...

<u>September 1782</u>   <u>Page 63</u>

...Solomon RYE, John TURNAGE, Robert WILSON, John CROWSSON, Lott STRICKLIN, Stephen COLE, William TERRY, William McDANIEL, George BOUNDS, Joseph RYE, and Nicholas STONE who upon their oaths do say that they find for the plaintiff the sum of twenty eight pound specie and so they say all &c.

Thomas CRAWFORD and William WALL Commissioners of said county of the confiscated property came into this court and resigned &c.

State)
vs.)
John McKAY) Treason &c
Daniel McKAY)
John McKAY (miller))
Dugal KERMICAL) In which suit the following jury was sworn (vizt) John MASK, Solomon RYE, John TURNAGE, Robert WILSON, John CROWSSON, Lott STRICKLIN, Stephen COLE, William TERRY, William McDANIEL, George BOUNDS, and Joseph RYE, Nicholas STONE upon their oath say that the defendants is not guilty of any species of treason &c.

September 1782 *Page 64*

John McKAY (miller), Daniel McKAY, John McKAY, Dugal KERMICAL, and Malcom McMILLON came into this court, and took the oath of allegiance ~~to this s~~ as prescribed by law as denizens of this state &c.

State)
vs.)
John FARLEY, John BARNES) Treason
George GRAHAM, John GRAHAM)
Right FAULK) In which suit the aforegoing jury was sworn and on their oaths do say that the defendants is not guilty of any species of treason and so they say all.

John FARLEY, John BARNES, George GRAHAM, John GRAHAM and Right FAULK came into this court and took the oath \of allegiance as/ prescribed by law as citizens to this state &c.

State) Petty larceny bound in the sum of £100
vs.) Wm. WALL & Wm. WATKINS)
Charles CARTER) securities each in the sum of £50) £100-0

Sarah McKINSEY and John WEBB bound over as witnesses Sarah McKINSEY in the sum of £40 John WEBB her security in the sum of £20-0.

September 1782 *Page 65*

Isaiah STEELY bound over to the next court for petty larceny in the sum of £100-0-0. James BOUND and Charles CROWSSON his securities each in the sum of £50-0-0.

Richmond County NC Court Minutes, 1779-1786   41

John COLE, James WATSON, Robert WEBB, John CROWSSON bound over as evidences against Isaiah STEELY each in the sum of £50-0-

Court adjourned untill tomorrow 8 o'clock.

Met according to adjournments.
    Present   Charles MEDLOCK   )
                   James COLE   ) Esqrs.
                   Benjamin COVINGTON   )

State   )
    vs.   )
Isable BURT Administratrix   ) Treason
of Wm. BURT deceased for   )
~~Treason~~ In which suit the following jury was sworn (vizt) John MASK, Solomon RYE, John TURNAGE, Robert WILSON, Lott STRICKLIN, Stephen COLE, Nicholas STONE, Randolph HALEY, Daniel SNEED, John SNEED, Charles HUCKABY, and Joseph RYE who upon their oaths do say that the estate of the said William BURT deceased in the hands of Isable BURT Adminstratrix of the deceased is liable to confiscation agreeble to act of assembly and so they say all &c.

On motion of Spence? McCOY Esqr. an appeal granted & Morgan BROWN Randolph McDANIEL securities each in the sum of one hundred pounds specie &c.

September 1782   *Page 66*

State   )
    vs.   ) Treason
Daniel McDANIEL   ) In which suit the following jury was sworn (vizt) John MASK, Solomon RYE, John TURNAGE, Robert WILSON, Lott STRICKLIN, Stephen COLE, Nicholas STONE, John CROWSSON, Randolph HALEY, Daniel SNEED, John SNEED and Joseph RYE upon their oaths do say that the defendant is not guilty of any species of treason and so they say all &c.

State   )
    vs.   ) Treason
Richard LEVERETT   ) In which suit the following jury was sworn to (vizt) John MASK, Solomon RYE, John TURNAGE, Robert WILSON, Lott STRICKLIN, Stephen COLE, Nicholas STONE, Randolph HALEY, John SMITH, Daniel SNEED, John SNEED and Charles HUCKABY upon their oaths do say that the defendant is not guilty of any species of treason and so they say all &c.

State   )
   vs.   ) Treason
Benjn. POWEL) In which suit the aforegoing jury was sworn and upon their oaths do say that the defendant is not guilty of any species of treason and so they say all &c.

State   )
   vs.   ) Treason
James BOSTICK) In which suit the aforegoing jury was sworn and upon their oaths do say that the defendant is not guilty of any species of treason & so they say all &c.

September 1782   *Page 67*

State   )
   vs.   ) Treason
Malcom McMILLON) In which suit the following jury was sworn to (vizt) John MASK, Solomon RYE, John TURNAGE, Robert WILSON, \John CROWSSON,/ Lott STRICKLIN, ~~Stephen~~ \John/ COLE, Nicholas STONE, Randolph HALEY, John SMITH, Daniel SNEED, \Wm. TERRY/ and ~~Charles HUCKABY~~ \Joseph RYE, Stephen COLE/ and upon their oaths do say that the defendant is not guilty of any species of treason & so they say all &c.

State   )
   vs.   ) Treason
Thos. PERKHILL) In which suit the aforegoing jury was sworn and upon their oaths do say that the defendant is not guilty of any species of treason and so they say all &c.

State   )
   vs.   ) Treason
Thos. HATHCOCK) In which suit the aforegoing jury was sworn and upon their oaths do say that the defendant is ~~not~~ guilty ~~of any species~~ of treason and so they say all & agreeable to act of assembly &c.

State   )
   vs.   ) Treason
John THORNTON) In which suit the aforegoing jury was sworn and upon their oaths do say that John THORNTON is guilty agreeable to the act of assembly and so they say all &c.

State   )
vs.   ) Treason
Thos. CLERK) In which suit the aforegoing jury was sworn and upon their oath do say that the defendant is not guilty of any species of treason and so they say all &c.

September 1782   Page 68

State   )
vs.   ) Treason &c
Zacherias JOHNSON) In which suit the aforegoing jury was sworn upon their oaths do say that the defendant is not guilty of any species of treason and so they say all &c.

State   )
vs.   ) Treason &c
Duncan McFARLAND) In which suit the aforegoing jury was sworn and upon their oaths do say that the defendant is guilty of treason agreeable to act of assembly and so they say all &c.

Ordered that William LOVE Esqr. be allowed the priviledge to build a water grist mill on the north east side of the Pee Dee River at the place where Samuel WILLIAMS formerly had one at Blewitt's Falls &c.

On motion ordered that John COLEMANs mill \built/ on Mountain Creek be a publick grist mill &c.

State   )
vs.   )
Jacob FALCONBURY)
Thoroughgood PATE) Treason
Moses BOWMAN   )
Lenoir BREWER   )
Randolph McDANIEL) In which suit the following jury was sworn (vizt) Solomon RYE, John TURNAGE, Robert WILSON, John CROWSSON, Lott STRICKLIN, Stephen COLE, Nicholas STONE, Wm. McDANIEL, George BOUNDS, James BOUNDS, Wm. HUSBANDS and Richd. POWEL? upon their do [!] say that the defendants is not guilty of treason &c.

September 1782   Page 69

Jacob FALCONBURY, Thoroughgood PATE, Moses BOWMAN, Lenoir BREWER came into this court and took, the oath of allegiance prescribed by law as denizens of this state &c.

State)
vs.)
John PEEK) Treason
Dugal BLUE)
Sion ODOM) In which suit the aforegoing jury was sworn who upon their do say Dugal BLUE and Sion ODOM is not guilty of any species of treason so as to forfeit their estates & that John PEEK is guilty and so they say all &c. On motion in arrest of judgment as to John PEEK.

John HUNT came into court and was discharged from his recognizance &c.

State)
vs.)
Shadrack WILLIAMSON, Charles FRAZER)
Owen SLAUGHTER, Wm. BROWN) Treason
Thomas JOWERS, Samuel USHER)
Wm. JOWERS, Izra BOSTICK)
Barnaby SKIPPER, Jacob MORRIS) In which suit he following jury was sworn (vizt) Solomon RYE, John TURNAGE, Robert WILSON, John CROWSSON, Lott STRICKLIN, Stephen COLE, Nicholas STONE, Wm. McDANIEL, George BOUNDS, Wm. HUSBANDS, Daniel HICKS and Richard POWEL, who upon their oaths do say that Charles FRAZER Owen SLAUGHTER,...

September 1782   Page 70

...William BROWN, Thomas JOWERS, Samuel USHER, William JOWERS, Izra BOSTICK, Barnaby SKIPPER, and Jacob MORRIS is not guilty of any kind of treason so as to forfeit their estates and that Shadrack WILLIAMSON is guilty and so they say all &c. On motion in arrest of judgment as to Shadrack WILLIAMS[!] (reasons filed).

Charles FRAZER, Owen SLAUGHTER, Wm. BROWN, Thos. JOWERS, Samuel USHER, Wm. JOWERS, Izra BOSTICK, John THORNTON, Barnaby SKIPPER, and Jacob MORRIS came into this court and took the oath of allegiance as prescribed by law as denizens of this state &c.

Ordered that the Sheriff summon the following persons (vizt) James MERIDETH, Wm. McDANIEL, Wm. WATKINS, Laurance EVERIT, Henry ADCOCK, Thomas GIBSON, Nelson GIBSON, John COLE Sr., Thos. DOCKERY, Joseph HALL Jr., John EZZEL?, Nathl. HARRINGTON, Jesse BOUNDS, Zacha. MOREMAN, William WEBB, James EASTERLING, Josias LYONS, Simon THOMAS, Darby HANAGAN, Jacob MANGRUM, Daniel HICKS, Thomas CURTIS, Silas HALEY, Isam HALEY, Charles ROBERTSON...

September 1782

...Thomas BLEWITT, John POWERS, Samuel COVINGTON, John COVINGTON Jr., Matthew COVINGTON, George SATERFIELD, James HUNTER, Thomas EVERITT, Timothy HURLEY, Wm. THOMAS Jr., and Joseph HINES as jurior to the next court and make return thereof &c.

Stephen \COLE/ came into this court and qualified as administrator upon the estate of Isreal MEDLOCK deceased and gave bond and security agreeable to law, and ~~made a~~ returned an inventory of the deceased estate upon oath.

Ordered that the Sheriff sell all the perishable estate of Isreal MEDLOCK deceased & make return thereof to the next court &c.

Court adjourned untill court in course.

Test Wm. LOVE Clk.   Charles MEDLOCK)
                        John SPEED   )
                        Wm. LEGGATE   ) Esqrs.
                        Benjn. COVINGTON)

December 1782

At a County Court of Pleas and Quarter Sessions began and held for the County of Richmond held at the Court House therein on the last Monday in December Anno Dom. 1782.

Present   Charles MEDLOCK)
            Benjn. BEARD   )
            James COLE   ) Esqrs.
            John BOUND   )

December 1782

Ordered that John SWAY? Sr. be exempted from this time forward of paying a county tax in this county &c.

Benjn. BEARD Esqr. came into this court and qualified as administrator upon the estate of Solomon ALRED late of this county deceased returned an inventory of the deceased estate and gave bond & security agreeable to law &c.

Ordered that the Sheriff sell all the perishable estate of Solomon ALRED deceased and make return to the next court &c.

Ordered that Henry ADCOCK be exempted from serving as a jurior this term &c.

John LONG and Wm. WATKINS bound during the setting of this term, to give evidence against Wm. WALSH each in the sum of £50-0.

Court adjourned untill tomorrow 10 o'clock.

Court met according to adjournment.
    Present   Charles MEDLOCK   )
                    Henry Wm. HARRINGTON)
                    Robert WEBB   )
                    James COLE   ) Esqrs.
                    John JONES   )
                    John BOUNDS   )

December 1782

A deed from Thomas HATHCOCK to David SNEED Sr. and proved by the oath of Hendley SNEED ordered to be registred &c.

A deed from Thomas HALCOCK [*HATHCOCK*] to Hendly SNEED and proved in open court by the oath of Solomon SNEED ordered to be registred &c.

A deed from William LEGATE and wife to John MARTIN and proved in open court by the oath of William SMITH ordered to be registred.

Ordered that Isem HALEY be exempted from serving as a jurior this term &c.

Grand Jury pannelled and sworn (vizt) John COLE foreman, Wm. McDANIEL, Thomas GIBSON, Natheniel HARRING[TON?], Jesse BOUNDS, Darby HANAGAN, Wm. WEBB, Thomas BLEWITT, Silas HALEY, Timothy HURLEY, Joseph HINES, Zacherias MOREMAN, Nelson GIBSON, Wm. THOMAS, Josas LYON &c.

Izra BOSTICK came into this court and qualified as administrator upon the estate of James PRICE and gave bond and security agreeable to law &c in the sum of fifty pounds.

The Sheriff made a return of the sale Isreal MEDLOCK deceased estate to the amount of thirty five pounds fourteen shilling specie £35-14.

December 1782

Robert WEBB   )
    vs.   ) Petition
James COTTON) Upon which petition the court ordered the following jury to be sworn (vizt) Charles ROBERTSON, Wm. WATKINS, Samuel

Richmond County NC Court Minutes, 1779-1786 47

COVINGTON, Matthew COVINGTON, James HUNTER, John COVINGTON Jr., James BOUNDS, Wm. SMITH, Stephen COLE, Solomon SNEED, Isreal SNEED and John PEMBERTON who upon their oaths do say that they assess damages to the plaintiff the sum of fourty pounds specie and so they say all &c.

Ordered that the Sheriff summon the following persons to appear at the next court and shew cause if any they have why they should not be fined for their nonattendance at this court as juriors (vizt) John IZZARD, Jacob MANGRUM, James MERIDETH, Thos. DOCKERY, John POWERS, Thos. EVERITT, and Daniel HICKS and make return to the next court &c.

Ordered that the Sheriff sell all the perishable estate of James PRICE deceased and make return to the next court &c.

Robert WEBB)
   vs.) Petition
Alexander McLEOUD) In which case the ~~following~~ \aforegoing/ jury was sworn ~~(viz)~~ who upon their oaths do assess damages to the plantiff the sum of one hundred...

December 1782   Page 75

...and thirty nine pounds nine shilling specie and so they say all &c.

Court adjourned untill tomorrow 9 o'clock.

Court met according to adjournment &c.
    Present   Charles MEDLOCK)
                  James COLE   ) Esqrs.
                  John BOUNDS)

A deed from Alexander MARTIN to John MARTIN and proved in open court by the oath of John COLE Sr. ordered to be registered &c.

Barnaby SKIPPER) Defendant bound over to this court in the sum of £50.
   vs.   ) River JORDON & Thomas BROWN security each in
Robert SPEED   ) the sum of £25.   Forfeited

Same) Defendant bound over to this court in the sum of £50-0.
   vs.   ) River JORDON & Thomas BROWN security each in the sum of
Same) £25-0.   Forfeited

George HILL, Hugh McCOLLERT and Aron KNIGHT evidences against Robert SPEED each in the sum of £20-0.

John McINNISE bound over on evidence against Robert SPEED in the sum of £20-0.

December 1782   Page 76

Sarah CROWSSON administratrix   )
of Jehuele CROWSSON decd.   )
    vs.   )
Matthew TERRY, Wm. BRIGMAN   ) Petition
John MARTIN, Daniel McNEAR   )
John WATSON, Matthew WATSON   ) Upon which petition the court ordered the following jury to be sworn (vizt) Charles ROBERTSON, Wm. WATKINS, Samuel COVINGTON, Matthew COVINGTON, James HUNTER, John COVINGTON Jr., James BOUNDS, Simon THOMAS, James EASTERLING, Joseph HALL, Randolph HALEY, George CARTER upon their oaths to say that they assess damages for the plaintiff the sum of twenty three pounds eight shilling specie and so they say all &c.

A deed from John MATTHEWS to Robert WEBB Esqr. and proved in open court by the oath of Wm. JARNIGAN ordered to be registred &c.

A deed from Jonathon LEWALLEN to Robert Esqr. [*Robert WEBB?*] and proved in open court by the oath of William LEGGET ordered to be registred.

A deed from Jonathon LEWALLEN to Robert WEBB Esqr. and proved in open court by the oath of Wm. LEGGATE ordered to be registred.

A deed from Jonathon LEWALLEN to Robert WEBB Esqr. and proved in open court by the oath of Wm. LEGATE ordered to be registred.

December 1782   Page 77

A deed from William WEBB to Robert WEBB Esqr. and proved in open court by the oath of William COULTER ordered to be registred &c.

A deed from John BOUNDS Esrq. to Robert WEBB Esqr. and proved in open court by the of [!] Wm. WEBB, ordered to be registred &c.

Court adjourned untill tomorrow 10 o'clock.

Court met according to adjournment.
    Present   Charles MEDLOCK   )
                   Robert WEBB   )
                   Henry Wm. HARRINGTON   ) Esqrs.
                   John JONES   )

Ordered that George SATERFIELD be exempted from serving as a jurior this term &c.

The Last Will and Testament of William HALEY Sr. late of this county was exhibited in open court and proved in open court and proved [!] by the oath of Benjn. THOMAS who saw the other subscribing witnesses assign their names thereto, and after the said will was exhibited and duly proved Silas HALEY and William HALEY Jr. Executors came into this court and was duly qualified as executors thereto agreeable to law &c.

A deed from William HALEY Sr. To Milley HALEY and proved in open court by Benjn. THOMAS ordered to be registred.

December 1782   **Page 78**

A deed from Robert THOMAS to David PARISH and proved in open court by the oath of William WALSH ordered to be registred.

The Sheriff returned the amount of the sale of James HUTCHENS estate in specie to the amount of eleven pounds sixteen shillings and three pence &c. £11-16-3.

The Sheriff returned the account of the sale of John McGUIRE estate to the amount of twenty nine pounds fifteen shillings and three pence &c. £29-15-3.

A deed from Zacherias SMITH and wife to John COLEMAN and proved in open court by the oath of James TERRY ordered to be registred.

A deed from Zacherias SMITH and wife to John COLEMAN and proved in open court by the oath of James TERRY ordered to be registred.

A deed from William BAKER to John COLEMAN and proved in open court by the oath of Wm. LOVE ordered to be registred &c.

A deed from Isem HALEY to Henry Wm. HARRINGTON and acknowledged in open court ordered to be registred.

Court adjourned untill tomorrow 10 o'clock.

Court met according to adjournment.
      Present   James COLE   )
                          John SPEED   ) Esqrs.
                          John BOUNDS   )

December 1782

On motion made, it is ordered by the court that the following affadavit which has been made in open court by Jacob COCKRAHAM an inhabitant of this county be entered into the records of this court, in order to perpetuate the same on behalf of Daniel McPHERSON heir at law, to Alexander McPHERSON late of this county deceased. The said Jacob COCKRAHAM came into open court and being first sworn on the Holy Evangelists of God, sayeth that before the decease of the said Alexander McPHERSON he the deponent, heard the said Alexander McPHERSON anounce, declare and say that Daniel McPHERSON was his first cousin, and the nearest of kin to him; and that as such, in case the said Daniel outlived him the said Alexander McPHERSON he the said Daniel McPHERSON should inherit all his estate the said Daniel being then present and the said deponent saith, that the said Daniel lived with the said Alexander McPHERSON for the space of two years and ever was acknowledged ~~by~~ and deemed to be the deceased blood relation and first cousin and further this deponent saith not & sworn to in open court &c.

Ordered that the aforegoing affadavit be registred in the registers office of this county.

Ordered that Wm. LOVE have leave to build a water grist mill on the north prong of Solomon's Creek at the old mill place agreeable to his petition.

December 1782

Ordered that James COLE and Charles MEDLOCK be a committee to settle with the collectors for the county and publick taxes for the year 1780 and ~~eighty~~ 1781 and make report tomorrow &c.

Court adjourned untill tomorrow 8 o'clock.

Court met according to adjournment.
    Present   Charles MEDLOCK)
                    James COLE   ) Esqrs.
                    John SPEED   )

Ordered that the Sheriff summon William HUNTER, John COVINGTON and William McDANIEL to attend at the next Salisbury Superior Court as a vinire &c.

John DICKSON came into court and was bound over to the next court in the sum of £100-0-0. Richd. DICKSON and Kader? LASETER security for his appearance each in the sum of £50-0.

Ordered that the Sheriff summon John WALL, Thomas BROWN, Daniel THOMAS, Daniel SMITH, Daniel McDANIEL, Wm. BOLTON, Hugh LEATON?, Samuel CURTIS, Wm. HICKS, Barnaby SKIPPER, James BAGGETT Sr., Solomon SNEED, Hendley SNEED, John SNEED, Joseph RYE, Solomon RYE, Robert WILSON, Randolph HALEY, Benjn. MOREMAN, Wm. WATKINS Sr., Wm. NEWBERY Sr., Wm. WOODLE Kader KENDON?, John TURNAGE, Edward BROWN, Wm. COTTENGAME, David SNEED...

December 1782   *Page 81*

...Daniel SNEED, David SNEED Sr. and William EASTERLING to attend as juriors at the next court and make return thereof.

Collectors of the publick and county taxes for the years 1780 and 1781

To publick and county tax	£96929 - 6
Credit by collectors commisn. @ £3 prct	2897 - 17 - 6
Due to county and public	£94031 - 8 - 6
The net? proceeds of the publick tax for 80 and 81 is	£89660 - 5 - 6
Do County	4371 - 3
	£94031 - 8 - 6

Wm. WALL Collector of the uper districts his part to publick and county is   £33994 - 4
Commissions @ £3 prct. deducted out is   1019 - 16 - 6
    32974 - 7 - 6
Credit by money and ticket   32974 - 7 - 6

John SPEED Esqr. of the lower districts ditto publick and county is   £62935 - 2
Commissions @ £3 prct.   1878 - 1
    61057 - 1
Credit by money and ticket   61057 - 1

County tax for 1780 is   £2830 - 10
Ditto   for 1781 is   £1540 - 13
    £4371 - 3

December 1782   *Page 82*

Ordered that Dudley MASK Esqr. be appointed Collector of the uper district of this county beginning at [*blot*] Mr. Wm. BLEWITTs and runing with the Catfish Road to the widow McKATHAs, including the uper end of the county &c.

Ordered that John WALL Esqr. be appointed collector of the lower district of this county agreeable to the foregoing line &c.

Ordered that the county tax be one shilling and four pence in the hundred pound, of taxable property for the year 1782.

Ordered that Jesse COULTER be discharged from his recognizance &c.

Court adjourned untill court in course.

      Charles MEDLOCK)
Test. Wm. LOVE Clk. John SPEED) Esqrs.
      James COLE   )

March 1783

At a County Court began and held for the County of Richmond at the Court House therein on the last Monday in March in the year of our Lord Anno Dom. 1783.

 Present Charles MEDLOCK)
      Robert WEBB) Esqrs.
      John SPEED   )

March 1783

A deed from George COLLINS to Anguish NICHOLSON acknowledged in open court, ordered to be registred &c.

A deed from William WATKINS Sr. To John WATKINS acknowledged in open court, ordered to be registred &c.

A deed from Daniel SNEED to John WATKINS acknowledged in open court ordered to be registred &c.

A deed from Luke ROBERTSON to John ROBERTSON acknowledged in open court, ordered to be registred &c.

Ordered that Daniel McDANIEL be exempted from serving as a jurior this term &c.

A deed from John COCKRAHAM to Luke ROBERTSON and proved in open court by the oath of Luke ROBERTSON Jr. ordered to be registred &c.

The Last Will and Testament of John ROE late of this county deceased was proved in open court by the oath of Joseph HINES Esqr. who saw the other witnesses subscribe their names thereto, and after the said will and testament was exhibited in open court and proved Susanna ROE wife and relict of the said John ROE deceased and Executrix to the said will as therein named came into this court and was duly qualified as Executrix thereto according to law &c.

March 1783   Page 84

John CRAWFORD and John WALL Esqr. and Davis [David?] SNEED Sr. came into this court and renewed their allegiance.

Ordered that John EZEL and Daniel HICKS be excused from a fine [blot] for their not attending as juriors at the last court &c.

John WALL Esqr. came into and [!] qualified as a Justice of the Peace &c.

Daniel HICKS came into this court and made oath as a garnishee that he had no property in his hands of Jethro MOREs, at the time a certain attachment of Patrick BOGGAN's was levied on that account &c.

Grand Jury sworn (vizt) Moses CHAMBERS foreman, Wm. COTTENGAME, Daniel SMITH, Daniel THOMAS, Solomon SNEED, Hendley SNEED, John SNEED, Randolph HALEY, Wm. WOODLE, David SNEED Sr., Daniel SNEED, David SNEED Jr., Wm. EASTERLING, and Wm. WATKINS Sr.

Court adjourned till tomorrow 10 o'clock.

Met according to adjournment.
    Present   Charles MEDLOCK)
                    John WALL   ) Esqrs.
                    Robert WEBB   )

March 1783   Page 85

Wm. WATKINS Jr. bound over unto this court by Charles MEDLOCK Esqr. in the sum of £50-0 for petit larceny. Robert WEBB Esqr. security in the sum of £50-0. David SNEED Sr. Prosecutor in the sum of £50-0.

John DICKSON bound over unto next court and to be of good behaviour in the mean time in the sum of £50-0. John WALL Esqr. security in the sum of £50-0.
                                                          Released &c.

A deed from George WEBB and wife to Henry ADCOCK proved in open court by the affirmation of Archelus MOREMON ordered to be registred &c.

A deed from Henry ADCOCK and wife to Thos. CRAWFORD and proved in open court by the affirmation of Archelus MOREMON ordered to be registred &c.

A Did. Po. to issue to South Carolina in behalf of John BARNES in the suit of John NORTON to take the examination of Nihemiah RANDOLPH before [blank] Esqr. and make return to the next court &c.

A deed from Luke ROBERTSON to Hugh LEATON? and proved in open court by the oath of Jesse JONES ordered to be registred &c.

March 1783   *Page 86*

A deed from Natheniel WILLIAMS to Nelson GIBSON proved in open court by the oath of Thos. GIBSON ordered to be registred &c.

A deed from Solom. GROSS to Solomon SPRAWLS; proved in open court by the oath of Wm. PICKITT ordered to be registred &c.

James WATSON, Irvine McINTOSH, John PARNEL came into this court and took the oath of allegiance prescribed by law as free denizens of this state &c.

Ordered that Duncan McFARLAND be appointed overseer of the road that leads from the Polley Bridge at Gum Swamp to the line of Bladen County crossing Shew-Heel at the rockey ford, and that all the hands in Captain CARMICALs company work thereon &c.

Ordered that John BOUNDS Esqr. be appointed overseer of the road that leads from the Court-House to the Polley Bridge on Gum Swamp, and all the hands contiguous work thereon &c.

Ordered that Daniel SNEED be appointed Captain of the Patroll from Solomon's Creek to Hitchcock Creek and that David Jr. [!] Benjn. MOREMAN, Randolph HALEY and John SNEED be his company.

March 1783   *Page 87*

Ordered that Thos. EVERITT be excused from paying a fine [blot] for his nonattendance as a jurior at the last court &c.

Ordered John EZEL be appointed Capt. of the Patroll from Hitcock to Cartledges Creek, and that Christopher and Richd. REYNOLDS, Peter MOLTON?, John CAMPBLE Jr. and Laurance EVERITT be his company &c.

Richmond County NC Court Minutes, 1779-1786

Ordered that Edward WILLIAMS \Esqr./ be appointed Capt. of the Patroll from Cartledges Creek to Mountain Creek and Thomas HINES, John HILYARD, John LYONS, Wm. SEAMONS and Richd. ADAMS be his company &c.

Ordered that Wm. LOVE Esqr. be appointed Captain of the Patroll from Mountain Creek to Little River and that Hugh LEATON, Walter LEAK, John HEWS, Solomon GROSS, and Wm. McDANIEL be his company &c.

Ordered that Duncan McFARLAND be appointed Capt. of the Patroll in Capt. CARMICALs company and that Malcom BLUE, John McINNISE Malichi DEES, Duncan McBRIDGE, Daniel McINNISE, John McPHERSON, and Daniel CARMICAL be his company &c.

March 1783   Page 88

Benjamin BEARD Esqr. Administrator of Solomon ALRED made a return of the sale of the said estate upon oath to the amount of seventeen pounds eight shilling and six pence &c £17-8-6.

A deed from John MASON to Mary McKASKILL proved in open court by the oath of John McCALMON ordered to be registred.

Wm. HUNTER laid in his claim and was allowed the sum of seven pounds two shillings and a penny £7-2-1.

A deed from Vinson DAVIS to John HORRY proved in open court by the oath of Joseph HINES ordered to be registred &c.

Wm. PICKETT   ) Case
   vs.   ) Attcht.
Daniel McINNISE) In which suit the following jury was sworn (viz) Thomas BROWN, Wm. HUNTER, John CROWSSON, Darby HANAGAN, John JAMES, James POSTON, Wm. SMITH, Wm. COULTER, Joseph HINES, James BAGGETT, Charles HUCKABY, Nicholas [! *Nicholas STONE?*] upon their oaths do say assess damages the plaintiff to the amount of eleven pounds and the cost? and so they say all &c.

Court adjourned till tomorrow 9 o'clock.

Met according to adjournment.

March 1783

Present   Charles MEDLOCK   )
               John BOUNDS   ) Esqrs.
               Benjn. COVINGTON)

A deed from Charles ROBERTSON to Benjn. POWEL acknowledged in open court ordered to be registred.

A deed from Stephen PARKER and wife to Norman McLEOD? proved in open court by the oath of Wm. JORDON ordered to be registred &c.

A Did. Po. to issue to Bladen \and Cumberland Counties/ to take the examination of sundry witnesses in behalf of John McCRANEY, &c.

Ordered that Darby HANAGAN be appointed Capt. of the Patroll, in Capt. EASTERLINGs company, and that Samuel PATE, John BETHIGH Wm. PEARCE, Shadrick WILLIAMSON, Stephen PATE, and Sion ADAM be his company &c.

Charles ROBERTSON)
     vs.   ) Genl. Issue
Solo. GROSS   ) In which suit the following jury was sworn (vizt) Thos. CRAWFORD, Alexander GORDON, John CROWSSON, Wm. WEBB, Solomon DEARMAN, Wm. WALL, Wm. McGUIRE, Wm. WATKINS, Solomon SPRAWLS, Lott STRICKLIN, George BOUNDS, Hugh LEATON, upon their oaths do say that they assess damages for the plaintiff the sum of thirteen pounds fifteen shillings and six pence with cost and so they say all &c.
£13-15-6.

March 1783

Wm. GAINER)
     vs.   ) Attcht.
Matthew TERRY) In which suit the aforegoing jury was sworn and upon their oaths do say that they assess damages for the plaintiff the sum of sixteen pound specie and cost and so they say all &c.

Mary BLUE and Dugal BLUE came into this court and prayed letters of administration upon the estate of John BLUE and gave bond and security in the sum of one hundred pounds and was duly qualified as administrator &c.

Ordered that the Sheriff sell all the perishable estate of John BLUE late if this county deceased and make return to the next court.

Dudley MASK Esqr. came into court and gave bond and security agreeable to law as collector of the uper district of this county &c.

Alexand GORDON came into this court and made oath as garnishee that he had no property of Murdock McDANIELs in his hands at the time Robert WEBB Esqr. had his attachment levied in \his/ hands against the \said/ McDANIEL &c.

John BULL came into court and was discharged from his recognizance.

Did. Po. to issue to Bladen County to take the examination of Robert WILSON in behalf of the State against Silas OVERSTREET, &c.

March 1783 — Page 91

Isaac BRIGMAN came into this court and was bound over to the next Salisbury Superior Court, to answear a charge of murder and treason in the sum of £100-0.

Solomon DEARMON and Nicholas GREEN securities each in the sum of £50-0.

On motion Wm. MASK was allowed his ticket containing the sum of £6-0-0.

Court adjourned untill tomorrow 9 o'clock.

Court met according to adjournment.
    Present   Charles MEDLOCK   )
               Benjn. BEARD   )
               Benjn. COVINGTON   ) Esqrs.
               John BOUNDS   )

Daniel McDANIEL) Att't.
    vs.   ) Def. Inq.
Charles CHEARS) In which suit the following jury was sworn (viz) Solomon DEARMAN, Solomon RYE, Hugh LEATON, Wm. WATKINS, John CROWSSON, John COLE, William WALL, Walter LEAK, Isaac YATES, Thomas CRAWFORD, Zacherias MARTIN, Josiah LYON, upon their oaths do say that they assess damages for the plaintiff the sum of [blank] and so they say all.

March 1783 — Page 92

Dudley MASK Esqr. Commissioner in the uper district of this county came into this court and settled his accounts as Commissioner of the specific tax for the year 1781 as followeth:

Assessment in the uper district is	£142553 - 14
Deduction of money and money at interest	14431 -
Amount of the assessment is	£128122 - 14
	Barrels B. Peck
At one peck of corn prct. is	64 - 2 - 2
By commissions at £5 prct.	3 - 1
	61 - 1 - 2
By insolvents allowed by court	3 - - 2
Balance due to the publick	58 - 1 - 0

The ballance due from the collector to the public upears to be fifty eight barrels and one bushel of corn as pr. settlement.

State)
vs.) Ind. Petty Lar.
Kedar LASETER) In which suit the following jury was sworn (vizt) Solomon DEARMAN, Solomon RYE, Hugh LEATON, Wm. WATKINS, John CROWSSON, William WALL, Walter LEAK, Isaac YATES, Thomas CRAWFORD, Jesse BOUNDS, Daniel McDANIEL, and George BOUNDS upon their oaths do say that the defendant is not guilty in manner & form as charged in the bill of indictment and so they say all &c.

March 1783   Page 93

Ordered that the Sheriff [!] James HICKS, Duncan McFARLAND, Solomon DEARMAN, Sterling WILLIAMSON, Daniel McKAY, Daniel KERMICAL, Dugal BLUE, Thomas SUMMERLAND, Solomon RYE, Silas HALEY, Thomas MOREMAN, John JAMES, Wm. TERRY, John COLE, Stephen COLE, Josias LYON, Daniel McDANIEL, Solomon GROSS, Wm. WALL, Thomas CRAWFORD, Joseph HINES, Simon THOMAS, John COVINGTON, Henry COVINGTON, Wm. JERNIGAN, John COLEMAN, Walter LEAK, John MASK, Wm. MASK, and Jesse BOUNDS to serve as juriors at the next court and make return thereof &c.

John LONG Jr. came into this court as garnishee and upon \oth/ says that he has a fiddle in his hands the property of Wm. CHEVES.

Ordered that the collector of the uper district of this county deposit the enumerated articles to be received in the payment of taxes for the year 1782 at Colo. Edward WILLIAMS &c.

Ordered that Sterling WILLIAMSON be appointed to serve as Constable the insuing year &c.

Did. Po. to issue to Cumberland County to take the examination of Wm. COCKRAHAM before Wm. LEAK Esqr.

March 1783　　　　　　　　　　　　　　　　Page 94

Ordered that the collector of the lower district of this county deposit the enumerated articles to be received in the payment of taxes for the year 1782 at John WALL Esqr. &c.

Ordered that Aron NIGHT be appointed to serve as Constable the insuing &c.

Court adjourned untill court in course.

Test. Wm. WALL Clk.
　　　　　　Charles MEDLOCK　）
　　　　　　Benjn. COVINGTON　） Esqr.
　　　　　　John BOUNDS　　　）

June 1783

At a County Court of Pleas and Quarter Sessions began and held for the County of Richmond at the Court House therein on the last Monday in June Anno Dom. 1783.
　Present　　Charles MEDLOCK　　　　）
　　　　　　Henry Wm. HARRINGTON　） Esqrs.
　　　　　　John SPEED　　　　　　　　）

Ordered, that the court proceed upon balloting for the several officers necessary to serve in this county for the insuing year on Wednesday the third day in this term &c.

Ordered that Solomon GROSS be excused from serving as a jurior this term &c.

June 1783　　　　　　　　　　　　　　　　Page 95

Grand Jury sworn (vizt) John COVINGTON Sr. foreman, Henry COVINGTON, Jesse BOUNDS, John MASK, Wm. JERNIGAN, Walter LEAK, Daniel McDANIEL, Stephen COLE, Wm. TERRY, John JAMES, Silas HALEY, Solomon RYE, Thos. SUMMERAL, Sterling WILLIAMSON, Solomon DEARMAN and Duncan McFARLAND &c.

Court adjourned untill tomorrow 9 o'clock.

Court met according to adjournment.
　Present　　Charles MEDLOCK　）
　　　　　　Robert WEBB　　　　）
　　　　　　James COLE　　　　　） Esqrs.
　　　　　　Benjn. BEARD　　　　）
　　　　　　Benjn. COVINGTON　）

John EZEL bound over to this term for an assault &c in the sum of £100-0-0. Edward ALMOND security in the sum of £100-0. Wm. WALL prosecutor in the sum of £50-0.

Evidences bound (vizt) John WALL Esqr. Lott STRICKLIN and Matthew COVINGTON each in the sum of £50-0.

A deed from John COVINGTON Jr. to Archabold McMILLON proved in open court by the oath of John SPEED Esqr. ordered to be registred &c.

June 1783   *Page 96*

A deed from Valentine MORRIS to Elisha PARKER proved in open court by the oath of Robert WEBB Esqr. ordered to be registred.

Ordered that Daniel HICKS be sited to appear before this court now seting at the Court House on thirday the day in this term in order to settle with the court the estate of Nicholas STONE deceased.

John EZEL bound over to the next court for an assault &c in the sum of £50-0.

Edward ALMOND security in the sum of £50-0. John WALL Esqr., Lott STRICKLIN, Burrell STRICKLIN and Matthew COVINGTON in ~~the sum of~~ evidences ~~in~~ each in the sum of £25-0-0.

John EZEL bound over to the next court for a contempt in the sum of £50-0. Edward ALMOND security in the sum of £50-0. John WALL Esqr., Lott STRICKLIN, Burrell STRICKLIN and Matthew COVINGTON evidences each in the sum of £25-0-0.

Ordered that John CRAWFORD Esqr. be appointed Surveyor of this county protemporary untill furth provission be made by act of assembly &c.

June 1783   *Page 97*

Ordered that Elisabeth POSTON daughter of Robert POSTON deceased be bound unto John WALL Esqr. untill she arrive to the age of eighteen years, she now being fifteen year and nine months old &c.

Ordered that Walter LEAK be appointed overseer of the road from the ford of Little River to the middle of Mountain Creek bridge and the hands contiguous work thereon &c.

Ordered that the Sheriff bring the children of Mary MAYFIELD and Lucy? JONES to the next court to be dealt with according as the law directs &c.

Richmond County NC Court Minutes, 1779-1786   61

Court adjourned untill tomorrow 9 10 o'clock.

Court met according to adjournment.
Present   Charles MEDLOCK   )
            Benjn. BEARD   )
            John SPEED   ) Esqrs.
            Benjn. COVINGTON   )

A deed from Isum HALEY and wife to Joseph HINES proved in open court by the oath of Morgan BROWN ordered to be registred.

Ordered that Henry ADCOCK be appointed overseer of the road in room of Duncan McFARLAND.

A deed from James POSTON to John McCAUL proved in open court by the oath of Joseph HINES? ordered to be registred &c.

June 1783   Page 98

A deed from Micajah PUCKITT to Wm. PUCKITT and proved in open court by the oath of James PUCKITT ordered to be registred.

Ordered that Edward WILLIAMS Esqr. be appointed to serve as Sheriff the insuing year.

Ordered that Benjamin COVINGTON be appointed Ranger for the County of Richmond.

Ordered that Morgan BROWN Esqr. be appointed Attorney for the State in this county during good behavior.

John DICKSON came into this court and was discharged from his recognizance.

Henry Wm. HARRINGTON Esqr.   )
           vs.   )
John MASON, Solomon SPRAWLS,)
John BENNETT, Wm. BENNETT   ) Case
Daniel McCAUL, David McCAUL   )
Christopher McCRAY   ) In which suit the following jury was sworn (vizt) Joseph HINES, Darby HANAGAN, Wm. HUNTER Sr., Daniel HICKS, James POSTON, Daniel SMITH, Ezra BOSTICK, David SNEED Jr., John SMITH, John PEMBERTON, George BOUNDS, and Jacob MANGRUM who upon their oaths do say that the assess damages for the plaintiff the sum of seven hundred pounds specie and so they say all &c.

June 1783   *Page 99*

Ordered that John CRAWFORD, Charles MEDLOCK and John SPEED Esqrs. be ordered to appraise the estate of John DONALDSON deceased and make return to court &c.

[blot] Joseph STRICKLIN bound over to the next court for petty larceny in the sum of £50-0-0. Silas OVERSTREET security in the sum of £50-0.

Henry Wm. HARRINGTON Esqr.)
    vs.)
John JINKINS, George SLAUGHTER) [blot] Case
Samuel USHER, Thos. USHER)
George COLLINS   ) In which suit the aforegoing jury was sworn who upon their oaths do say that they assess damages for the plaintiff the sum of two hundred eighty pounds specie against John JINKINS and George COLLINS — and that George SLAUGHTER, Thos. USHER and Samuel USHER is not guilty of the charge of trespass brought against them and so they say all &c.

Court adjourned untill tomorrow 9 o'clock.

Met according to adjournment.
    Present   Benjn. BEARD   )
                       James COLE   )
                       John BOUNDS   ) Esqrs.
                       Benjn. COVINGTON)

June 1783   *Page 100*

The Last Will and Testament of George FREEMAS was exhibited to this court and and duly proved by the oath of John COLE and Josiah FREEMAN, who saw the witness assign his name thereto–and after the said Last Will and Testament of George FREEMAN late of this county deceased was exhibited in open court and duly proved Elisabeth FREEMAN and George BOUNDS the Executors therein named came into this court and and was duly qualified as executors thereto according to law &c.

Thos. BROWN)
    vs.   ) Att't.
Rice? HENDERSON   ) Def. Inqy.
Nicholas HENDERSON) In which suit the following jury was sworn Daniel HICKS, Thos. CRAWFORD, Moses CHAMBERS, John COLE Sr., James BOUNDS, William HUSBANDS, John SMITH, Thos. BLEWITT, Nicholas STONE, Natheniel HARRINGTON, Ezra BOSTICK, Wm.

WEBB, upon their oaths do say that they find damages for the plaintiff the sum of seventeen pounds four shillings specie and so they say all &c.

John McCOY)
vs.) Case
Moses BOWMAN) In which suit the...

June 1783   *Page 101*

...aforegoing jury was sworn who upon their oaths do say that they find for the plaintiff one penny and six pence cost and so they say all &c.

Benjn. BEARD Admr.)
of Solomon ALRED decd.) Case debt
vs.)
Wm. ASHLEY) In which suit the aforegoing jury was sworn who upon their oaths do say that they find for the plaintiff one pound and the cost and so they say all &c.

A deed from John WALL and wife to Thos. CRAWFORD proved in open court by the oath of James COLE ordered to be registred.

Ordered that the Sheriff be allowed the sum of fifteen pounds specie from March court 1782 to June court 1783.

Ordered that the Clerk be allowed the sum of twenty pounds specie from March court 1782 to June court 1783.

John CRAWFORD)
vs.) Debt
Wm. NEWBERY) In which suit the aforegoing jury was sworn and upon their oaths do say that they find for the plaintiff the sum of twenty pounds eleven shillings and six pence and interest till paid and so they say all &c.

June 1783   *Page 102*

Ordered that the Sheriff summon Thos. GIBSON, Nelson GIBSON, Laurance OBRYAN, Thos. ADAMS, Richd. ADAMS, Timothy HURLEY, John DAWKINS, Samuel DAWKINS, Moses CHAMBERS, George SATERFIELD, James HUNTER, Simon THOMAS, Daniel THOMAS, Daniel SMITH, Josias LYON, Wm. HUSBAND, John JAMES Jr., John PARNEL, Thos. BLEWITT, John CROWSSON, Thos. EVERITT, Hendly SNEED, David SNEED Sr., David SNEED Jr., John SNEED, Isreal SNEED, Daniel SNEED, Daniel HICKS, Wm. WATKINS, Derby HANAGAN, John BARNS, John COVINGTON Jr., Matthew COVING-

TON, Lott STRICKLIN, Isaac YATES, James YATES, as juriors at the next court and make return thereof &c.

Ordered that Isaac WILLIAMSON be appointed to serve as Constable the insuing year.

Ordered that Thomas BROWN be appointed to serve as Constable the insuing year.

Ordered that Moses CHAMBERS, Thos. BLEWITT and Walter LEAK be appointed to serve at Salisbury Superior on the fifteenth day of September next as a venire.

Ordered that James COLE Esqr. be appointed to take the inventorys of all the inhabitants from the lower end of the county up to Maskes Creek and from the head of said creek along the old road to Coles Bridge.

June 1783   *Page 103*

Ordered that John SPEED Esqr. be appointed to take the inventory of all the inhabitants from Maskes Creek to Hitchcock Creek, and from the head of said creek a direct course to the Cumberland line.

Ordered that Benjn. BROWN Esqr. be appointed to take the inventory of all the inhabitants from Hitch-cock Creek up to Bigg Mountain Creek and to extend out upon direct lines from heads of said creeks to the Cumberland line &c.

Ordered that Dudley MASK Esqr. be appointed to take the inventory of all the inhabitants from Bigg Mountain Creek to the uper end of the county &c.

Ordered that John WALL, Benjn. BEARD and John CRAWFORD Esqrs. be appointed assessors for the year 1783 and make return to the next court &c.

John CRAWFORD, Charles MEDLOCK and John SPEED Esqrs. appraisers of John DONALDSON estate late of this county deceased made their return of their appraisement of the said estate to the amount of eleven hundred and eighty eight pounds one shilling and ten pence specie &c.

June 1783   *Page 104*

A bond from Wm. HUSBAND to Thos. CRAWFORD in the sum of one hundred and fifty pounds specie and attested by John SPEED and James COLE Esqrs. bearing date the third day of July 1783 to make good the title of a tract of land &c.

Robert WEBB Esqr. comes into this court and made a resignation of his entry takers appointment.

Ordered that Thomas CRAWFORD be appointed Entry Taker for this county upon giving bond and approved security agreeable to law &c.

John BOUNDS came into this court as garnishee and upon oath says that he has nothing in his hands of the property of Wm. CHEVES &c.

Ordered that John COLE Sr. be appointed overseer of the road from his bridge to the cross road and the hands contiguous work thereon.

Ordered that William SMITH be appointed overseer of the road from Falling Creek to the cross road and the hands contiguous work thereon &c.

Ordered that Wm. LOVE be allowed the sum of one pound for one book found for the use of the county &c.

June 1783   Page 105

Court adjourned untill court in course.
        Charles MEDLOCK)
Test Wm. LOVE Clk. James COLE   ) Esqrs.
        John BOUNDS)

September 1783

At a County Court began and held for the County of Richmond at the Court House therein on the last Monday in September Anno Dom. 1783.
  Present Charles MEDLOCK)
       James COLE   ) Esqrs.
       John SPEND [SPEED])

A deed from Derby HANAGAN to James PHILLIPS acknowledged in open court ordered to be registred &c.

Ordered that the widow McKATHA be discharged from paying a fourfold tax for the year 1780, 1781 and 1782 upon the assessment of £300-0.

On motion Samuel GARLAND Esqr. from Virginia one of the Execr. of George JEFFERSON deceased came into this court and returned an inventory in part of the said JEFFERSON's estate &c.

Ordered that one negroe of John CRAWFORD be put in the lowest class by reason of bodily infirmities.

September 1783

A grand jury &c. Derby HANAGAN foreman, Thos. GIBSON, Nelson GIBSON, Laurance OBRYAN, Timothy HURLEY, Simon THOMAS, Daniel THOMAS, Daniel SMITH, John JAMES Jr., Hendley SNEED, David SNEED Jr., John SNEED, Isreal SNEED, Daniel SNEED, and Daniel HICKS &c.

Peggy DICKSON came into court and made oath that the child she now has by the name of Dorcas, is a bastard, and Josiah FREEMAS is the father of her child (to wit Dorcas) and is likly to become chargable to the parish &c.

Court adjourned untill tomorrow 10 o'clock.

Met according to adjourment.
    Present   Charles MEDLOCK)
                   James COLE   ) Esqrs.

A deed from John JINKINS to William McDANIEL proved in open court by the oath of Owen SLAUGHTER Jr. ordered to be registred.

A deed from James SANDERS to Wm. McDANIEL proved in open court by the oath of Owen SLAUGHTER Jr. ordered to be registred.

A deed from John JINKS [JINKINS?] to William McDANIEL proved in open court by the oath of Daniel McDUFFEE, ordered to be registred.

A deed from Thomas JOWERS to Wm. McDANIEL proved in open court by the oath of Daniel McDUFFEE ordered to be registred.

September 1783

A deed from Joseph PLEDGER to William EASTERLING proved in open court by the oath of James EASTERLING ordered to be registred.

A deed from John BOUNDS to Henry ADCOCK ~~proved~~ \acknowledged/ in open court ~~by the oath of~~ ordered to be registred.

A deed from Benjn. HERRING to Henry Wm. HARRINGTON Esqr. and acknowledged in open court ordered to be registred.

Thomas CRAWFORD)
    vs.   ) Case Def. Inqy.
John NORTON   ) In which suit the following jury was sworn (vizt) James HUNTER, Thos. ADAMS, Samuel DAWKINS, John PARNEL, Thomas EVERITT, William WATKINS, John COVINGTON Jr., Lott

STRICKLIN, Isaac YATES, James YATES, Richard HILL, Matthew COVINGTON who upon their oaths to say that they find for the plaintiff the sum of nine pound twelve shillings specie & cost and so they say all &c.

A deed from Daniel HICKS and wife to Samuel CURTISS acknowledged in open court ordered to be registred.

Court adjourned untill tomorrow 10 o'clock.

Met according to adjournment.
 Present James COLE   )
       John SPEED   )
       Benjn. COVINGTON) Esqrs.
       John BOUND   )

September 1783   Page 108

A Did. Po. to issue to Bladen to take the examination of John MARTIN, James WILSON and James SMILEY in behalf of John CURRY, in the suit of John PARNEL, and subpa. to issue for Sarah McMILLON, Anguish McMILLON of this county &c.

Solomon GROSS)
 vs.   ) Att't.
Alexander McDANIEL) In which suit the following jury was sworn (vizt) James HUNTER, Thos. ADAMS, Samuel DAWKINS, John PARNEL, Thomas EVERIT, William WATKINS, Wm. HUNTER, Charles HUCKABY, James YATES, Richd. HILL, Edmund BROWN, and Matthew COVINGTON who upon their oaths do say that they find for the plaintiff the sum of twenty five pound six shillings with cost of suit <u>suit</u> and so they say all &c.

Wm. SEALS   )
 vs.   ) Case
Murdock McDANIEL) In which suit the aforegoing jury was sworn who upon their oath do say that they find for the plaintiff the sum of fifteen pounds specie and so they say all.

Ordered that Joseph Sr. [!] be exempted from paying a publick or county taxes by reason of his age and infirmity.

Owen SLAUGHTER Sr. came into this court and made oath that he was not ready to come to tryal in the suit Henry Wm. HARRINGTON against him &c.

September 1783

Robert WILSON)
    vs.   ) Case
Wm. HUNTER) In which suit the following jury was sworn (vizt) Thos. ADAMS, Samuel DAWKINS, John PARNEL, Thomas EVERIT, Wm. WATKINS, Charles HUCKABY, James YATES, Richd. HILL, Edmund BROWN, Matthew COVINGTON, Wm. COLTER, and Wm. McGUIRE upon their oaths do say that they find for the plaintiff the sum of twenty one pounds eighteen shilling specie and six pence cost and so they say all &c.

Henry Wm. HARRINGTON)
    vs.   ) Judi'l. Att't.
John COCKRAHAM) In which suit the following jury was sworn (vizt) James HUNTER, Thos. ADAMS, Samuel DAWKINS, John PARNEL, Thos. EVERIT, William WATKINS, Wm. HUNTER Sr., Charles HUCKABY, James YATES, Richd. HILL, Edmund BROWN, and Matthew COVINGTON upon their oaths do say that they find for the plaintiff the sum of two hundred pound & six pence cost and so they say all &c.

Ordered that Solomon DEARMAN be appointed overseer of the road beginning two miles and a half beyond the Chalk Fork out of the road that lead from Cole Bridge to Haley's Ferry, and thence along the old bridle path to James cowpens, thence to the head of the Juniper and thence to Betty's Bridge on Drowning Creek and the hands [blot] contiguous work thereon &c.

September 1783

Jacob COCKRAHAM)
    vs.   ) Case
John McCRANEY) In which suit the aforegoing jury was sworn, and upon their oaths do say that they find for the plaintiff the sum of ninty six pounds specie and six pence cost and so they say all &c.

Did. Po. to issue to So. Carolina in the behalf of James POSTON in the suit of Benjn. HERRING to take the examination of sundry witnesses &c.

Rachel ROE came into this court and was fined the sum of two pounds ten shilling for bearing of a bastard child and entred unto? bound with Solomon GROSS security for maintaining the child and keeping it off the parish.

Ordered that Samuel CHAPPLIN orphan of Wm. CHAPLIN deceased now the age of eight years old, the first day of January next insuing be bound unto John USSERY untill he arrive to the age of twenty one.

Richmond County NC Court Minutes, 1779-1786

Ordered that Wm. CHAPLIN orphan of Wm. CHAPLIN deceased now the age of eleven years old this present term, be bound unto Susanna ROE, untill he becomes the age of twenty one.

Ordered that Joseph SIMKINS be appointed to serve as Constable the insuing year &c.

Court adjourned untill tomorrow 10 o'clock.

September 1783   Page 111

Court met according to adjournment.
    Present   Charles MEDLOCK   )
                   Henry Wm. HARRING[!]) [HARRINGTON]
                   Dudley MASK   ) Esqrs.
                   John BOUND   )
                   Benjn. COVINGTON   )

A deed from Wm. THOMAS to Simon [!] and proved in open court by the oath of Benjn. COVINGTON Esqr. ordered to be registered.

Farquar McCRAY)
    vs.   ) Case
Joseph SIMKINS) In which suit the following jury was sworn (vizt) James HUNTER, Thomas ADAMS, Samuel DAWKINS, John PARNEL, Thos. EVERITT, John COVINGTON Jr., Lott STRICKLIN, James YATES, Richd. HILL, Matthew COVINGTON, William DAWKINS, and John LONG who upon their oath do say that they find for the defendant and so they say all &c.

A deed from James POSTON to John SPEED Esqr. proved in open court by the oath of John WALL Esqr. ordered to be registered &c.

John JOWERS)
    vs.   ) Att't. Def. Inqy.
Wm. HUNTER Jr.) In which suit the following jury was sworn (vizt) Thomas ADAMS...

September 1783   Page 112

...Samuel DAWKINS, John PARNEL, Thomas EVERITT, John COVINGTON Jr., Lott STRICKLIN, James YATES, Richard HILL, Matthew COVINGTON, Wm. DAWKINS, John LONG, Edmund BROWN, upon their oaths do say that they find for the plaintiff the sum of twelve pounds specie and six pence cost and so they say all &c.

A deed from John CHILES to Jonathon NEWBERY proved in court by the oath of Wm. NEWBERY, ordered to be registered.

Edward WILLIAMS Esqr. came into this court and qualified as Sheriff the insuing year and gave bond, and security, also as County Treasurer and Commissioner of the Publick Property &c.

Duncan McFARLAND bound over to the next court for an assault upon Moses JOHNSON in the sum of £50-0. Stephen COLE security in the sum of £50-0.

Duncan McFARLAND bound over to the next court for assaulting Moses JOHNSON in the sum of £50-0. Stephen COLE security in the sum of £50-0.

Court adjourned untill tomorrow 10 o'clock.

Met according to adjournment.
    Present   Charles MEDLOCK   )
                    Henry Wm. HARRINGTON) Esqr.
                    Benjn. COVINGTON   )

<u>September 1783</u>   <u>Page 113</u>

A deed from James POSTON to ~~Morgan BROWN~~ John POWERS, proved in open court by the oath of Morgan BROWN, ordered to be registered &c.

A deed from James POSTON to John CAMPBLE proved in open court by the oath of Charles MEDLOCK Esqr. &c.

Edward WILLIAMS Esqr. came into this court, as garnishee to declare what property he has in his hand of the estate of Charles HARBERT who says upon oathat he is indebted to the said Charles HARBERT, (at the time an attch't. of Henry Wm. HARRINGTON Esqr. was levied in hands) the sum of one hundred pounds specie on a promissory note due in January or February one thousand seven hundred and eighty five, and confessed judgment, for the sum above mentioned with stay of execution, till, [blank]

Wm. JORDON)
    vs.   ) Case
John DAVIS   ) In which suit the following jury was sworn (vizt) James HUNTER, Thos. ADAMS, Samuel DAWKINS, John PARNEL, Thos. EVERITT, Wm. WATKINS, John COVINGTON Jr., Lott STRICKLIN, James YATES, Richard HILL, Matthew COVINGTON, and William WEBB, upon their oath do say that they find for the defendant and so they say all.

September 1783 *Page 114*

Edward WILLIAMS Esqr. came into this court and protested against the insufficiency of the goal [*jail*].

Ordered that Zacherias MOREMAN be appointed overseer of the road from Haley ferry over Hitchcock at Mr. WADEs mill to the fork in the road near Colo. CRAWFORDs and that Jesse BOUND, Wm. JARNIGAN, Archibald MOREMAN, John EZEL, Robert WEBB, Edward ALMOND, Robert WILSON, John HALL, Jacob LAMPLEY?, Lott STRICKLIN, Thomas ADCOCK, Thos. MOREMAN, John MOREMAN, Peter MOLTON, & Isem HALEY work thereon &c.

John CRAWFORD, Benjn. BEARD and John WALL Esqr. assessors, for the year 1783 for this county made a return of their assessment to the amount of fifty two thousand six hundred and ninty two pounds eleven shilling — the court reviewed their return and allowed the said assessors the sum of two dollars pr. day each for six days.

Court adjourned till tomorrow 10 o'clock.

Met according to adjournment.
    Present   Charles MEDLOCK)
                     James COLE   ) Esqrs.
                     Robert WEBB   )

John SPEED Esqr. collector of the lower district of this county came into this...

September 1783 *Page 115*

...court and settled his accounts as commissioner of the specific tax for the year 1781.

The amount of the assessment in the lower district is	£218405 - 9 - 5
Money and money upon interest deducted out is	9647 - 7 - 4
Neat proceeds of assessment is	£208758 - 2 - 1

The tax on £208758-2-1 at one peck of corn ~~pret.~~ amounts in corn to be as follows:

	Barrels B. P.
	115 - 3 - 1
Credit by commission at 5 prct.	5 - 3 - 3
	109 - 4 - 2
By insolvents allowed by the court	8 - 2 - 1
Due to the publick	101 - 2 - 1

There appears to be due from John SPEED Esqr. as collector to the publick one hundred and one barrels two bushels and a peck of corn as pr. settlement.

A deed from Edward WILLIAMS as Sheriff to William JOHNSON, acknowledged in open court ordered to be registred.

Charles MEDLOCK Esqr. came into this court and settled upon oath for his collection of the specific tax for the year 1782.   turn over

September 1783   Page 116

Total amount of the assessment for the year 1782 is	£45706 - 3
At one bushel of corn prct. Is	457 -
To supernumeries	18 - 3
	475 - 3
Credit by insolvents allowed by court	72 -
Due the publick	403 - 3

From the settlement with the collector there appear due to the publick for the specific tax for the year 1782 four hundred and three bushels and three pecks of corn as pr. settlement &c.

Ordered that the Sheriff summons Richard ADAMS, John JONES, Wm. JERNIGAN, George BOUND, Jesse BOUNDS, Wm. WEBB, Silas HALEY, John CRAWSSON, Wm. HUSBANDS, Joseph GADD Jr., John COLEMAN, John LONG Sr., Wm. MORE, Joseph HALL, John HALL, John COVINGTON Sr., Henry COVINGTON, Wm. HUNTER Sr., Dun RYE, David SNEED Sr., Josias LYON, Wm. TERRY, Wm. McGUIRE, Wm. McDANIEL, Wm. SMITH, Nathl. HARRINGTON, Laurance EVERITT, Thos. CRAWFORD, Isem HALEY, Zachs. MOREMAN as juriors to attend at the next court and make return thereof.

John COLEMAN was allowed upon his vinire tickitt the sum of £5-4.

Benjn. DUMAS was allowed upon his vinire tickitt the sum of £5-13.

September 1783   Page 117

Sampson WILLIAMS (Constable) exhibited his claim to court for summoning of sundry persons to give in their list of taxable property, and was allowed the sum of twelve shillings &c.

John WATSON (Constable) exhibited his claim for attending at four several courts as constable and was allowed the sum of three pounds ten shilling &c.

Morgan BROWN Esqr. was allowed the sum of four pounds for serving this court as attorney for the state &c.

Ordered that Zacherias McDANIEL be appointed Collector in the uper district of this county upon giving bond agreeable to law &c.

Ordered that John WALL Esqr. be appointed Collector in the lower district of this county upon giving bond agreeable to law &c.

Ordered that the following rates be laid upon all liquors (vizt) West India Rum pr. half pint 1s./4d. French or norward ditto 1s./ Brandy pr. half pint 1s./ Whiskey ditto 0/8d. Crab cider pr. quart 8d. Forward ditto 6d &c.

September 1783   Page 118

September Court 1783
Good dinner with two dishes 1/8. Breakfast 1/. Supper 1/. Lodging with clean sheets /6d. Pasturage 24 hours 1/. Stableage pr. night /6d. Corn pr. quart /3d. Fodder pr. bundle /2d. Oats pr. quart /3d.

Charles MEDLOCK Esqr. came into court and was allowed per his vinire tickitt £7-14.

Ordered that the county tax be two shilling specie in the hundred pound for the year 1783.

Ordered that the Sheriff sell two head of cattle the property of Wm. BAKER and make return to the next court &c.

Ordered that Thomas BLEWITT be appointed guarden to the children of Nicholas STONE deceased.

Court adjourned untill court in course.
       Charles MEDLOCK)
Test. Wm. LOVE Clk. John SPEED   ) Esqrs.
       Jame COLE   )

December 1783

State of No. Carolina
At a County Court of Pleas and Quarter Session began and held for the County of Richmond at the Court House therein on the last Monday in December...

December 1783   Page 119

December court 1783
...Anno Dom. one thousand seven hundred eighty three.

Present   Charles MEDLOCK) Esqr.

Court adjourned untill tomorrow 9 o'clock.

Court met according to adjournment.
        Present   Charles MEDLOCK   )
                       Henry Wm. HARRINGTON) Esqr.
                       Robert WEBB   )

A deed from Little Bird SHEPHERD and wife to Duncan McCAUL proved in open court by the oath of Robert WEBB, ordered to be registered.

A deed from Thomas MEGGINSON to Nicholas CHRISTIAN proved in open court by the oath of Jesse CHRISTIAN ordered to be registred.

On motion of Thomas MEGGENSON tis ordered by the court that the probate of the Last Will and Testament of John WALTERS deceased untill March court 1784 it being suggested to the court that there is a younger will of the said John WALTERS then the one now in the possession of Colo. Jacob SHEPHERD &c.

A deed from John HUTCHENS to John DEGARNETT Esqr. proved in open court by the oath of David CAUDLE, ordered to be registred.

A deed from James PATTERSON to Jesse BOUNDS proved in open court by the oath of George BOUNDS ordered to be registred.

December 1783   *Page 120*

December Court 1783
Ordered that a road be opened from the river head \near John MASK/ to Hilyard Ford on Pee Dee and that said ford be kept open, and that James MERIDITH Jr. with his own hands, John MASK's and Dudley MASK's hands keep the same in good repair &c.

On motion John CRAWFORD Esqr. for Letters of Administration upon the estate of John TURNER deceased late of this county which being granted came into this court and qualified as administrator and gave bond agreeable to law &c.

The Last Will and Testament of Timothy HURLEY late of this county deceased was exhibited in open court and proved by the oath of Elias GARNER and James ROGERS, and after the said will was approved off by the court Moses HURLEY came into this court and was duly qualified as executor thereto agreeable to law &c.

Grand Jury sworn John CRAWFORD foreman, Wm. JARNIGAN, Wm. WEBB, Silas HALEY, John LONG Sr., John COVINGTON, Henry COVINGTON, Wm. HUNTER, Wm. TERRY, Wm. McDANIEL, Nathl. HARRINGTON, Laurance EVERITT, Dun RYE, Jesse BOUND, and Richd. ADAMS &c.

December 1783   *Page 121*

December Court 1783
On motion of Nancy McLEOD for Letters of Administration of the estate of Daniel McLEOUD late of this county deceased, which be granted she came into this court and qualified as Administratrix and gave bond and security agreeable to law &c.

Ordered that the Sheriff sell all the perishable part of the estate of Daniel McLEOUD and make return to the next court &c.

Court adjourned till tomorrow 9 o'clock.

Court met according to adjournment.
    Present   Charles MEDLOCK   )
                         John BOUNDS   ) Esqrs.
                         Benjn. COVINGTON)

Andrew KILLET bound over to this present court by Charles MEDLOCK Esqr. John SNEED prosecutor bound in the sum of £40-0.

John KILLET and Solomon KILLITT bound over to this present court by Charles MEDLOCK Esqr. each in the sum of £100) 200

Wm. HUSBAND and Stephen PETTUS securites each in the sum of £100) 200

Thos. COLLINS and George COLLINS Jr. bound to this present term by Charles MEDLOCK Esqr. each in the sum of £100) 200

December 1783   *Page 122*

December Court 1783
George COLLINS Sr. Arthur DEES security each in the sum of £100.

Arthur DEES bound as prosecutor against the above persons in the sum of £100.

George CARTER bound to this court for petty larceny by Benjn. BEARD Esqr. in the sum of £100-0. John McCAUL Jr. Sampson WILLIAMS bound as witness against George CARTER \each/ in the sum of £50.

William MOODY bound to this court for petty larceny by Charles MEDLOCK Esqr. in the sum of £50-0. John WALL, Edward WILLIAMS securities for Wm. MOODY each in the sum of £25.

Daniel THOMAS, William BLEWITT witness against Wm. MOODY each in the sum of £25.

Wm. MOODY came into this court and gave Richd. FARR and Edward WILLIAMS as securities for his appearance at the next court to answear a charge of petty larceny himself bound in the sum of one hundred pounds and his securities each in the sum of fifty pounds.

Daniel THOMAS, William BLEWITT bound to give evidence against Wm. MOODY each in the sum of £25.

A deed from Benjn. MANOR to Edward SMITH proved in open court by the oath of Robert WEBB ordered to be registred &c.

December 1783   *Page 123*

December Court 1783
David LOVE Esqr.   )
    vs.   ) Att't. Def. Inqy.
Wm. BAKER   ) In which suit the following being sworn (vizt) George BOUNDS, Wm. HUSBANDS, John CROWSSON, Thomas CRAWFORD, Walter LEAK, Matthew COVINGTON, Joseph RYE, David SNEED Jr., Daniel THOMAS, Moses CHAMBERS, Daniel McDANIEL, and John PARNEL upon their oaths do say that they find for the plaintiff the sum of five pounds six shillings debt and interest and so they say all &c.

A deed from Henry ADCOCK and wife to Robert WEBB Esqr. proved in open court by the oath of Joseph DEVONPORT, ordered to be registred &c.

A deed from Matthew COVINGTON to Wm. THOMAS proved in open court by the oath of Thomas CRAWFORD ordered to be registred.

Andrew KELLET bound over for is appearance during this present term in the sum of one hundred pounds &c. Wm. WATKINS and Wm. COULTER securities each in the sum of £50-0.

Henry Wm. HARRINGTON Esqr.)
   vs.   ) Attch.
Charles HARBERT   ) In which suit the aforegoing jury was sworn who upon their oaths do say that they find for the plaintiff the sum of thirty six pound ten shilling and so they say all &c.

December 1783   Page 124

December Court 1783
John BETHIGH, Elisabeth BREWER, John COOK bound to the next court to give evidence against Nancy CASTLEHAM each in the sum of fifty pounds and John BETHIGH security for Elisabeth BREWER &c.

A deed from John CRAWFORD to Alexander McDANIEL acknowledged in open court, ordered to be registred &c.

A deed from Archelous MOREMAN and wife to Robert WEBB, proved in open court by the oath of John EZEL ordered to be registred.

A deed from Jesse BOUND and wife to Robert WEBB Esqr. proved in open court by the oath of Wm. WEBB, ordered to be registred.

A bond from John CHILES to Henry Wm. HARRINGTON Esqr. (and others) Comissioners appointed for the County of Richmond and proved in open court by the oath of Moses HURLEY ordered to be registred.

Charles ROBERTSON)
   vs.   ) Case
John COLEMAN   ) In which suit the following jury was sworn (vizt) George BOUND, John CROWSSON, Wm. HUSBAND, Thomas CRAWFORD, Walter LEAK, Matthew COVINGTON, Joseph RYE, Daniel THOMAS, Moses CHAMBERS, Daniel McDANIEL, John PARNEL, and John SNEED who upon their oath do say that they find for the plaintiff the sum of six pounds twelve shillings and eight pence with six pence cost and so they say all.

December 1783   Page 125

December Court – 1783
Court adjourned till tomorrow morning 9 o'clock.

Court met according to adjournment.
     Present   Henry Wm. HARRINGTON)
                       John SPEED   ) Esqrs.
                       Benjn. COVINGTON   )

Mary McCOY came into this court and qualified as Administratrix upon the estate of John McCOY late of this county deceased and entred into bond with John SPEED Esqr. in the sum of one hundred pounds &c.

Ordered that the Sheriff sell all the perishable estate of John McCOY deceased & make return to the next court &c.

Edward WILLIAMS Esqr. came into this court, and qualified as Adminstrator upon the estate of Wm. CHAPLIN late of this county decd. and entred into bond and security in the sum of two hundred pounds &c.

Ordered that the Sheriff sell all the perishable estate of Wm. CHAPLIN deceased and make return to the next court &c.

Ordered that Edward ALMOND be allowed the sum of thirty shillings for serving as constable three days at June court and three day at September court &c.

December 1783   Page 126

December Court – 1783
Ordered that a logg house to receive tob.? [*tobacco?*] as a ware-house be erected at Haley's ferry agreeable to the act of assembly in such case made and provided &c.

Ordered that Colo. Charles MEDLOCK and Silas HALEY be appointed inspectors for the ware house at Haley's ferry.

George COLLINS and Thos. COLLINS came into this court and was discharged from their recognizance.

Ordered that Burrell STRICKLIN be allowed the sum of two pounds ten shillings for serving as constable at two court &c.

Court adjourned till tomorrow 9 o'clock.

Court met according to adjournment.
    Present   Charles MEDLOCK)
                   Robert WEBB   )
                   Benjn. COVINGTON) Esqrs.
                   John BOUNDS   )

Ordered that Silas HALEY be appointed overseer of the road from the fork of the road near to Colo. MEDLOCKs to Haley's ferry, and from thence to the school house at the fork of Clerks Road, and John CRAWFORD Esqr. hand, John MOREMAN, Thos. MOREMAN, Benjn. MOREMAN, Will. MORE-

MAN, Andrew MOREMAN, Randolph HALEY, Lott STRICKLIN, Irvine McINTOSH, Alexander McKASKILL, Kennith McKASKILL, Daniel McCASKILL, and General HARRINGTONs hands work thereon &c.

December 1783   Page 127

December Court – 1783
Ordered that the Sheriff summons Silas HALEY, Benjn. COVINGTON and James MERIDETH as a vinire for Salisbury Superior Court to be t held on the fifteenth day of March next and make return thereof &c.

Ordered that the Sheriff summon Thos. SUMMERAL, Darby HANAGAN, Wm. EASTERLING, James EASTERLING, Nathl. WILLIAMS, Daniel HICKS, Randolph HALEY, James BAGGETT, Isreal SNEED Jr., David SNEED Sr., Hendley SNEED, John SNEED, Zachs. MOREMAN, Henry ADCOCK, Stephen COLE, Daniel THOMAS, Daniel SMITH, Nicholas STONE, Thomas BLEWITT, Simon THOMAS, Joseph HINES, Jonathon NEWBERY, John COLEMAN, Walter LEAK, John PEMBERTON, John COLE Sr., Wm. WATKINS, Wm. WATKINS Jr., Thomas WATKINS, Wm. MIMS to serve as juriors at the next court and make return thereof &c.

State   )
  vs.   ) Indt. Trespass
Andrew KILLET) In which suit the following jury was sworn (vizt) George BOUNDS, John CROWSSON, Wm. HUSBANDS, Thomas CRAWFORD, Matthew COVINGTON, Moses CHAMBERS, Thomas GIBSON, Stephen COLE, Samuel COVINGTON, John COLE, Benjn. THOMAS, and Randolph HALEY who upon their oaths do say that they find the defendant guilty of a trespass and so they say all &c.

December 1783   Page 128

December Court – 1783
On motion of Wm. HUNTER Jr. in the suit of Robert WILSON against there appears error in the judgment – ordered to be set aside.

State   )
  vs.   ) Indt. Larceny
John KILLET   ) In which suit the following jury was sworn (vizt) George BOUNDS, John CROWSSON, Wm. HUSBANDS, Thomas CRAWFORD, Matthew COVINGTON, Moses CHAMBERS, Thomas GIBSON, Stephen COLE, Samuel COVINGTON, John SNEED, John COLE, and Benjn. THOMAS, who upon their oaths do say that the said John KILLET is guilty in manner and form as charged in the bill of indictment and so they say all &c.

State   )
    vs.   ) Indt. Larceny
Charles COLLINS) In which suit the aforegoing jury was sworn and upon their oaths do say that the said Charles COLLINS is guilty in manner and form as charged in the bill of indictment and so they say all &c.

A deed from Wm. HALEY to Silas HALEY proved in open court by the oath of Benjn. THOMAS ordered to be registered &c.

On motion of Silas HALEY tis ordered by the court that he have leave to keep an ordinary upon giving bond and security.

On motion of John SPEED Esqr. tis ordered by the court that he have leave to keep an ordinary upon giving bond and security.

December 1783   Page 129

December Court – 1783
Ordered that a road be cleared out the nearest and best way from the Court House to John BOUNDS and from thence to the Polley Bridge and that the hands on the two Falling Creeks work thereon.

Court adjourned untill court in course.
                        Charles MEDLOCK   )
Test. Wm. LOVE Clk.   John BOUNDS   ) Esqrs.
                        Benjn. COVINGTON   )

March 1784

At a County Court of Pleas and Quarter Sessions began and held for the County of Richmond at the Court House therein on the last Monday in March Anno Dom. 1784.
    Present   Charles MEDLOCK)
               John SPEED   ) Esqrs.
               Robert WEBB   )

Ordered that Wm. WATKINS Sr. be discharged from his attendance as a jurior this court.

A deed from Luke ROBERTSON to John ROBERTSON proved in open court by the oath of Jesse JONES ordered to be registred.

The Last Will and Testament of Hugh LEATON late of this county deceased was exhibited in this court and duly proved by the oath of Wm. LOVE who saw the other witness assign the said will with himself – and after the said Last Will and Testament of Hugh LEATON dec'd....

March 1784   *Page 130*

March Court – 1784
...was exhibited and approved of by the said court Isreal SNEED, Jesse JONES and Mary LEATON the Executors therein named came into this court as was duly qualified as executors thereto according to law &c.

Grand Jury sworn (vizt) John COLE Sr. foreman, Wm. EASTERLING, Daniel THOMAS, Daniel HICKS, Randolph HALEY, Isreal SNEED, David SNEED Sr., John SNEED, Zachs. MOREMAN, Henry ADCOCK, Nicholas STONE, Thomas BLEWITT, Joseph HINES, Derby HANAGAN, Walter LEAK, and Daniel SMITH &c.

Court adjourned till tomorrow 10 o'clock.

Court met according to adjournment.
    Present   Charles MEDLOCK)
                      John SPEED   ) Esqrs.
                      Robert WEBB   )

A deed from Thomas TURNER to Malcom McPHERSON proved in open court by the oath of John CRAWFORD Esqr. ordered to be registred.

A deed from Robert WEBB Esqr. to Archelous MOREMAN, proved in open court by the oath of Jesse BOUND, ordered to be registred.

Ordered that Thomas STANDBACK have leave to keep an ordinary at Masks Ferry.

March 1784   *Page 131*

March Court – 1784
A deed from William BOLTON to Jonathon NEWBERY proved in open court by the oath of Owen SLAUGHTER Sr. ordered to be registred.

A deed of gift from John RAY to Marran RAY proved in open court by the oath of Alexander GORDON, ordered to be registred.

A deed from Richard LEAK to James CAMPBLE proved in open court by the oath of James CAMPBLE ordered to be registred.

Court adjourned untill tomorrow 10 o'clock.

Court met according to adjournment.
    Present   Charles MEDLOCK   )
                      John BOWN [! *BOUND*]) Esqrs.
                      Benjn. COVINGTON   )

A deed from Elisha LEWIS to John McFARLAND proved in open court by the oath of Duncan McFARLAND ordered to be registered.

On motion ~~of~~ William CRAWFORD Esqr. came into this court and was duly qualified to his license as an attorney at law &c.

On motion John McNARY Esqr. came into this court and was duly qualified to his license as an attorney at law &c.

March 1784   *Page 132*

March Court – 1784
State   )
    vs.   ) Indt. Larceny
\Thos./ ~~Wm.~~ MOODY) In which suit the following jury was sworn (vizt) Wm. WATKINS, Wm. MIMS, Nathl. WILLIAMS, James BAGGETT, John JAMES Jr., Charles ROBERTSON, Thomas GIBSON, Solomon RYE, George BOUND, Moses CHAMBER, Wm. HUSBANDS, John PEMBERTON, who upon their oaths do say that the said Wm.[!] MOODY is not guilty in manner and form as charged in the bill of indictment and so they say all &c.

A deed from Elisabeth HALES to John LONG Sr. acknowledged in open court ordered to be registred.

Did. Po. to issue to South Carolina in behalf of Tristam THOMAS in the suit of Thomas STEPHENS to take the examination of George HICKS, & John HODGE before Morgan BROWN Esqr.

A deed from Edward WILLIAMS to Benjn. INGRAM, acknowledged in open court ordered to be registred.

A deed from Matthew COVINGTON to Thomas EVERITT proved in open court by the oath of Wm. HUNTER Sr. ordered to be registred.

Henry LIGHTFOOT Esqr. came into this court and qualified as a practising attorney in this court &c.

March 1784   *Page 133*

March Court 1784
Alexander McNEEL bound in the sum of fifty pounds for his appearance at next court) £50. Thos. CRAWFORD and Wm. KELLEY his security each in the sum of twenty five pound) £50-.

A deed from James CAMPBLE to Robert WEBB Esqr. acknowledged in open court ordered to be registred &c.

Richmond County NC Court Minutes, 1779-1786

A deed from Robert THOMAS to Gelbert McNEAR proved in open court by the oath of Wm. EASTERLING ordered to be registred &c.

Court adjourned untill tomorrow 10 o'clock.

Court mett according to adjournment.
    Present   Charles MEDLOCK)
                      Dudley MASK   ) Esqrs.
                      Benjn. COVINGTON)

Ordered that Derby HANAGAN be appointed overseer of the road from Halls Bridge the nearest and best way from said bridge to the south line leading to the beauty spott and all the hands contiguous work thereon.

Ordered that Wm. MIMS be appointed overseer of the road from Halls Bridge to Richmond Court House the nearest and best was and all the hands contiguous work thereon &c.

Charles MEDLOCK Esqr. came into court and qualified as administrator upon the estate of John SMITH and gave bond in the sum of fifty pound and John SPEED Esqr. security.

March 1784   Page 134

March Court 1784
A deed from Robert WEBB Esqr. to Henry ADCOCK, proved in open court by the of [!] Jesse BOWND ordered to be registred.

A deed from Robert WEBB Esqr. to Hen\r/y ADCOCK proved in open court \by the oath of Jesse BOUNDS/ ordered to be registred.

A deed from Daniel McNEIL to Henry ADCOCK, proved in open court by the oath of Tillotson OBRYAN ordered to be registred.

On motion in indenture from Rachel BALDEN to Charles ROBERTSON for bringing out sundry orphans proved in open court by the oath of Jacob COCKRAHAM &c.

John PARNEL)
     vs.   ) Def. Inqy.
John CURRY) In which suit the following jury was sworn (vizt) Simon THOMAS, Wm. WATKINS, Wm. MIMS, Nathaniel WILLIAMS, James BAGGET, John PEMBERTON, John COLEMAN, Thos. CRAWFORD, Silas HALEY, Wm. WEBB, David SNEED Jr., George BOUNDS who upon their oaths do say that they assess damages for the plaintiff thirty one pounds sixteen shillings and cost and so they say all &c.

Robert WEBB Esqr.)
    vs.) Genl. Issue
Wm. COULTER) In which suit the following jury was sworn (vizt) Simon THOMAS, Wm. WATKINS, Wm. MIMS, Nathaniel WILLIAMS, James BAGGET, John PEMBERTON, John COLEMAN, Thos. CRAWFORD, Silas HALEY, David SNEED Jr., ...

March 1784   Page 135

March Court 1784
...George BOWND and John EZEL who upon their oaths assess damages for the plaintiff the sum of twenty five pounds and cost and so they say all &c.

Wm. COULTER)
    vs.) Genl. Issue
Wm. WEBB) In which suit the following jury was sworn (vizt) Simon THOMAS, Nathaniel WILLIAMS, James BAGGET, John PEMBERTON, John COLEMAN, Thos. CRAWFORD, Silas HALEY, David SNEED Jr., John EZEL, George BOUNDS and Joseph LASETER who upon their oaths assess damages for the plaintiff the sum of twenty five pounds and the cost and so they say all &c.

Ordered that, John PARNEL, James JAMES, Solomon QUICK, Andrew HENDRICKSON, Robert MALCOM, and Thos. MIMS, be exempted from working on the road, crossing at Halls Bridge, and to keep Mims Bridge in good repair &c.

Henry Wm. HARRINGTON Esqr.)
    vs.)
Owen SLAUGHTER Sr.) ~~Case~~ Genl. Issue
Owen SLAUGHTER Jr.)
Elisha COLLINS) In which suit the following jury was sworn (vizt) Simon THOMAS, Wm. WATKINS, Wm. MIMS, James BAGGET, John PEMBERTON, John COLEMAN, Thos. CRAWFORD, Silas HALEY, Wm. WEBB, David SNEED Jr., George BOWND and Nathl. WILLIAMS who upon their oaths do say that they find no course of action and so they say all &c.

Wm. WEBB)
    vs.) Case
John LONG Jr.) In which suit the following jury was sworn (vizt) Simon (THOMAS)...

March 1784   Page 136

March Court 1784

...THOMAS, Wm. WATKINS, Natheniel WILLIAMS, James BAGGET, John PEMBERTON, John COLEMAN, Thos. CRAWFORD, Silas HALEY, David SNEED Jr., George BOWND, John EZEL, and Joseph LASETER who upon their oaths do say that they assess damages for the plaintiff in the sum of twenty five pounds and so they say all &c.

Court adjourned untill tomorrow 9 o'clock.

Court met according to adjournment.
    Present   John BOWND   )
                    Benjn. COVINGTON) Esqrs.
Ordered that the Sheriff summon John HILYARD John COLEMAN, John PEMBERTON, Benjn. DUMAS, Wm. McGUIRE, Charles ROBERTSON, Wm. MASK, James MERIDETH, Solomon GROSS, Joseph GADD Jr., John LEVERIT, Thomas BLEWITT, Wm. NEWBERY, Jonathon NEWBERY, and Owen SLAUGHTER to lay of a road at Hillar's Ford on Pee Dee and make return thereof &c.

A deed from William WEBB & wife to Archabald McMILLON acknowledged in open court ordered to be registred &c.

John MASK bound over to the next court in the sum of £50-. Edward ALMOND security for Mask's appearance bound in the sum of £50-.

Stephen COLE   )
    vs.   ) Genl. Issue
John CROWSSON) In which suit the...

March 1784

March Court 1784
...following jury was sworn (vizt) Simon THOMAS, Wm. MIMS, Nathl. WILLIAMS, James BAGGET, John EZEL, Jesse BOUNDS, John COLEMAN, John PEMBERTON, William WEBB, John WALL, John CRAWFORD Esqr., and George DAWKINS who upon their oaths do assess damages for the plaintiff the sum of twelve pounds and cost and so they say all.

Ordered that Samuel MILLER be bound out to James HUNTER for the term of ten years &c.

Ordered that the Sheriff summon John COVINGTON Sr., John COVINGTON Jr., Wm. HUNTER Sr., Henry COVINGTON, Wm. TERRY, John CROWSSON, Wm. THOMAS Sr., Wm. THOMAS Jr., Richard ADAMS, Wm. McDANIEL, James BOSTICK, John MASK, Wm. MORE, Joseph GADD Jr., Charles ROBERTSON, James EASTERLING, Thos. SUMMERAL, Wm. WOODLE, John TURNAGE, John PARNEL,

Moses CHAMBERS, Thos. EVERITT, Thos. CRAWFORD, John WALL, Wm. JORNIGAN, Jesse BOWND, George BOWND, Benjn. INGRAM, Barnaby SKIPPER, & Sterling WILLIAMSON to serve as jurors at the next court and make return thereof &c.

Court adjourned untill court in course.

      Charles MEDLOCK)
Test. Wm. LOVE Clk. John SPEED)Esqrs.
      John BOWND)

June 1784   *Page 138*

June Court 1784
At a County Court of Pleas and Quarter Sessions began and held for the County of Richmond at the Court House therein on the last Monday in June in the VIII year of American independance Ann. dom. 1784.

  Present Charles MEDLOCK)
      Benjn. COVINGTON) Esqrs.
      John SPEED   )

A deed from William ROBERTS to John COLES Sr. proved in open court by the oath of James TERRY? ordered to be registred &c.

Ordered that Dugal McFARLAND be appointed to serve as Constable on the east side of Gum Swamp for the ensuing year &c.

Ordered that Jacob MANGRUM be appointed to serve as ~~Constable~~ overseer of the road that leads across the Polley bridge of Gum Swamp then to John BOWNDS, and all hands between the Juniper and Joes Creek work thereon.

Ordered that Jonathon NEWBERY be excused from a fine for his nonattendance as a juror at the last court &c.

Grand Jury sworn (vizt) Charles ROBERTSON, John COVINGTON Sr., John COVINGTON Jr., Wm. HUNTER Sr., Henry COVINGTON, Wm. TERRY, Wm. THOMAS Jr., Richard ADAMS, John MASK, James EASTERLING, Wm. WOODLE, John TURNAGE, Wm. JERNIGAN, Barnaby SKIPPER, and Sterling WILLIAMSON.

Court adjourned untill tomorrow 9 o'clock.

Met according to adjournment.

June 1784   Page 139

June Court 1784
    Present   Charles MEDLOCK)
                    John BOUND   ) Esqrs.
                    Benjn. COVINGTON)

A deed from Wm. NEWBERY and wife to John COLEMAN, acknowledged in open court by Wm. NEWBERY ordered to be registred.

A deed from Thomas JOHNSON and wife to Enoch HALL, proved in open court by the oath of Lewis HALL, ordered to be registred &c.

A deed from Richard PEMBERTON to John PANKEY, proved in open court by the oath of Edward WILLIAMS, ordered to be registred.

On motion of John SMITH, the indentures of Bird SHEPHERD, <u>was</u> proved in open court by the oath of Zacherias McDANIEL &c.

On motion a Did. Po. to issue to South Carolina to take the examination of Wm. WILLIAMS in behalf of Daniel McDANIEL &c.

Dugal KERMICAL)
    vs.   ) Att't. Def. Inqy.
Wm. CHEVES   ) In which suit the following jury was sworn (vizt) John CROWSSON, Thomas CRAWFORD, James BOSTICK, Wm. THOMAS, Daniel McDANIEL, Daniel SMITH, Wm. COTTENGAME, Samuel COVINGTON, Matthew COVINGTON, Lott STRICKLIN, Laurance EVERIT, and Jesse BOUNDS who upon their oath do say that they find for the plaintiff the sum of one penny and cost and so they say all &c.

June 1784   Page 140

June Court – 1784
Edward ALMOND)
    vs.   ) Att't.
John CAMPBLE   ) In which suit the aforegoing jury was sworn and upon their oaths do say they find for the plaintiff the sum of twenty eight pounds ten shilling and so they say all.

Wm. HUSBAND)
    vs.   ) Case
John LONG Sr.   ) In which suit the aforegoing jury was sworn and upon their oaths do say that they find for the plaintiff the sum of four pound ten shillings and cost and so they say all &c.

Two? deeds from George GRAHAM to Samuel COVINGTON, proved in open court by the oath of Wm. EASTERLING, ordered to be registred &c.

Ordered that Wm. PEARCE be appointed to serve as Constable the insuing year.

A deed from William SEAGO, to Wm. JOHNSON, proved in open court by the oath of Richd. ADAMS, ordered to be registred &c.

Ordered that Isam HALEY and Silas HALEY jointly have leave to keep a publick ferry across Pee Dee River at the place known by and called Haley's Ferry upon giving bond and security &c.

A deed from Zacherias SMITH to Samuel USHER, proved in open court by the oath of Joseph HINES ordered to be registred.

June 1784

June Court – 1784
A deed from Jacob COLLINS to Stephen PITCOCK proved in open court by the oath of James BURN, ordered to be registred &c.

A deed from Joseph SIMKINS to Solomon GROSS proved in open court by the oath of Joseph HINES ordered to be registred.

A deed from William and Sarah POSTON to [blot] \Elisabeth/ LEATON proved in open court by the oath of Solomon GROSS, ordered to be registred.

A deed from John LEVERITT to Solomon GROSS proved in open court by the oath of Edward WILLIAMS ordered to be registred.

A receipt from William CHAMBERS to Solomon GROSS, proved in open court by the oath of Allison GROSS, ordered to be registred &c.

Court adjourned untill tomorrow 9 o'clock.

Met according to adjournment.
    Present   Charles MEDLOCK)
                      Benjn. COVINGTON) Esqrs.
                      Robert WEBB   )

Court adjourned for half an hour and then to meet at the house of Phillip JAMES's.

Richmond County NC Court Minutes, 1779-1786   89

Court met according to adjournment.
    Present   Charles MEDLOCK)
                  Benjn. COVINGTON) Esqrs.
                  Robert WEBB   )

June 1784   *Page 142*

June Court 1784
Ordered that the following persons be a jury to lay of a road, from Hellen Ford on Pee Dee River (vizt) Benjn. DUMAS, James MERIDITH, Joseph GADD, Wm. MASK, Owen SLAUGHTER, Wm. NEWBERY, Jonathon NEWBERY, Wm. McGUIRE, Thomas BLEWITT, Charles ~~MEDLOCK~~ ROBERTSON, Thomas JOWERS, James BOSTICK, Wm. JOWERS, Wm. HENDLEY, Daniel McDANIEL and Benjn. POWEL, and make return to the next court &c.

Tristam THOMAS)
    vs.   ) Dittanue [*Detinue*]
Thos. STEPHENS) In which case the following jury was sworn (vizt) John CROWSSON, Thomas CRAWFORD, James BOSTICK, Wm. THOMAS, Jesse BOUND, Solomon GROSS, Laurance EVERITT, Benjn. INGRAM, Wm. MIMS, John JAMES, Wm. WEBB and John MATTHEW who upon their oaths do say that the defendant does detain a negroe boy named York, the property of Tristam THOMAS, the plaintiff and so they say all &c.

On motion of Henry LIGHTFOOT Esqr. Esqr. attorney for the defendant Thomas STEPHENS in the aforegoing suit, moves for an arrest of judgment &c.

A deed from Benjn. COVINGTON and wife to Thomas TURNER, acknowledged in open court ordered to be registered.

On motion a Did. Po. issue to Bladen County to take the deposition of James BEASLEY as an evidence to a deed given by John GRAHAM to Derby SMITHHEART &c.

June 1784   *Page 143*

June Court – 1784
On motion of William CRAWFORD Esqr. attorney in the suit of Jacob COCKRAHAM, vs. John McCRANEY, it is the opinion of the court, that the judgment stands confirmed agreeable to the verdict of the jury heretofore given, notwithstanding the motion of Henry LIGHTFOOT Esqr. made in objection thereto &c. Present on the bench Charles MEDLOCK, James COLE, Robert WEBB, and Benjn. COVINGTON Esqrs.

Court adjourned untill tomorrow 9 o'clock at the Court House.

Met according to adjournment.
    Present   Charles MEDLOCK)
                   James COLE   ) Esqrs.
                   John BOUNDS   )

Court adjourned for half an hour & to meet at the house of Phillip JAMES's.

Met according to adjournment.
    Present   Charles MEDLOCK   )
                   Henry Wm. HARRINGTON)
                   James COLE   ) Esqrs.
                   John BOUND   )

MALLET, AMIT & MALLET)
    vs.   ) Def. Inqy.
Wm. NEWBERY   ) In which suit the following jury was sworn (vizt) Jesse BOWNDS, Benjn. INGRAM, John CROWSSON, James BOSTICK, Wm. THOMAS, John MATTHEWS, James BOUNDS, George BOUNDS, James EASTERLING, Wm. HUNTER Jr. and Moses CHAMBERS who upon their oaths do say that they find for the plaintiffs the sum of twenty six pound nine shillings with cost of suit & so they say all &c.

June 1784   *Page 144*

June Court – 1784
Ordered, that the Clerk be allowed the sum of fifteen pounds for his ex oficio services settled by the court, from the year 1779 to March court 1782 in lieu of four thousand pound dollar bills &c.

Ordered that the Sheriff be allowed the sum of eleven pounds for his services from the year 1779 to March court 1782 in lieu of three thousand pounds settled by the court &c.

Walter LEAK, John PEMBERTON, Joseph HINES, Derby HANAGAN and William EASTERLING Esqr. came into court and qualified as Justices of the Peace for said county &c.

John CRAWFORD Esqr.)
    vs.   )
Edward WILLIAM Esqr.) Genl. Issue
Execr. of JEFFERSON   ) In which suit the aforegoing jury was sworn and upon their oaths do say that they find for the plaintiff the sum of thirty five pound, seven shilling and four pence and so they say all &c.

Richmond County NC Court Minutes, 1779-1786

Henry Wm. HARRINGTON Esqr.)
assignee of Wm. THOMAS)
vs.) Genl. Issue
Edward WILLIAMS Esqr. Execr.)
of G. JEFFERSON decd.) In which suit the aforegoing jury was duly sworn ~~except Solomon GROSS Tho~~ \except Solomon GROSS and Thos. CRAWFORD in his stead?/ and upon their oaths do say that they find for the plaintiff the sum of one hundred and thirty eight pounds ten shilling and so they say all.

June 1784 *Page 145*

June Court – 1784
Same)
vs.) Genl. Issue
Same) Juries verdict as the aforegoing for the sum of one hundred and thirty eight pound ten shillings and so they say all &c.

Same)
vs.) Genl. Issue
Same) The aforegoing jury sworn and their verdict as the aforegoing for the sum of one hundred and thirty eight pound ten shillings and so they say all &c.

Walter LEAK Esqr. was allowed the sum of five pounds fifteen shilling upon his vinire tickitt &c.

Ordered that Edward WILLIAMS Esqr. be appointed to serve as Sheriff the insuing year &c.

A deed from Wm. WEBB to James PATTERSON proved in open court by the oath of Robert WEBB Esqr. ordered to be registred &c.

Wm. HUNTER Jr.)
vs.) Genl. Issue
Duncan BLUE) In which suit the following jury was sworn (vizt) Jesse BOUND, Benjn. INGRAM, John CROWSSON, Thos. CRAWFORD, James BOSTICK, Wm. THOMAS, John MATTHEWS, James BOUND, George BOUND, James EASTERLING, Lott STRICKLIN, and Charles HUCKABY who upon their oaths do say that they find for the plaintiff the sum of nine pounds thirteen shillings and so they say all &c.

June 1784 *Page 146*

June Court 1784
A deed from Wm. COULTER to Daniel McDANIEL proved in open court by the oath of Lott STRICKLIN ordered to be registred.

Court adjourned untill tomorrow 9 o'clock at the Court House.

Met according to adjournment.
Present   Charles MEDLOCK)
                 James COLE   )
                 John SPEED   ) Esqrs.
                 Benjn. COVINGTON)

The Collectors came into this court and settled their accounts for the taxes for the year 1783 as pr. account filed &c.

Ordered that John COVINGTON Jr. have leave to build a water grist mill on Bridge Creek on his own land at the lower end, &c.

On motion of Wm. CRAWFORD Esqr. for the admission of a will of John WALTERS deceased to probate, the court, adjudged on argument that it was improper to admit it to proof.

A deed from Wm. HALL to Joseph HALL, proved in open court by the oath of John WALL, ordered to be registred.

In the suit Tristam THOMAS vs. Thomas STEPHENS, in which suit there was a...

June 1784   Page 147

June Court – 1784
...judgment obtained for a negroe boy named York, which judgment was arrested, by the defendants attorneys and upon arguing the reasons they were ajudged insufficient, and the judgment, confirmed, in consequence of which judgment, the said STEPHENS and THOMAS, came into court and compremised another suit for damages, and each man to pay his own cost, in the last suit, and the said STEPHEN agreed to deliver up the said negroe York, without any further contention.

Nathen JONES bound over to the next court in the sum of £25-. Lott STRICKLIN Ditto in the sum of -12-10.

Henry Wm. HARRINGTON Esqr.)
Execr. of Samuel WISE   ) Genl. Issue
     vs.   )
Andrew HENDRICKSON   ) In which suit the following jury was sworn (vizt) Henry ADCOCK, David SNEED Sr., Moses CHAMBERS, Wm. MIMS, John SNEED, Wm. THOMAS, Thos. CRAWFORD, James BOSTICK, Jesse BOUNDS, Benjn. INGRAM, \George BOUND/ and John

CROWSSON who upon their oaths do say that they find for the plaintiff the sum of forty pounds and so they say all &c.

Court adjourned untill tomorrow 9 o'clock.

Met according to adjournment.
  Present Charles MEDLOCK)
        John BOUND   ) Esqrs.
        John SPEED   )

June 1784   *Page 148*

June Court – 1784
Ordered that the following rates be allowed for the insuing year upon liquors &c (vizt)

  Good West India rum pr. half pint ------------------------- £0-9-4
  French or norward rum ditto --------------------------------- 1-0
  Brandy   do. ---------------------------------- 1-0
  Crab cyder pr. quart --- 8
  Forward cyder do. --- 6
  Whiskey pr. half pint --- 8

  Good dinner with two dishes --------------------------------- 1-4
  Breakfast --- 1-0
  Supper -- 1-0
  Lodging with clean sheets ------------------------------------- 6

  Pastorage --- 6
  Stableage pr. night -- 6
  Corn pr. quart -- 2
  Fodder pr. bundle -- 2
  Oats pr. quart -- 2

Ordered that the Sheriff summons Wm. LOVE, Thomas CRAWFORD and Silas HALEY to attend at Salisbury Superior Court as a Vinire on the fifteenth day of September next and make return thereof &c.

Ordered that the Clerk be allowed the sum of four pounds for furnishing the county with a blank book for the use of the register's office.

Ordered that the Clerk be allowed the sum of two pounds for two books for the use of the county records &c.

June 1784   *Page 149*

June Court 1784

Ordered that the Sheriff summons Dun RYE, Thomas MOREMAN, Benjn. MOREMAN, John MOREMAN, Andrew MOREMAN, Zacherias MOREMAN, Lott STRICKLIN, David SNEED Jr., Randolph HALEY, Isreal SNEED, Hendley SNEED, John SNEED, Benjn. SKIPPER, Arthur DEES, Joseph HALL Jr., Thomas SUMMERAL, Edmund BROWN, Jacob MANGRUM, Thomas GRAVES, Wm. McDANIEL, Thos. BLEWITT, John WALL, Nicholas STONE, Henry ADCOCK, William MORE, Laurance EVERITT, Joseph GADD Jr., Thomas GIBSON, Nelson GIBSON, Laurance OBRYAN, John JAMES Jr., Samuel DAWKINS, Isaac YATES, Benjn. DEES, Solomon DEARMAN, Gilbert McNEAR, and as a jury to serve at the next court and make return thereof &c.

On motion of Henry LIGHTFOOTT and Wm. CRAWFORD Esqrs. ordered by the court, that the attachment Solomon GROSS vs. Preseellar [*Priscilla?*] McFERSHON administratrix of Alexand McFERSHON deceased formerly set aside be reinstated or brought forward on the docket.

Ordered that Wm. LOVE, Edward WILLIAMS and James BOSTICK be appointed to praise the estate of Hugh LEATON deceased and make return to the next court &c.

June 1784 *Page 150*

June Court 1784
Ordered that Isreal SNEED Jr. be appointed overseer of the road from Falling Creek to Solomon's Creek and that Gilbert McNAIR, David SNEED Senr., Daniel SNEED, David SNEED Jr., Phillip SNEED, Temperance SNEED's hands, George GULLETT, Allen McKASKILL Senr., Allen McKASKILL Jr., Keneth McKASKILL, Irvine McINTOSH, John CRAWFORD Esqr. hands, and Zacherias BELL work thereon &c.

Ordered that William HUNTER Jr. have leave to keep an Ordinary at his own house the insuing year upon giving bond and good security &c.

A deed from Edward WILLIAM Sheriff to William TERRY acknowledged in open court ordered to be registred &c.

Ordered that Joseph SIMKINS be allowed? for serving nine days at this court and at March court for his services agreeable to law &c.

Ordered that Charles MEDLOCK Esqr. have leave to build a water grist mill near the mouth of the Bigg Beaver Dam, and that it be a publick mill &c.

No. 1) Ordered Wm. EASTERLING and Darby HANAGAN be appointed to take the inventorys from the lower end of the county up to Maskes Creek and from the head thereof, to Coles Bridge.

June 1784   *Page 151*

June Court 1784
No. 2) Ordered that Henry Wm. HARRINGTON be appointed to take the inventorys from the south line up to the Hitch-cock and up the said creek to Falling Creek, and up Falling Creek to the head thereof, then across to Maskes Creek, then down the said creek to the south line &c.

No. 3) Ordered that Robert WEBB and Benjamin COVINGTON Esqrs. be appointed to take the inventorys from the mouth of Hitchcock up to Falling Creek, then to the head thereof, thence to Coles Bridge, then up Drowning Creek opposite to the head of Cartledges Creek then down the said creek to the mouth thereof &c.

No. 4) Ordered that Joseph HINES Esqr. be appointed to take the inventorys from Cartledge Creek to Mountain Creek, back to the county line.

No. 5) Ordered that Walter LEAK Esqr. be appointed to take the inventorys from Mountain Creek to Little River back to the county line &c.

No. 6) Ordered that John PEMBERTON Esqr. be appointed to take the inventorys from Little River to the uper end of the county &c.

Ordered that James BAGGET Jr. be appointed to serve as Constable the insuing year.

June 1784   *Page 152*

June Court 1784
Ordered that John BOUNDS have leave to keep a publick ferry over D\r/owning Creek at the place known by the name of Overstreets Bridge upon giving bond and security &c.

Ordered that Herod CLARK be appointed overseer of the road from Cornelius's Pond to Overstreet's Bridge crossing the Shew-Heel at the Rockey Ford, and all the hands contiguous work thereon &c.

Sarah BEVERLY bound to this court in the sum of – £20-. Isaac WILLIAMSON the same as her security – £20-. Simon PARKER prosecutor in the sum of £20-.

Wm. HATHCOCK, Mary HATHCOCK witnesses each in the sum of £20 – £40-. Hendley SNEED security each in the sum of £20-.

Court adjourned untill court in course

Test. Wm. LOVE Clk.
Charles MEDLOCK)
John BOUNDS)
John SPEED) Esqrs.
Henry Wm. HARRINGTON)

September 1784   Page 153

September Court 1784
At a County Court of Pleas and Quarter Sessions began and held for the County of Richmond on the last Monday in September Anno Dom. 1784 and in the ninth year of American independence.

Present   Charles MEDLOCK)
           Robert WEBB   ) Esqrs.
           James COLE   )

Ordered that Solomon GROSS be allowed the previledge to keep an Ordinary at Richmond court house upon giving bond & good security &c.

A deed from Samuel MIMS to James JAMES, and proved in open court by the oath of Wm. MIMS, ordered to be registered &c.

A deed from Elisabeth LEATON to Solomon GROSS proved in open court by the oath of Mun? GROSS ordered to be registred &c.

Grand Jury sworn Laurance OBRYAN foreman, John MOREMAN, Randle HALEY, Isreal SNEED, Hendley SNEED, John SNEED, Joseph HALL, Thos. SUMMERAL, Jacob MANGRUM, Wm. McDANIEL, Nicholas STONE, Henry ADCOCK, Laurance EVERITT, Nelson GIBSON, John JAMES.

September 1784   Page 154

September Court 1784
Court adjourned until tomorrow 10 o'clock.

Court met according to adjournment.
    Present   Charles MEDLOCK   )
               Henry Wm. HARRINGTON)
               Benjn. COVINGTON   ) Esqrs.
               John PEMBERTON   )
               Joseph HINES   )

A deed from Thomas ROBERTSON to Wm. BETTY and proved in open court by the oath of Lewis HALL ordered to be registred.

Richmond County NC Court Minutes, 1779-1786   97

A deed from Jacob COCKRAHAM to James SMITH and proved in open court by the oath of Charles ROBESON, ordered to be registred.

A deed from Jacob COCKRAHAM to James SMITH and proved in open court by the oath of Charles ROBESON ordered to be registred.

Solomon GROSS)
    vs.)
Priscellar McFERSHON admx.)
Alexr. McFERSHON decd.) In which suit the following jury was sworn jury was sworn (vizt) Benjamin SKIPPER, Dun RYE, Arther RYE, Joseph GADD, Samuel DAWKINS, Isaac YATES, Benjamin DEES, Solomon DEARMAN, Gilbert McNEAR, Stephen COLE, Wm. HUNTER Sr. & John CRAWFORD who upon their oaths do say that they find for the plaintiff the sum of…

September 1784   Page 155

September Court 1784
…thirty one pounds one shilling and four pence and so they say all &c.

A deed from John MASON to Murdock CHISM and proved in open court by the oath of John WEBB, ordered to be registred.

Court adjourned untill tomorrow 10 o'clock.

Court Met according to adjournment.
    Present   James COLE)
                 John BOUND)
                 Wm. EASTERLING) Esqrs.
                 John PEMBERTON)

A deed from Wm. ASHLEY \& wife/ to Sampson SELLERS and proved in open court by the oath of Alexr. McCRAY ordered to be registred.

A deed from Wm. ASHLEY & wife to Sampson SELLERS and proved in open court by the oath of Alexr. McCRAY ordered to be registred.

A deed from Jacob COCKRAHAM & wife to Sampson SELLERS and proved in open court by the oath of Wm. McDANIEL ordered to be registred &c.

On motion of Benjamin DUMAS Senr. ordered that a gift be admitted to record in behalf of his children, ordered to be registred &c.

September 1784

September Court 1784
A deed from John SMITH to James PATTERSON and proved in open court by the oath of James WATSON ordered to be registered.

John MASK)
    vs.) Genl. Issue &c.
Joseph LASETER) In which suit the following jury was sworn (vizt) Dun RYE, John WALL, Joseph GADD, Samuel DAWKINS, Isaac YATES, Solomon DEARMAN, Gilbert McNEAR, Benjn. DEES, Arther DEES, Benjn. SKIPPER, Wm. HUNTER and William JARNIGAN who upon their oaths do say that they find for the defendant and so they say all &c.

A deed from John POWERS to Stephen PARKER and acknowledged in open court by the said John POWERS ordered to be registered.

A deed from John POWERS to Hartwell AYERS, acknowledged in open court ordered to be registered &c.

A deed from John POWERS to Hartwell AYERS, acknowledged in open court ordered to be registered &c. [*repeat sic*]

A deed from River JORDON to John SPEED Esqr. acknowledged in open court ordered to be registered.

September 1784

September Court 1784
A deed from River JORDON to John SPEED Esqr. acknowledged in open court ordered to be registered.

A deed from Neil SMITH & Allen SMITH to John SPEED Esqr. and proved in open court by the oath of Alexr. WATSON ordered to be registered.

On motion of Colo. Samuel GARLAND from Virginia and Colo. Ed. WILLIAMS of Richmond County, executors of George JEFFERSON decd. came into court, and made return of sundry accounts in part of settling of the Jeffersons estate upon their oaths as pr. accounts filed &c.

Court adjourned untill tomorrow 9 o'clock.

Court met according to adjournment &c.
    Present   Charles MEDLOCK)
                    James COLE   ) Esqrs.
                      Benj. COVINGTON)

A deed from Archibald GRAHAM, to Daniel GRAHAM, proved in open court by the oath of Duncan McFARLAND ordered to be registred &c.

Wm. EASTERLING, Walter LEAK, Joseph HINES, John PEMBERTON, and Derby HANAGAN Esqr. made their returns to court.

A deed from Edward ALMOND to John EVANS acknowledged in open court ordered to be registred &c.

September 1784   Page 158

September Court 1784
Henry Wm. HARRINGTON)
    vs.   ) Deft. Inqy.
John McCAUL   ) In which suit the following jury was sworn (vizt) Dun RYE, John WALL, Joseph GADD, Samuel DAWKINS, Isaac YATES, Solomon DEARMAN, Gilbert McNEAR, Benjn. DEES, Arther DEES, Benjn. SKIPPER, Wm. HUNTER Sr., Thos. CRAWFORD who upon their oaths do say that they find for assess the plaintiff damage the sum of one penny & cost and so they say all &c.

Henry Wm. HARRINGTON)
    vs.   ) Deft. Inqy.
Duncan McCAUL   ) In which suit the aforegoing jury was sworn who upon their oaths do say that they assess damages for the plaintiff thirty pounds and cost and so they say all &c.

State   )
    vs.   ) I. A. B.
Moses CHAMBERS   ) In which suit the following jury was sworn (vizt) Dun RYE, John WALL, Joseph GADD, Gilbert McNEAR, Benjn. DEES, Arther DEES, Benjn. SKIPPER, Thos. CRAWFORD, and Richd. ADAMS who upon their oaths, do say that they find the defendant not guilty and so they say all &c.

September 1784   Page 159

September Court 1784
A deed from Elisabeth HALES and Thos. MOODY to Thos. CHILES and proved in open court by the oath of Solom GROSS ordered to be registred.

State   )
    vs.   ) I. A. B.
Thomas Plumr. WILLIAMS) In which suit the following jury was sworn (vizt) Wm. WALL, Dun RYE, John WALL, Joseph GADD, Samuel DAWKINS, Isaac YATES, Solomon DEARMAN, Gilbert McNEAR, Benj.

DEES, Arther DEES, Benjn. SKIPPER, and Thos. CRAWFORD who upon their oaths do find the defendant guilty in manner and form as charged in the bill and so they say all &c.

Court adjourned untill tomorrow 9 o'clock.

Court met according to adjournment
    Present   Charles MEDLOK)
                    John BOUND   ) Esqrs.
                    Derby HANAGAN)

State   )
  vs.   ) I. A. B.
John PEMBERTON) In which suit the following jury was sworn (vizt) Dun RYE, John WALL, Joseph GADD, Samuel DAWKINS, Isaac YATES, Solomon DEARMAN, Gilbert McNEAR, Benj. DEES, Arther DEES, Benjn. SKIPPER, Moses CHAMBERS and John CRAWFORDEsqr. upon their oaths do find that the defendant is not guilty in manner and form as charged in the bill and so they say all.

September 1784   *Page 160*

September Court 1784
Ordered that Owen SLAUGHTER Senr. be appointed overseer of the road, from Mountain Creek to Little River and all the hands from Coleman's Road, Little River, Mountain Creek & Pee Dee, work thereon &c.

A deed from John CROWSSON and wife to Demsey PITMAN and proved in open court by the oath of William HUSBAND, ordered to be registred &c.

On motion ordered that John PANKEY have leave to build a water grist mill on Mountain Creek, between the lower end of his plantation and the uper end [*blot*] thereof &c.

John LONG Jr.)
    vs.   ) Genl. Issue
Alexr. McCRAY) In which suit the following jury was sworn (to wit) Dun RYE, John WALL, Joseph GADD, Samuel DAWKINS, Isaac YATES, Solomon DEARMAN, Gilbert McNEAR, Benj. DEES, Arther DEES, Benjn. SKIPPER, Wm. HUNTER Senr. and John CRAWFORD who upon their oaths do say that they find for the plaintiff the sum of seven pounds with cost and so they say all.

Wm. LOVE)
vs.) Def. Inqy.
Wm. BRIGMAN) In which suit the aforegoing jury was sworn and find for the plaintiff the sum of fourteen pound \ten shilling/ and cost & so they say all £14-10.

September 1784   *Page 161*

September Court 1784
Gilbert McNEAR)
vs.) Genl. Issue
Wm. HUSBANDS) In which suit the following jury was sworn (to wit) Dun RYE, John WALL, Joseph GADD, Samuel DAWKINS, Isaac YATES, Solomon DEARMAN, Benj. DEES, Arther DEES, John CRAWFORD, William HUNTER, Benjn. SKIPPER, and William HUNTER Sr. who upon their oaths do say that they find for the defendant and so they say all &c.

State)
vs.) I. A. B.
John MASK) In which suit the following jury was sworn (to wit) Dun RYE, John WALL, Joseph GADD, Samuel DAWKINS, Isaac YATES, Solomon DEARMAN, Gilbert McNEAR, Benjn. DEES, Arther DEES, Benjn. SKIPPER, Wm. HUNTER Senr. and John CRAWFORD Esqr. who upon their oaths, do say that they find the defendant guilty in manner and form as charged in the bill and so they say all &c.

Ordered that Green Pond William THOMAS be appointed overseer of the road, from the Court House, in room of Derby HANAGAN &c.

Ordered that Wm. HUNTER Jr. be appointed overseer of the road from the Court House to the so. fork of Cartledge Creek and all the hands contiguous there to work thereon &c.

September 1784   *Page 162*

September Court 1784
Ordered that Henry ADCOCK have leave to build a water grist mill on the Rockey Fork of Hetchcock Creek about three hundred yards above John GRISSOM's old mill place &c.

On motion of Robert WEBB Esqr. ordered that the piece taken out of his ear by accident be admitted to the records of this court.

A deed from Daniel McDUFFEE to Wm. William McDANIEL acknowledged in open court ordered to be registered.

Court adjourned untill tomorrow 9 o'clock.

Court met according to adjournment.
Present   James COLE   )
              John BOUND   )
              Benjn. COVINGTON) Esqrs.
              Derby HANAGAN)

A deed from Solomon GROSS to Joseph SIMKINS acknowledged in open court ordered to be registred.

Ordered that Solomon GROSS be appointed overseer of the road, from the fork of the road, near Dry Creek, along the old road, near or above Coleman's mill, and from thence to where it goes into the road by Edwin INGRAM and the Widow DUDLEY's old place and that all the hands contiguous work thereon.

Ordered that Zacherias MARTIN be cited to court to shew cause whe he does not pay ~~the~~ fees in the suit DOBBINS vs. GEORGE.

September 1784   Page 163

September Court 1784
Ordered that the following persons be summoned to attend as juriors at the next court (vizt) Daniel HICKS, John MOREMAN, Andrew MOREMAN, Isem HALEY, Lott STRICKLIN, William WEBB, William JERNIGAN, Jesse BOUNDS, George BOUNDS, Thomas EVERITT, Daniel THOMAS, Daniel SMITH, Jonathon NEWBERY, John PANKEY, John COLEMAN, James BOSTICK, ~~John COLEMAN~~, Joseph TARBUTTON, Thomas JOWERS, Daniel McDANOLD, Wm. MORE, James MERIDETH, Peter USSERY, Richard ADAMS, Peter USSERY, Thomas ADAMS, John COVINGTON Senr., Henry COVINGTON, William HUNTER Sr.?, John CROWSSON, Thomas BLEWITT, and make return to the next court &c.

Ordered that Isaac YATES be appointed overseer of the road in room of John BOUNDS Esqr. and that the following hands work on the said road, (vizt) Donald & John CURRY, Elias GARDENER, Richd. DIXON, and his son, George BOUND, Samuel DAWKINS and all the hands that worked under the said BOUNDS, &c.

Edward WILLIAMS Esqr. came into court and qualified as Sheriff for the insuing year &c.

September 1784   Page 164

September Court 1784

Ordered that Jonathen NEWBERY be appointed overseer of the road in room of Ed. WILLIAMS Esqr.

Ordered that John JAMES Jr. be appointed overseer of the road from Wm. WATKINS ford on Hetchcock Creek to Crawford Old Road, and that the following hands work thereon (vizt) Thos. WATKINS, Wm. WATKINS Senr. \& his/ hands, Francis COLE, Peter COLE, & William WEBB work thereon &c.

Ordered that John McALESTER be appointed overseer of the road, from Falling Creek to the cross roads, and all the hands contiguous work thereon.

Ordered that Solomon GROSS be appointed Collector of the uper district, of said county, beginning at the mouth of Hitch-cock and running up the main creek to the head thereof, the a direct line to the nearest part of the county line &c.

Ordered that George MEDLOCK be appointed Collector in the lower district (agreeable to the aforeing line mentioned in the uper district) to the lower end of the county &c.

Ordered that the Clerk be allowed the sum of fifteen pounds for his e last years services &c.

September 1784   Page 165

September Court 1784
Ordered that the county tax for the year one thousand seven hundred & eighty four be four shillings on every poll tax and four shilling on every three hundred acres of land, or in proportion to a less or greater quantaty &c.

Ordered that Silas HALEY be appointed overseer of the road, from the fork in the road by Colo. MEDLOCKs, crossing at the land ford on Solomon's Creek, to Haley's Ferry, from thence into the road at the old school house, and that all the hands that heretofore were under the said Haley work thereon &c.

Ordered that Thos. CRAWFORD be appointed overseer of the road from Aulds ferry to said Crawfords, and that said Crawfords, John WALL, and Robert WEBB's hands, John EVANS, Benjn. EVERITT, & Adrey HICKS work thereon &c.

Court adjourned untill court in course.
        Charles MEDLOCK
Test. Wm. LOVE Clk. John BOUND
        Derby HANAGAN

December 1784

December Court 1784
At a County Court of Pleas and Quarter Sessions began and held for the County of Richmond, at the Court House therein on the last Monday in December in the year one thousand seven hundred and eighty four, and in the ninth year of American independance &c.
    Present   Charles MEDLOCK) Esqr.

Court adjourned untill tomorrow 10 o'clock.

Court met according to adjournment.
    Present   Charles MEDLOCK   )
                   John BOUND   )
                   Robert WEBB   ) Esqrs.
                   Benjn. COVINGTON)

Grand Jury sworn &c.
John COVINGTON Senr. Foreman, Wm. WEBB, Wm. JERNIGAN, Jesse BOUNDS, ~~John~~ \George/ BOUNDS, Thos. EVERITT, Daniel THOMAS, Simon THOMAS, Daniel SMITH, John PANKEY, Daniel McDANIEL, Henry COVINGTON, Wm. HUNTER Sr., & Thos. BLEWITT &c.

On motion of Alexr. CAMPBLE ordered that he have leave to keep an ordinary in Rockingham Town, upon giving bond & security &c.

December 1784

December Court 1784
On motion. A deed of gift from Duncan McCAUL Senr. to his grand daughter Mary McCAUL provided in open court by the oath of Wm. McDONALD, ordered to be registred &c.

A deed from Walter SLAUGHTER to Richard CAMPBLE, and proved in open court by the oath of Robert WEBB Esqr. ordered to be registred &c.

Court adjourned untill tomorrow 10 o'clock.

Court met according to adjournment.
    Present   Charles MEDLOCK)
                   John BOUNDS   ) Esqrs.
                   Dudley MASK   )

A deed from Edward WILLIAMS Esqr. Sheriff of said county to Isaac YATES acknowledged in open court ordered to be registred &c.

A deed from John CRAWFORD Esqr. acknowledged in open court ordered to be registred &c.

A deed from Thos. ADAMS to Alexr. McCRAY proved in open court by the oath of Duncan McCRAY ordered to be registred &c.

December 1784   *Page 168*

December Court 1784
A deed from John McDONALD to Owen McCAULEY & Peggy McCAULEY, proved in open court by the oath of James WATSON ordered to be registred &c.

A deed from George WEBB to John SMITH proved in open court by the oath of Daniel McNIEL, ordered to be registred &c.

Jacob COCKRAHAM)
    vs.) Deft. Inqy.
Anguish MELOY) In which suit the following jury was sworn (vizt) Daniel HICKS, George COLE, Jonathen NEWBERY, Thos. JOWERS, James MERIDETH, Peter USSERY, Richd. ADAMS, John CROWSSON, William WATKINS, John JAMES, Thos. CRAWFORD, William WALL, who upon their oath do say that they find for the plaintiff fifty pounds & so they say all &c.

William HUNTER Jr.) Genl. Issue
    vs.) P. P.?
Moses PETTUS) In which suit the aforegoing jury was sworn, and say upon their oaths that they find for the plaintiff twenty pounds and so they say all &c.

A deed from John WATSON to Roger McNAIR and proved in open court by the oath of Iver? CURRY ordered to be registred.

December 1784   *Page 169*

December Court 1784
John LEVERITT)
    vs.) Genl. Issue
Randolph McDONALD) In which suit the aforegoing jury was sworn, and say upon their oaths that they find for the defendant and so they say all &c.

A deed from Joseph RYE to Henry Wm. HARRINGTON Esqr. and proved in open court by the oath of George MEDLOCK ordered to be registred &c.

A deed from Joseph RYE to John JONES, and proved in open court by the oath of George MEDLOCK ordered to be registred &c.

A deed from Sampson WILLIAMS to Wm. McDONALD, proved in open court by the oath of Thos. ADAMS ordered to be registred &c.

A deed from Simon THOMAS to Daniel THOMAS and acknowledged in open court ordered to be registred.

A deed from Micheal AULD to Wm. SMITH proved in open court by the oath of John AULD Esqr. ordered to be registred &c.

Court adjourned untill tomorrow 10 o'clock.

December 1784 *Page 170*

December Court 1784
Court meet according to adjournment.
    Present   Robert WEBB   )
                   John BOUNDS   )
                   Walter LEAK   ) Esqr.
                   Derby HANAGAN)

A deed from Thomas TURNER to Neil McNAIR and proved in open court by the oath of Archabald CAMPBLE ordered to be registred &c.

Ordered that Leviny LEWIS be fined agreeable to law in the sum of twenty five shillings, and remain in custody of the Sheriff untill the fine paid &c.

A deed from George WEBB to Iver CURRY and proved in open court by the oath of Roger McNEAR who was present when Allen MARTIN and Jehuele CROWSSON the subscribing witness's who assigned their names to the above deed ordered to be registred &c.

A deed from River JORDON to Henry Wm. HARRINGTON Esqr. as proved in open court by the oath of George MEDLOCK ordered to be registred &c.

A deed from Solomon RYE to Henry Wm. HARRINGTON Esqr. and proved in open court by the oath of George MEDLOCK ordered to be registred &c.

Ordered that a road be laid of leading from Pates Mill, to cross Gum Swamp at the old muster ground, and the hands...

December 1784   *Page 171*

December Court 1784
...to lay out the said road is Hendley SNEED, Solomon SNEED, Daniel McKASKILL, Zachs. JOHNSON, Simon PARKER, Elisha COTTENGAME, Wm. COTTENGAME, Nicholas GREEN, Wm. WOODLE, Matthew WOODLE, Jacob MORRIS, & Isaac WILLIAMSON work thereon &c.

Nancy McINNISE)
    vs.   ) Genl. Issue
Wm. HUNTER Sr.) In which suit the following jury was sworn (to wit) Daniel HICKS, Jonathen NEWBERY, Thomas JOWERS, Richd. ADAMS, Thos. ADAMS, Nicholas STONE, John JONES Sr., Joseph TARBUTTON, John PARNEL, Nathl. HARRINGTON, William MIMS, Isreal SNEED, Jr. who upon their oath do say that they find for the plaintiff the sum of eight pounds and so they say all.

On motion of Wm. CRAWFORD Esqr. reasons in arrest of judgment filed &c.

A deed from Solomon GROSS to John DEGARNOT and acknowledged in open court, ordered to be registered &c.

Ordered that the following persons be appointed to lay of a road ~~from~~ agreeable to the former order at Hilyards Ford and that James MERIDETH, Joseph GADD Sr., Joseph GADD Jr., Hardy STEPHENS, Walter LEAK, Charles ROBESON, John BOSTICK, James BOSTICK, Daniel McDANIEL, Benjn. POWEL, Wm. McGUIRE, James SMITH, Wm. NEWBERY, Jonathen NEWBERY, & John PANKEY & make return at the next court &c.

December 1784   *Page 172*

December Court 1784
Court adjourned untill tomorrow 10 o'clock.

Court met according to adjournment.
    Present   Charles MEDLOCK)
                   Darby HANAGAN   ) Esqrs.
                   Dudley MASK   )

On motion Wm. PUCKITT Esqr. was appointed guarden to John COLEMAN Jr. and gave bond in the sum of two hundred pounds specie &c.

A deed from John SPEED to John PONDER, acknowledged in open court ordered to be registred &c.

Christian McCRAY)
    vs.   ) Genl. Issue
George CARTER   ) In which suit the following jury was sworn (to wit) Daniel HICKS, John WALL, Wm. HUNTER, Henry ADCOCK, Laurance OBRYAN, Robert WILSON, Joseph TARBUTTON, John CRAWFORD, John JAMES, Solomon SNEED, John COLE Senr., Thos. CRAWFORD, who upon their oaths do say that they find for the plaintiff five twelve [!] shillings and so they say all &c.

A deed from Anguish NICHOLSON to Daniel MARTIN, proved in open court by the oath of Roger KINZIE ordered to be registred &c.

December 1784   *Page 173*

December Court 1784
A deed from Robert WEBB Esqr. & wife to John JONES acknowledged in open court ordered to be registred &c.

A deed from John THOMAS to John JONES and proved in open court by the oath of Henry Wm. HARRINGTON Esqr. ordered to be registred.

Ordered that Morgan BROWN Esqr. be allowed the sum of thirteen pounds for serving as County Sole<u>seter</u> for December court 1783 March court 1784 including his services during his appointment &c.

Nancy McINNISE)
    vs.   ) Genl. Issue
Wm. HUNTER Jr.) In which suit the following jury was sworn (to wit) Daniel HICKS, Jonathen NEWBERY, Thos. JOWERS, Richd. ADAMS, Henry ADCOCK, Robert WILSON, Thos. ADAMS, Joseph TARBUTTON, John JAMES, Solomon SNEED, Thos. CRAWFORD, John PARNEL, who upon their oaths do say that the find for the defendant, and so they say all &c.

Ordered that Solomon GROSS be appointed Patro<u>ll</u> from Rockingham to the mouth of Hitch-cock & to Haleys Ferry for the <u>i</u>nsuing year &c.

December 1784   *Page 174*

December Court 1784
Court adjourned untill tomorrow 9 o'clock.

Court met according to adjournment.

Present   Charles MEDLOCK)
                    Robert WEBB   )
                    James COLE   ) Esqrs.
                    John BOUND   )

Edward WILLIAM assignee)
of Henry LIGHTFOOT   )
   vs.   )
Elisabeth HALEY &   )
Thos. MOODY   ) In which suit the following jury was sworn (to wit) Joseph TARBUTTON, Daniel HICKS, Jonathon NEWBERRY, Thos. JOWERS, Richard ADAMS, Thos. ADAMS, John COVINGTON Jr., Daniel SMITH, Thomas CRAWFORD, William HUNTER Senr., David SNEED Jr., Robert WILSON who upon their oaths do say that the find for the plaintiff the sum of sixty one pounds six shillings and so they say all &c.

Wm. McGUIRE)
   vs.   ) Def. Inqy.
Richd. POWEL)
Thos. JINING   ) In which suit the aforegoing was sworn and find for the plaintiff the sum of twelve pounds twelve shillings and two pence & so they all &c.

December 1784   *Page 175*

December Court 1784
Jacob FALCONBURY   )
Executor of Wm. BAKER) Genl. Issue &c
   vs.   )
John COLEMAN   ) In which suit the aforegoing jury was sworn and say on their oaths that they find for the plaintiff the sum of one hundred and one pounds eighteen shillings and so they say all.

Ordered that the Sheriff summons the following persons to attend as a jury at the next court (to wit) James BOSTICK, Peter USSERY, James BAGGET, Samuel DAWKINS, John DAWKINS, Solomon DEARMAN, Isaac YATES, Wm. TERRY, Wm. JERNIGAN, Andrew MOREMAN, Lott STRICKLIN, John COLEMAN, John COLE Sr., Thos. GIBSON, Nelson GIBSON, Tillotson OBRYAN, Henry ADCOCK, John McCALMON, John EZEL, Wm. McDONALD, John SMITH, James SMITH, Benjn. POWEL, Solomon SPRAWLS, Luke ROBERTSON, Matthew COVINGTON, Nathl. HARRINGTON, John JAMES Jr., Wm. MIMS, Silas HALEY, John SNEED, Isreal SNEED Jr., David SNEED Senr., John WALL, Laurance EVERITT, John ROBESON & make return at the next court &c.

December 1784

December Court 1784
James BOLTON)
    vs.) Def. Inqy.
John KIMBOROUGH) In which the aforegoing jury was sworn except, Thos. JOWERS, which Randle HALEY was in lieu and upon their oaths do say that they find for the plaintiff the sum of fifty pounds and so they say all.

Ordered that Wm. McGUIRE be appointed Constable from Little River to the uper end of the county &c.

Ordered that Stephen BOUNDS be appointed overseer of the road from the crossroads to Coles bridge and all the hands contiguous work thereon &c.

Ordered that Wm. LOVE, Silas HALEY & Thomas CRAWFORD, be appointed to attend as a vinire at Salisbury in March next &c.

Ordered that the Clerk be allowed the sum of five pounds for extra services agreeable to act of assembly.

Ordered that Joseph SIMKINS be allowed the sum of three pound twelve shilling \for two courts/ agreable to his accounts filed&c.

December 1784

December Court 1784
Ordered that Joseph SIMKINS be allowed the sum of four pounds sixteen shillings for his services for two court agreable to his accounts filed &c.

Ordered that Benjn. MOREMAN be appointed overseeer of the road in room of Silas HALEY &c.

Ordered that John EVANS & Adrey HICKS be annexed to Colo. CRAWFORDs order.

Court adjourned untill court in course.
                              Charles MEDLOCK
    Test Wm. LOVE Clk.   Robert WEBB
                              John BOUND
                              James COLE

March 1785
March Court 1785
At a County Court of Pleas and Quarter Sessions began and held for the County of Richmond at the Court House therein on the last Monday in

March one thousand seven hundred and eighty five in the ninth year of American independence &c.
 Present Charles MEDLOCK)
      Robert WEBB   ) Esqrs.
      Josephe HINES)

March 1785   *Page 178*

March Court 1785
A deed from Natheniel SANDERS to John McFARLAND and proved in open court by the oath of Duncan McFARLAND ordered to be registred &c.

A deed from Thomas GIBSON to Donald McKOY, acknowledged in open court ordered to be registred &c.

A deed from Archelus MOREMAN to Henry Wm. HARRINGTON Esqr. acknowledged in open court ordered to be registred &c.

Luke ROBESON and Obedience his wife late the relict of Wm. ADAMS, deceased came into court and prayed letters of administration and was granted by the court, and gave Solomon GROSS & Richard LEVERITT bail for their performance, in the sum of seven hundred pounds specie &c.

Ordered that Wm. JARNIGAN be excused from serving as a juror at this present term.

Grand jury sworn, John COLE Sr. foreman, James BOSTICK, Peter USSERY, Isaac YATES, Wm. TERRY, Lott STRICKLIN, Thomas GIBSON, Nelson GIBSON, Henry ADCOCK, John SMITH, Luke ROBESON, Nathl. HARRINGTON, John JAMES Jr., John SNEED & David SNEED Jr. &c.

Court adjourned untill tomorrow 9 o'clock.

March 1785   *Page 179*

March Court 1785
Court met according to adjournment.
 Present Charles MEDLOCK)
      John SPEED   ) Esqrs.
      Walter LEAK   )

Ordered that Anguish McALESTER be appointed overseer of the road in room of Herod CLARK, that leads over the Shew-Heel at the Rockey Ford &c.

Ordered that a road be laid of the nearest and best way from the south line near Summerals mill – to cross at or near Greens? old muster ground on Gum Swamp, from thence to cross Jordon's Creek at Murphys cowpens, from thence a direct course to cross Downing Creek at or near Farleys Bridge and that Duncan McFARLAND, Archabald McMILLON, Alexr. WATSON, Malcom BLUE, Robert McNAIR, Dugal McFARLAND, John RAY, John BRICE, Alexr. GORDON, Thomas TURNER, Moses HODGES, Dugal BLUE, James SMILEY, John DOVE, Moses TURNER, be appointed to lay of the same and make return to the next court &c.

A deed from Solomon FISHER & wife to Duncan McKOY, and proved in open court by the oath of Neil MARTIN ordered to be registered &c.

Court adjourned untill 2 o'clock p.m.

Court met according to adjournment.

March 1785   *Page 180*

March Court 1785
A deed from Farquard McCRAY Senr. to Farquard McCRAY Jr. and proved in open court by the oath of Alexr. McKOY ordered to be registered &c.

Thos. SMITH)
    vs.) Def. Inqy.
Wm. McQUEEN) In which suit the following jury was sworn (to wit) Samuel DAWKINS, John DAWKINS, Solomon DEARMAN, Tillotson OBRYAN, Wm. MIMS, Isreal SNEED Jr., George DAWKINS, James JAMES, Dugal McFARLAND, Luke WILLIAMS, Robert WILSON & Jesse BOUNDS who upon their oaths do say that the find for the plaintiff the sum of eight pounds and so they say all.

Anguish McDANIEL)
    vs.)
Wm. McQUEEN) In which suit the aforegoing jury was sworn and find for the plaintiff the sum of five pounds twelve shilling specie & so they say all.

Court adjourned untill tomorrow 10 o'clock.

Court met according to adjournment.
    Present   Charles MEDLOCK)
                    Dudley MASK)
                    Walter LEAK) Esqrs.
                    Joseph HINES)
                    John BOUNDS)

March 1785 — Page 181

March Court 1785
A deed from Unity LOUGE? to John MARTIN and proved in open court by the oath of John DOVE ordered to be registred &c.

Wm. HUNTER Jr.)
vs.) Genl. Issue
Moses CHAMBERS) In which suit the following jury was sworn (to wit) James SMITH, Samuel DAWKINS, John DAWKINS, Solomon DEARMAN, Tillotson OBRYAN, William MIMS, Isreal SNEED, Daniel SNEED, Robert WILSON, John PARNEL, James BOUNDS, Daniel CARMICAL, who upon their oaths do say that the find for the defendant, three pounds nine shillings and nine pence & so they say all &c.

A deed from Luke ROBESON to James PHILLIPS and acknowledged in open court ordered to be registred &c.

A deed from Benjn. COVINGTON & wife to John McFARLAND acknowledged in open court ordered to be registred, &c.

On motion the Last Will & Testament of James PHILLIPS deceased was proved in open court by the oath of Joseph HINES who saw the other subscribing witnesses assign their names thereto ordered to be admitted to record, &c. After the aforegoing will and testament was...

March 1785 — Page 182

March Court 1785
...exhibited in open court and duly proved Solomon PHILLIPS one of the executors there named came into open court and was duly qualified according to law &c.

A deed from John DUNHUM [*DURHUM?*] & wife to Joseph HINES Esqr. and was duly proved in open court by the oath of George JOWERS, ordered to be registred &c.

A deed from William EASTERLING to John MURPHY, acknowledged in open court ordered to be registred &c.

Court adjurned untill tomorrow 10 o'clock.

Court met according to adjournment.
    Present   Robert WEBB)
                   John BOUND) Esqrs.
                   Joseph HINES)

A deed from Wm. SMITH to Archabald McKOY and proved in open court by the oath of Donald McKOY ordered to be registred.

James SMITH, discharged from his attendance as a juror at this court &c.

On motion of John McNARY Esqr. and upon his affidavit being attorney for the plaintiff in the suit James ROCHEL vs. Wm. HUNTER the suit was reinstated and brought forward &c.

March 1785   *Page 183*

March Court 1785
State   )
    vs.   ) Presentment
Thos. Plumer WILLIAMS) In which traverse the following jury was sworn (to wit) Samuel DAWKINS, John DAWKINS, Solomon DEARMAN, Tillotson OBRYAN, Wm. HUNTER, John McALESTER, ~~John DUNBAR,~~ John DUNBAR, John CROWSSON, Wm. WEBB, James BOUNDS, Richard ADAMS, and William WATKINS who upon their oaths do say that they find the defendant not guilty in manner and form as charged in the presentment & so they say all &c.

State   )
    vs.   ) Presentment
Solomon GROSS) In which suit the following jury was sworn (to wit) Stephen COLE, Randle HALEY, Gilbert McNAIR, Roger McNAIR, Benjn. POWEL, Daniel SNEED, John COVINGTON Jr., Josiah FREEMAN, John DAWKINS, Wm. KELLEY, John COLEMAN, Silas HALEY, who upon their oaths do say that they find the defendant guilty in manner and form as charged in the presentmentand so they say all &c.

State   )
    vs.   ) Presentment
Alex BIGHAM) In which suit the aforegoing jury was sworn and find the defendant guilty in manner & form as charged in the presentment &c.

March 1785   *Page 184*

March Court 1785
State   )
    vs.   ) Presentment
Moses CHAMBERS) In which suit the aforegoing jury was sworn & find the defendant guilty in manner and form as <u>as</u> charged in the presentment and so they say all &c.

Nathl. HARRINGTON bound over in behalf of the State vs. George CARTER? in the sum of – £50.

State)
   vs.) Presentment
Moses CHAMBERS) In which suit the aforegoing jury was sworn and find the defendant guilty in manner & form as charged in the presentment for a common drunkard, and so they say all &c.

State)
   vs.) Presentment
Moses CHAMBERS) In which suit the aforegoing jury was sworn & find the defendant guilty in manner and form as charged in the presentment &c.

Demsey PITMAN came into court and was bound for his appearance at the next court in the sum of –) £50-. Richd. LEVERITT and Thos. Plummer WILLIAMS securities each in the sum of £25 –) £50.

March 1785

March Court 1785
Henry Wm. HARRINGTON)
   vs.) Deft. Inqy.
Alexr. McCRAY) In which suit the aforegoing jury was sworn and find for the plaintiff one penny and cost & so they say all &c.

Henry Wm. HARRINGTON)
   vs.) Deft. Inqy.
James USSHER) In which suit the aforegoing jury was sworn & find for the plaintiff one penny & cost and so they say all &c.

Ordered that there be a bridge built over Hetchcock-Cock Creek, between the mouth of Falling Creek and Crowssons mill, and that Charles MEDLOCK, Benjn. COVINGTON, Joseph HINES, Wm. LOVE and Robert WEBB Esqrs. be appointed to fix on the place to set the bridge and make return to the next court.

Ordered that a bill of sale be admitted to record, from Elisabeth HUTCHENS to her daughter Mary HUTCHENS proved in open court, ordered to be registred, &c.

March 1785

March Court 1785

John McINNISE)
    vs   ) Genl. Issue
John LONG   ) In which suit the following jury was sworn (to wit) Samuel DAWKINS, John DAWKINS, Solomon DEARMAN, Tillotson OBRYAN, Wm. MIMS, Wm. HUNTER Jr., John McALESTER, John DUNBAR, John CROWSSON, Wm. WEBB, James BOUNDS, Richd. ADAMS, who upon their oaths do say that they find for the defendant, and so they say all &c.

A deed from John BETHIGH and wife to Malcom McKASKILL and proved in open court by the oath of Derby HANAGAN, ordered to be registred.

Court adjourned untill 8 o'clock tomorrow.

Court met according to adjournment.
    Present   John BOUNDS)
                  Walter LEAK   ) Esqrs.
                  Joseph HINES)

A deed from Alexr. McKOY to Henry Wm. HARRINGTON Esqr. acknowledged in open court ordered to be registred &c.

A deed from Thomas GADDY & wife to Alexr. WATSON, and proved in open court by the oath of Dugal BLUE, ordered to be registred &c.

March 1785   *Page 187*

March Court 1785
James PUKITT   )
    vs.   ) Payment & Release &c
Thomas CARTER) In which suit the following jury was sworn (vizt) Samuel DAWKINS, John DAWKINS, Solomon DEARMAN, Tillotson OBRYAN, Wm. MIMS, John DUNBAR, Wm. HUNTER, Wm. SMITH, Adrey HICKS, George BOUNDS, John McALESTER, Thomas JOHNSON, who upon their oaths do say, that they find for the plaintiff five pounds, five shillings and so they say all &c.

A deed from John ROBESON, & wife to Natheniel CHAIRS, proved in open court by the oath of James BOSTICK ordered to be registred &c.

John SPEED)
    vs.   ) Genl. Issue
John CHILES) In which suit the following jury was sworn (vizt) Samuel DAWKINS, John DAWKINS, Solomon DEARMAN, Tillotson OBRYAN, Wm. MIMS, John COLEMAN, George BOUNDS, Wm. HUNTER, Wm. SMITH, Wm. WATKINS, John WATKINS, John McALESTER, who

upon their oaths do say that they find for the plaintiff the sum of eight pounds and so they say all &c.

March 1785 — Page 188

March Court 1785
On motion Thomas ~~BLEWITT~~ \CRAWFORD/ exhibited his claim and was allowed the sum of six pounds and four pence &c.

State)
   vs.) Ind. A. B.
River JORDON) In which suit the aforegoing jury was sworn and say that they find the defendant guilty as charged in the bill, and so they say all &c.

John CHILES)
   vs.) Genl. Issue
Thos. JININGS) In which suit the aforegoing jury was sworn, and find for the plaintiff the sum of six pounds eight shilling with interest from the time it was due untill paid and so they say all &c.

A deed from William BAKER and wife to William SEAGO proved in open court by the oath of Thos. ALMOND ordered to be registred &c.

A deed from Henry ADCOCK and wife to Malcom BLUE, acknowledged in open court ordered to be registred &c.

A deed from Edward SMITH to John EZEL proved in open court by the oath of James CAMPBLE ordered to be registred.

March 1785 — Page 189

March Court 1785
Burwell LENAIR)
   vs.) Genl. Issue &c
Luke ROBESON) In which suit the aforegoing jury was sworn, and say they find for the plaintiff the sum of ten pounds thirteen shilling with interest from the time it became due untill paid and so they say all &c.

Silas HALEY)
   vs.) Genl. Issue &c
Josiah LYON) In which suit the aforegoing jury was sworn and say they find for the plaintiff the sum of forty pounds six shillings and four pence and so they say all &c.

On motion of John McNARY Esqr. attorney in behalf of the defendant moves for an arrest of judgment and the reasons to be filed &c.

Court adjourned untill 2 o'clock p.m.

Court met according to adjournment.
  Present Charles MEDLOCK)
        John SPEED   ) Esqrs.
        Joseph HINES)

A deed from Robert SPEED to Zacherias MARTIN proved in open court, ordered to be registered &c.

Ordered that Aron NIGHT have leave to keep an Ordinary in the county aforesaid and gave Daniel HICKS be his security &c.

March 1785   *Page 190*

March Court 1785
John WHITE)
  vs.   ) Genl. Issue
John COPLAND) In which suit the aforegoing jury was sworn, and say they for the plaintiff the sum of five shilling and so they say all.

Sarah CROWSSON)
  vs.   ) Genl. Issue
John COLE Jr.) In which suit the following jury was sworn (to wit) Samuel DAWKINS, John DAWKINS, Solomon DEARMAN, Tillotson OBRYAN, William MIMS, John COLEMAN, Wm. SMITH, Wm. WATKINS, John WATKINS, John SNEED, Wm. HUSBANDS, Samuel COVINGTON who upon their oaths do say they find for the plaintiff and so they say all &c.

On motion of Wm. CRAWFORD Esqr. attorney in behalf of the defendant reasons in arrest of judgment to be filed &c.

Court adjourned untill tomorrow 10 o'clock.

Court met according to adjournment.
  Present Charles MEDLOCK)
        Dudley MASK   ) Esqrs.
        Joseph HINES   )

Wm. HUNTER Jr. vs. James ROCHEL, Did. Po. to Roan County to take the examination John BOWEN? and Ephrain POTTS for Plaintiff &c.

James ROCHELS vs. James JININGS Did. Po. to So. Carolina to take the examination of Robert DICKSON.

Ordered that Wm. THOMAS be appointed overseer of the Catfish Road from Blewitts Ferry to the Rockey Fork and all the hands contiguous work thereon.

March 1785

March Court 1785
Ordered that Thomas GIBSON be overseer of the road from the Rockey Fork to Coles Bridge and all the hands contiguous work thereon &c.

Ordered that Benjn. POWEL be appointed overseer of the road from Masks Ferry to Little River at Rayfords Ford &c.

Ordered that Daniel CARMICAL be appointed overseer of the road in room of Herod CLARK &c.

Ordered that James BAGGET, Andrew MOREMAN, John McCALMON, John EZEL, Benjn. POWEL, Solomon SPRAWLS, Matthew COVINGTON, John WALL, Laurance EVERITT and John ROBESON be fined Ni Si, and that a citation issue to have them summoned to the next court to make their excuse &c.

Burwell STRICKLIN was allowed the sum of one pound twelve shillings for his serving as Constable at December court 1784 and forty shillings for serving five days at March court 1785.

Ordered that Sarah CROWSSON be allowed the sum of five pounds for keeping a base born child, for one year from this term &c.

Joseph STRICKLIN was allowed the sum of forty eight shilling for his attendance as Constable six days at March court 1785.

Ordered that the following persons appointed a jury to serve at the next June court (to wit) John HALL, Joseph HALL, Wm. COTTENGAME, Thos. SUMMERAL, Richd. ADAMS, Wm. WEBB, Daniel McDANIEL, Randolph HALEY, John TURNAGE, John MATTHEWS, Darius BURNS,...

March 1785

March Court 1785
...Hendley SNEED, Wm. WOODLE, Elisha COTTENGAME, Wm. JERNIGAN, Zachs. MOREMAN, Nathl. CHAIRS, John MASK, James PATTERSON, Benjn. DUMAS Senr., Benjn. DUMAS Jr., Andrew DUMAS, Hardy STEPHENS, Joseph TARBUTTON, Owen SLAUGHTER Senr., Francis COLE, Thomas BLEWITT, Nicholas STONE, Laurance EVERITT, David SNEED Senr., Daniel HICKS, Robert WILSON, Shadrick

BAGGET, Thos. CRAWFORD, John WALL, Jesse BOUND, and make return to the next court &c.

Ordered that James SMITH be appointed overseer of the road from the Grassy Islands to the road crossing Naked Creek, from thence to the road that is the county line, thence to the new bridge and all the hands contiguous work thereon &c.

Ordered that John COLE Jr. be commited to goal [*jail*], and there to remain until he pay five pounds, or gives sufficient security for the payment of the above said sum at the expiration of one year from this term.

Court adjourned untill court in course.

Test Wm. LOVE Clk. Signed

Charle MEDLOCK   )
Joseph HINES   )
John BOUND   ) Esqrs.
Benjn. COVINGTON)

June 1785

At a County Court of Pleas and Quarter Sessions began & held for the County of Richmond at the Court House therein on the last Monday in June in the ninth year of American independence Anno Dom. 1785.
    Present – Charles MEDLOCK Esqr.

Court adjourned untill tomorrow 9 o'clock.

Met according to adjournment &c.

June 1785

June Court 1785
    Present   Charles MEDLOCK)
                   Walter LEAK   ) Esqrs.
                   Derby HANAGAN   )

Andrew MOREMAN appeared before the court upon a citation as a dilinquent juror, and his fine was remitted &c upon paying the clerks fees &c.

A deed from Thomas CHILES to Richd. LEVERITT, proved in open court by the oath of John McALESTER, ordered to be registred.

A deed from George COLLINS to James SMITH, acknowledged in open court, ordered to be registred &c.

Ordered that James SMITH be appointed overseer of the road from the fork of the Grassy Island Road, to Graham's Fork and all the hands contiguous work thereon.

Ordered that Randolph McDANIEL be appointed overseer of the road from Graham's Fork to the road that divides the county and all the hands contiguous work thereon.

Ordered that Anguish McNEIL be appointed to serve as Constable the insuing year in lieu of Dugal McFARLAND on the east side of Gum Swamp.

June 1785 — Page 194

June Court 1785
Ordered that John MATTHEWS be appointed overseer of the road, that leads from the south line, near Summerals Mill, crossing Joes Creek, the Beaver dam, and Gum Swamp at a ford about half a mile below, Greens Old Muster Ground, to Roger McNAIRs, & all the hands in Capt. EASTERLINGs district excepting those who have worked at the Polley bridge, to work on the said road, under the said overseer.

Ordered that Duncan McFARLAND be appointed overseer of the road, that leads from Roger McNAIRs on the Gum Swamp, crossing Jordons Creek at the old cowpens, Juniper at Rays Mill, Shew-Heel above Bobs Ford a small distance, and Drowning Creek at or near where Farleys Bridge formerly stood, and all the hands in the uper part of the district east of Gum Swamp work thereon &c.

George CARTER bound over to this court in the sum of for Pet. Lar.) £100-. Richd. ADAMS security jointly with him &c.

A deed from Philemon THOMAS & wife to John COLE Senr. proved in open court by the oath of John SPEED Esqr. ordered to be registred.

A deed from John HALL to Joel HALL acknowledged in open court, ordered to be registred &c.

June 1785 — Page 195

June Court 1785
Grand Jury sworn – John WALL foreman, Daniel McDANIEL, Wm. WEBB, Randolph HALEY, John TURNAGE, John MATTHEWS, Darius BURN, Hendley SNEED, Nathl. CHEARS, John MASK, James PATTERSON, Owen SLAUGHTER Senr., Thomas BLEWITT, Nicholas STONE, Daniel HICKS, Thos. CRAWFORD, & Jesse BOUNDS.

State)
vs.) Ind. Pet. Lar.
George CARTER Jr.) In which suit the following jury was sworn (vizt) John HALL, Joseph HALL, Wm. COTTENGAME, Wm. WOODLE, Elisha COTTENGAME, Wm. JARNIGAN, Benjn. DUMAS Jr., Joseph TARBUTTON, Laurance EVERITT, Robert WILSON, John COVINGTON, & George BOUNDS who upon their oaths do say that they find the defendant guilty in manner and form as charged in the bill and so they say all &c.

On motion of Wm. CRAWFORD Esqr. attorney for defendant entred his reasons in arrest of judgment &c.

On motion of Nathl. CHEARS ordered that his mark be entred upon the records (to wit) a crop & hole in the right ear, & an uper square in the left &c.

On motion of Moses PETTUS, ordered that the loss of a piece of his ear bitt off in a sudden affray be entred on the records of this court &c.

June 1785   *Page 196*

June Court 1785
James JOHNSON)
vs.) Case &c
Dugal McMILLON) In which suit the aforegoing jury was sworn, and upon their oaths do say that they find for the plaintiff and assess his damages to seventeen pounds and cost and so they say all &c.

On motion of John McNARY Esqr. attorney for defendant, offered his reasons in arrest of judgment, which was argued, and over ruled, then John McNARY Esqr. in behalf of the defendant, prayed an appeal from the judgment of the court on the reasons in arrest of judgment, John McNARY Esqr. & Alexr. McLEOD bail for the appeal in the sum of thirty four pounds &c.

Court adjourned untill tomorrow 9 o'clock.

Court met according to adjournment.

    Present   Charles MEDLOCK)
                    James COLE)
                      John BOUNDS) Esqrs.
                      Derby HANAGAN)

Wm. HUSBANDS)
    vs.   ) Case
John LONG Jr.   ) In which suit the following jury was sworn (vizt) John HALL, Joseph HALL, Wm. COTTENGAME, Wm. WOODLE, Elisha COTTENGAME, Wm. JARNIGAN, Benjn. DUMAS Jr., Joseph TARBUTTON, Laurance EVERITT, Joseph FREEMAN, \Robert WILSON,/ Wm. HUNTER Jr. who upon their oaths do say that they find for the plaintiff one penny & six pence cost and so they say all.

June 1785   *Page 197*

June Court 1785
Kathrine MORRISON)
    vs.   ) Case Assumpsit
Wm. HUSBAND   ) In which suit the aforegoing jury was sworn and upon their oaths do say that they find for the plaintiff and assess her damages to four pounds and cost & so they say all &c.

On motion of John McNARY Esqr. he offered reasons in arrest of judgment the reasons being argued and adjudged by the court to be insufficient &c.

Zacherias HAGGAN)
    vs.   ) Trespass
John HARRY   ) In which suit the aforegoing jury was sworn, who upon their oaths do say they find for the plaintiff and assess his damages to twenty seven pounds & cost and so they say all &c.

A deed from Wm. NEWBERY & wife to John COLEMAN, acknowledged in open court ordered to be registred.

On motion of George BOUND, ordered that he have his mark recorded as followeth, a crop & slit in the right ear &c.

Ordered that William LOVE, Edward WILLIAMS and Jame BOSTICK be appointed to appraise Hugh LEATON decd. estate – and made their report of the appraisement of the said estate to the amount of two hundred & eighty seven pounds twelve shillings specie &c.

June 1785   *Page 198*

June Court 1785
James BOLTON bound over to this present court by James COLE Esqr. in the sum of) £100. Richd. POWEL security in the sum of – £50-. John McDONALD ~~security~~ prosecutor in – £50-.

Bexley John LAMBDAN)
    vs.)
The executors of G. JEFFERSON Dd.) In which suit the aforegoing jury was sworn and on their oaths do find for the plaintiff and assess his damages to six pounds, sixteen shillings and six pence with cost of suit & that he receive interest on five pounds twelve shilling and six pence of the judgment from July 1778 untill paid & so they say all &c.

Ordered that Solomon GROSS be appointed administrator upon the estate of Wm. USSERY decd. upon his qualifying & giving bond and security agreeable to law &c.

Ordered that Thomas BLEWITT be appointed guardian to Uriah STONE, Benjamin STONE, William STONE and Rebeckah STONE orphans of Nicholas STONE deceased and to give bond in the sum of one thousand pounds.

Court adjourned untill tomorrow 9 o'clock.

M<u>ee</u>t according to adjournment.
    Present   Charles MEDLOCK)
                       Dudley MASK   ) Esqrs.
                       Darby HANAGAN)

The Last Will and Testament of John WALTERS deceased was exhibitted in open court by the executors therein named. Ordered that the same be admitted to record…

June 1785   *Page 199*

June Court 1785
…and was <u>according</u> proved in open court by the oaths of James BOSTICK & Sampson SELLERS – it being the same will that was formerly laid over the court not being satisfied to have it admitted to record untill this present court &c.

After the Last Will and Testament of John WALTERS deceased was exhibitted in open court & duly proved as aforesaid George WALTERS, one of the executors therein named came into open court and was duly qualified as executor thereto agreeable to law &c.

Ordered that George MEDLOCK be allowed the sum of sixteen pounds fifteen shillings and five pence for involvement in his collection for the year one thousand seven hundred & eighty four.

Lovick STEELY bound over to this court in the sum of – £100-0. James HUNTER witness vs. STEELY in the sum of £50-0. Wm. COULTER prosecutor in the sum of – £50-0.

James LONG bound to this court in the sum of £100-0. Wm. WATKINS & Wm. HUNTER Jr. each in the sum of as securities – £50-0.

Micheal DOCKERY bound in the sum of – £50-0. Wm. HUNTER & Wm. WATKINS securities each in the sum of £50 25 –) £100 50-.

The above acknowledged before Charles MEDLOCK Esqr.

John McDONALD bound as a witness against Richd. POWEL in the sum of £50-0.

June 1785 Page 200

June Court 1785
Edward WILLIAMS Esqr. Sheriff made return of the amount of the sales of the estate of Wm. ADAMS deceased to the amount of seven hundred & thirty six pounds two shillings specie &c. £736-2.

A deed from William ASHLEY to Alexander McKOY proved in open court by the oath of Sampson SELLERS ordered to be registred.

George MEDLOCK came into court and made his settlement of the county tax for the year one thousand seven hundred & eighty four &c.

Ordered that Richd. LEVERITT be appointed to serve as Sheriff the insuing year &c.

State   )
    vs.   ) Presentment &c.
Thos. DOBBINS) In which suit the following jury was sworn (to wit) John HALL, Joseph HALL, William COTTENGAME, Wm. WOODLE, Elisha COTTENGAME, Wm. JARNIGAN, Benjn. DUMAS Jr., Joseph TARBUTTON, Laurance EVERITT, Robert WILSON, John COVINGTON, & George BOUNDS, and on their oaths do say that they find the defendant guilty in manner and form as charged in the presentment & so they say all &c – whereupon Wm. CRAWFORD Esqr. attorney for the defendant offered his reasons in arrest of judgment. The reason when argued the court were of opinion that the reasons was insufficient – & fined accordingly.

June 1785

June Court 1785
Dudley MASK Esqr. came into court and qualified that he was a witness to a Power of Attorney from John DICKERSON to Benjn. POWEL &c.

Thos. DOBBINS came into court and bound in the sum of fifty pound for his appearance tomorrow &c –) £50-0. Wm. CRAWFORD Esqr. & Solo. GROSS securities for his appearance each in the sum of twenty five –) £50-0.

Court adjourned untill tomorrow 9 o'clock.

Met according to adjournment.
    Present   James COLE   )
                        John BOUNDS)
                        Walter LEAK   ) Esqrs.
                        Darby HANAGAN)

A deed from James POSTON to John McCAUL proved in open court by the oath of Duncan McCAUL, ordered to be registred.

James P. WILSON   )
      vs.   ) Case &c
Duncan McFARLAND) In which suit the following jury was sworn (to wit) Joseph HALL, Wm. COTTENGAME, William WOODLE, Elisha COTTENGAME, Benjn. DUMAS Jr., Joseph TARBUTTON, Laurance EVERITT, Robert WILSON, Wm. HUNTER Jr., Wm. MIMS, Wm. HUNTER Senr., & Isaac YATES who upon their oaths do say that they find for the plaintiff and assess his damages to sum of twelve pounds and interest untill paid agreeable to the note & cost of suit & so they say all.

June 1785

June Court 1785
Ordered that the following hands be annexed to work on the road that Wm. HUNTER Jr. is overseer of (to wit) John COVINGTON, Henry COVINGTON, Wm. HUNTER Senr., Wm. COULTER, James HUNTER, John JAMES, John STEELY, Moses CHAMBERS, Wm. WATKINS Jr., Joseph LASETER, John CROWSSON, & Wm. BOUNDS.

Miles KING Esqr.)
      vs.   ) Debt &c
Walter LEAK Esqr.) In which suit the following jury was sworn (to wit) Joseph HALL, Wm. COTTENGAME, Wm. WOODLE, Elisha COTTENGAME, Wm. JARNIGAN, Benjn. DUMAS Jr., Joseph TARBUTTON, Laurance EVERITT, Robert WILSON, Wm. HUNTER Jr., and Isaac

YATES and on their oaths do say they find for the plaintiff & assess his damages to the sum of fourteen pounds three shillings and four pence & cost of suit & so they say all &c.

On motion of Wm. CRAWFORD Esqr. offering his reasons for a new trial – the reasons be argued a a new trial was accordingly granted &c.

Gilbert McNEAR)
    vs.   ) Trespass &c
Wm. WATKINS) In which suit the following jury was sworn (to wit) Joseph HALL, Wm. COTTENGAME, Wm. WOODLE, Elisha COTTENGAME, Wm. JARNIGAN, Benjn. DUMAS Jr., Joseph TARBUTTON, Laurance EVERITT, Robert WILSON, Wm. MIMS, Isaac YATES & Wm. WALL who on their oaths do say that they find for the plaintiff defendant &c.

June 1785   *Page 203*

June Court 1785
Ordered that the following hands work under Captain SPEED from the province line to the fork of the road below Solomons Creek (to wit) Daniel HICKS, Wm. HICKS, John BONE, Benjn. SKIPPER, Barnaby SKIPPER, Zachs. MARTIN, George HILL, James BAGGET Jr., James BAGGET Senr., Shadrach BAGGET, James POWERS, Stephen LIVENBY, John BONE Jr., John DAVIS, & the hands of Elisabeth AYERS, Dun RYE, Solomon RYE, Absolum RYE, & Lewis AYERS &c.

Ordered that Daniel SNEED,...

> From here on to July term 1786 inclusive the minutes are found in "Rough Docket no. 2" here bind in.

[*remainder of page blank*]

June 1785   *[Page 204 blank] Page 205*

[*Rough draft bound in. Repeats from middle of p. 202 above (some variations)*]

...Laurance EVERITT, Robert WILSON, Wm. HUNTER Jr., Wm. MIMS, Isaac YATES who upon their oaths do say that they find for the plaintiff the sum of fourteen pound three shillings and four pence and so they say all.

On motion of Mr. Wm. CRAWFORD reasons entred for arrest of judgment a new tryal – reasons argued a new trial granted.

Gilbert McNEAR)
    vs.   ) Trespass
Wm. WATKINS) In which suit the following jury was sworn (vizt) Joseph HALL, Wm. COTTENGAME, Wm. WOODLE, Elisha COTTENGAME, Wm. JORNGAN, Benjn. DUMAS Jr., Joseph TARBUTTON, Laurence EVERITT, Robert WILSON, Wm. MIMS, Isaac YATES Wm. WALL who upon their oaths do say that they find for for the plaintiff the sum of defendant not guilty and so they say all &c.

Ordered that the following hands work under Capt. John SPEED, from the province line to the fork of the road below Solomons Creek (vizt) Daniel HICK, Wm. HICKS, John BONE, Benjn. SKIPPER, Barnaby SKIPPER, Zachs. MARTIN, George HILL, James BAGGET Jr., James BAGGET Senr., Shadrach BAGGET, James POWERS, Stephen LISENBY, John BONE Jr., John DAVIS, and the hands of Elisabeth HAIRS, Dunn RYE, Solomon RYE, Absolum RYE, & Lewis HAIRS &c.

June 1785   Page 206

Ordered that Daniel SNEED be appointed overseer of the road, from the fork below Solomons Creek to Rockingham and that the following hands work thereon (vizt) John WEST?, John CRAWFORD Esqr. hands, David SNEED Jr., Isreal SNEED Jr., the Widow SNEED hands, David SNEAD Senr., Gilbert McNEAR, John COLE Senr. hands, Roger NICHOLSON and the hands that lives in Rockingham &c.

Ordered that Silas HALEY is appointed overseer of the road from the fork of the road, below Solomons Creek, to the ferry, from thence out to the main road that leads to Rockingham, and that the following hands work thereon (vizt) General HARRINGTONs hands, Charles MEDLOCKs and Samuel LANEs hands, Allen McKASKILL, Keneth McKASKILL, Irvine McINTOSH, Findley McKASKILL &c.

H. Wm. HARRINGTON)
in trust of Jean Ann wife   ) Case
    vs.   )
John JORDON   ) In which suit the following jury was sworn (vizt) Joseph HALL, Wm. COTTENGAME, Wm. WOODLE, Elisha COTTENGAME, Wm. JERNIGAN, Benjn. DUMAS, Joseph TARBUTTON, Laurance EVERITT, Robert WILSON, Wm. HUNTER Jr., Wm. MIMS, Isaac YATES who upon their oaths do say that they find for the defendant and so they say all &c.

June 1785 — Page 207

Buckner NONCE? came into court as garnishee and made oath that he [scribble] [blank]

Thos. CHILES came into court as garnishee and made oath that he has about the sum of twelve pounds or more in his hands of the property of Colo. Peter PIRKINS and to shew the same? next court.

Wm. WALL)
   vs.   ) Case Miss Trial
John DUNBAR) ~~In which suit the aforegoing was jury was sworn (vizt) and say that they find for the plaint Miss Trial~~ &c.

~~State   )~~
~~   vs.   )~~
~~Brittain BRANCH)~~

Brittain BRANCH bound over to appear to the next court in the sum of £50 to give evidence in behalf of the state –) £50-0. Edward ALMOND, Wm. KELLEY securitys each in the sum of £25-0 –) £50-0-0.

Jame LONG bound over to the next court in the sum of £100, to answer unto the State) £50-0. Wm. WATKINS & Wm. WALL security each in the sum of fifty pounds) £100-.

June 1785 — Page 208

Micheal DOCKERY bound over to the next court in the sum of £50 –) £50-0. Solomon GROSS security in the sum of £25-0.

Court adjourned untill tomorrow 9 o'clock.

Court meet according to adjournment.
   Present   Charles MEDLOCK)
                 John BOUND   ) Esqrs.
                 Darby HANAGAN)

Isem HALEY \Executor of Benjn. MOREMAN/ came into court and made a settlement of the estate of said Moreman (vizt)

Benjn. MOREMAN estate pr. Isem HALEY Execr.		Dt.
To sundry's for my trouble in the arrangement? of the deceased estate		£6-0-0
		£5-18
	Ballance due HALEY	2

Credit by money recd. of John THOMSON	£ 2 - 0 - 0
By Zachs. PHILLIPS	1 -10
By George RENFROW	1 - 0
By Thomas LEVERITT	1 - 8
	5 -18

A ballance due appears to be due to HALEY the sum of two shilling &c.

Solomon GROSS came into court and exhibited his claim and was allowed the sum of seven pounds ten shillings &c – pr. account filed.

Ordered that Thoroughgood PATE be appointed to serve as Constable the insuing year in room of Wm. PEARCE.

Ordered that Isem HALEY Executor of Benjn. MOREMAN deceased, be allowed the sum of six pounds & six shillings for ~~for~~ his trouble in settleing and expenses in [blot]ing...

June 1785 *Page 209*

...the business of the said estate &c.

Ordered that Richd. ADAMS be appointed guardian Jame ADAMS and Wm. ADAMS, minors, children of Wm. ADAMS deceased and that he be bound in the sum of seven hundred pounds &c.

Ordered that Wm. DAWKINS be overseers of the road from Rockingham to Halls Bridge and that the following hands work thereon (vizt) John McINNISE, Alexander McLEOD, John McKOY, Samuel DAWKINS & son, John WATKINS, Wm. MIMS, John HADLEY, Isaac DAVIS, ~~Joh~~ Joel HALL, George ~~HALL~~ COLE, Robert MELSON work thereon.

A deed from John COLE Sr. to Henry William HARRINGTON, Robert WEBB & John COLE Commissioners in trust ~~for~~ for the publick, ~~for~~ \to/ the County of Richmond ~~County~~ and proved in open court by the oath of Charles MEDLOCK Esqr. ordered to be registred.

A deed from John JAMES Senr. to Henry William HARRINGTON, Robert WEBB & John COLE Sr. Commissioners in trust for the publick to the County of Richmond and proved in open court by the oath of Charles MEDLOCK Esqr. ordered to be registred.

John BOUND Eqr.)
    vs.) Def. Inqy.
Andrew GIBSON) In which suit the following jury was sworn (vizt) Joseph HALL, Wm. COTTENGAME, Wm. WOODLE, Elisha COTTENGAME, Wm. JERNIGAN, Benjn. DUMAS, Josph TARBUTTON, Laurance

EVERITT, Robert WILSON, Wm. HUNTER Jr., Isaac YATES, Wm. WALL who upon their oaths do say that they find for the plaintiff in the sum of ten pounds and six pence costand so they say all.

June 1785   *Page 210*

John WATKINS)
    vs.   ) Genl. Issue
Sol. GROSS   ) In which suit the aforegoing jury was sworn who upon their oaths do say that they find for the plaintiff the sum of forty pounds and six pence cost and so they say all.

On motion of Mr. John McNARY reason in arrest of judgment and filed &c – and argued the reasons thought by Henry Wm. HARRINGTON, John BOUND and Derby HANAGAN to be thought sufficient to arrest the judgment an appeal prayed and granted to the plaintiff ~~and~~ Wm. HUNTER Jr. and Wm. MIMS security in the sum of eighty pound – NB the appeal pray from the reason in arrest of judgment.

Ordered that the following persons be appointed to serve at the next court (vizt) Henry COVINGTON Sr., David SNEED Sr., John SNEED, Silas HALEY, John COVINGTON Sr., Thomas SLAY, Sterling WILLIAMSON, Alexander WATSON, John FARLEY Sr., John COVINGTON Jr., Wm. THOMAS Sr., Wm. THOMAS Jr., Wm. TERRY, Thos. GIBSON, Nelson GIBSON, George DAWKINS, John COLE, Wm. MIMS, James BOSTICK, Wm. HUNTER Sr., Daniel SMITH, Daniel THOMAS, Simon THOMAS, Thos. GROVES, Samuel PATE, Jacob MANGRUM, Gilbert McNEAR, Wm. WATKINS, John JAMES Jr., Moses HURLEY, John CROWSSON, James BOUNDS, George BOUNDS, George COLE, John COLE (Maryland), and make return thereof &c.

Ordered that John McCAULMAN be fined agred to law, upon his not attendance as a jurior at March court.

June 1785   *Page 211*

On motion of Mr. Wm. CRAWFORD Esqr. Nancy McINNIS, Wm. HUNTER for ~~an~~ \second/ appeal arguments heard, the appeal not granted, but execution to issue.

James HUNTER came into court and was bound over in the sum of £50. to give evidence in behalf of the state against Isaiah STEELY, Lovick STEELY and Jame LONG –) £50-0-0.

Ordered that the Sheriff summons Charles MEDLOCK, Derby HANAGAN and Benjn. DUMAS Sr. to serve at the next Salisbury Superior Court of Law and Equity to be held for the district aforesaid as a vinire and make return thereoff &c.

    Charles MEDLOCK
    John BOWND?
    James COLE
    Wm. EASTERLING [*original signatures*]

September 1785   Page 212

At a County Court of Pleas and Quarter Sessions began and held for the County of Richmond on the last Monday in September in the tenth year of our states independance anno Dom. 1785.

  Present Charles MEDLOCK   )
        Henry Wm. HARRINGTON) Esqrs.
        Wm. EASTERLING   )

Court adjourned untill tomorrow 10 o'clock.

Meet according to adjournment.

  Present Charles MEDLOCK   )
        Henry Wm. HARRINGTON)
        John BOUND   )
        Wm. EASTERLING   ) Esqrs.
        Derby HANAGAN   )
        Walter LEAK   )

Ordered that John FARLEY Sr. be excusd. from attending at this present session, upon the account of his wife being sick.

         Grand Jury
1 John SNEED   10 John CROWSSON
2 Nelson GIBSON   11 Wm. HUNTER Sr.
3 John COVINGTON Sr. 12 Samuel PATE
4 Henry COVINGTON 13 Gilbert McNEAR
5 George DAWKINS   14 Simon THOMAS
6 John COLE (Maryland) 15 Daniel THOMAS
7 John COVINGTON Jr. 16 George BOUND
8 Moses HURLEY   17 Jacob MANGRUM
9 Wm. THOMAS Sr.   18 John COLE

September 1785   Page 213

A deed from Abraham FREEMAN to George DAWKINS and proved in open court by the oath of John McALESTER ordered to be registred.

A deed from James EASTERLING to Thos. SLAY for three hundred acres of land, and proved in open court by the oath of Wm. EASTERLING ordered to be registred.

Richd. LIVERITT Esqr. came into court and qualified as Sheriff for the insuing year and gave bond in the sum of two thousand pounds and gave as security, Robert WEBB, William HUNTER Sr., Solomon GROSS, James PUCKITT Jr. and John BOUNDS.

Ordered that Edward WILLIAMS Esqr. be allowed the sum of thirty pounds for his ex oficio services &c.

Ordered that, the Clerk be allowed the sum of twenty pounds for his ex oficio \services/ for one year commencing from the last allowance.

Ordered that Benjn. ARNOLD be appointed to serve in Thoroughgood PATEs room, as Constable.

Court adjourned untill tomorrow 9 o'clock.

Court met according to adjournment.

Present	Charles MEDLOCK	)
	John BOUNDS	)
	Walter LEAK	) Esqr.
	Joseph HINES	)
	Wm. EASTERLING	)

September 1785   Page 214

A deed from William USSERY and Sarah USSERY, to Peter USSERY for two hundred & fifty acres of land and proved in open court by the oath of Robert LEVERITT ordered to be registred.

A deed from Thomas MASON to Solomon GROSS for one hundred acres of land \and proved in open court by the oath of Wm. McDANIEL/ ordered to be registred.

A deed from John MASON to Solomon SPRAWLS for fifty acres of land and proved in open court by the oath of Daniel SMITH, ordered to be registred. Tax paid.

Ordered that John COLE be appointed overseer of the road, in room of Stephen COLE, from the bridge to the fork of the road, and that his own hands and Demsy PITMAN work thereon &c.

John POWERS)
    vs.   ) Case
River JORDON) In which suit the following jury was sworn (vizt) Wm. MIMS, Wm. THOMAS Jr., Wm. WATKINS, Thos. SLAY, Daniel SMITH, Sterling WILLIAMSON, James BOUNDS, Thos. GIBSON, Alexr. WATSON, Wm. TERRY, Phillip JAMES, & Edward GRAHAM who upon their oaths do say that they assess damages for the plaintiff the sum of three pounds ten shilling and six pence cost, and so you say all.

A deed from Walter SLAUGHTER to Isem HALEY for thirty five acres, and proved in open court by the oath of Lott STRICKLIN ordered to be registred.

On motion a Did. Po. for Montgomery County for Wm. JOHNSON in behalf of James MERIDETH Sr.

September 1785   *Page 215*

River JORDON)
    vs.   ) Case
John POWERS) In which suit the aforegoing jury was sworn upon their oaths do say that they assess damages for the defendant and so they say all, &c.

Ordered that Jeramiah MINNASES? be appointed to serve as Constable the insuing year &c.

Wm. JOHNSON assignee)
of Wm. GAINER   ) Case
    vs.   )
Wm. HUSBANDS   ) In which suit the aforegoing jury was sworn and upon their oaths do say that they assess damage for the plaintiff the sum of twenty four pounds two shilling and four pence and so they say all &c.

Ordered that, Wm. BETTY be appointed overseer of the \road/ from Phillip JAMES to Bettys Bridge and that the following hands work thereon, Duncan McFARLAND, Dugal McFARLAND, Alexr. GORDON, Lacklin? McNIEL, John GRAHAM, John McFARLAND, Alexr. McINNISE, John WATSON, Alexr. WATSON, James DUNBAR, Rollin? DUNBAR, Alexr. MARTIN, work thereon &c.

Stephen COLE)
    vs.   ) Case
Dugal McMILLON) In which suit the following jury was sworn (vizt) Wm. MIMS, Wm. THOMAS Jr., Wm. WATKINS, Silas HALEY, Thomas SLAY, Daniel SMITH, Sterling WILLIAMSON, James BOUNDS, Thomas GIBSON, Alexander WATSON, Phillip JAMES,...

September 1785　　　　　　　　　　　　　　　　　　Page 216

...Edward GRAHAM, who upon their oaths do say that they assess damages for the plaintiff \the sum of twenty pounds/ and so they say all. Defendant dissatisfied with the judgment prays an appeal & granted.

A deed from Edward WILLIAMS Sheriff to Nancy McINNISE acknowledged in open court ordered to be registered &c. Tax not paid.

A deed from Wm. HALL to John COLE proved in open court by the oath of George COLE ordered to be registered. Tax paid.

A deed from Walter SLAUGHTER to John COLE and proved in open court by the oath of Solomon GROSS ordered to be registered. Tax paid.

A deed from Daniel HICKS to Thos. CURTIS and proved in open court, by the oath of Samuel CURTIS ordered to be registered. Tax paid. 2/ not paid.

Ordered that John COVINGTON Sr. be appointed overseer of the road in room of Wm. HUNTER Jr. for the insuing year.

Court adjourned untill tomorrow 9 o'clock.

Court meet according to adjournment.
　　Present　　Charles MEDLOCK　)
　　　　　　　John BOUNDS　　　)
　　　　　　　Walter LEAK　　　　) Esqrs.
　　　　　　　Derby HANAGAN　　)

A deed from John WALL & wife to Wm. HUNTER Jr. and proved in open court by the oath of Thos. CRAWFORD ordered to be registered &c.

September 1785　　　　　　　　　　　　　　　　　　Page 217

John PERSON　)
　　vs.　　　　)
John CHILES　) In which suit the following jury was sworn (vizt) Wm. MIMS, Wm. THOMAS Jr., William WATKINS, Silas HALEY, Thomas SLAY, Daniel SMITH, Sterling WILLIAMSON, James BOUNDS, Thos. GIBSON, Alexander WATSON, Wm. TERRY & Phillip JAMES who upon their oaths do say that they find for the Miss Tryal.

Ordered that Silvanus CHUN be overseer of the road from Leaks Ferry to Robert LEVERITs and the following hands work thereon (vizt) Richd. POWEL, James BOSTICK, Jeremiah CROUCH, James CROUCH, Thos. GEORGE, James SMITHs hands, John SMITH, Daniel McDANIEL, Joseph

TARBUTTON, Nathl. CHEARS, Abraham STOE?, Peter USSERY, Thos. PHILLIPS, Joseph LONG, Samuel USHER, Andrew SQUARES?, Jonathon & Jesse BALDINS? work thereon.

Wm. WALL)
    vs.) Case
John DUNBAR) In which suit the following jury was sworn (vizt) Wm. THOMAS Jr., Wm. WATKINS, Silas HALEY, Thos. SLAY, Daniel SMITH, Sterling WILLIAMSON, James BOUNDS, Thos. GIBSON, Alexander WATSON, Wm. TERRY, Phillip JAMES and Edward GRAHAM who upon their oaths do say, that they find for the plaintiff the sum of five pound & six pence ~~deft~~ and so they say all.

A deed from Solo. GROSS & wife to Thomas MEGINSON and proved in open court by the oath of John BOSTICK ordered to be registred.

September 1785   Page 218

~~A deed from John WALL, to Wm. HUNTER Jr. and proved in open court by the oath of Thomas CRAWFORD, ordered to be registred~~. Error.

Ordered that James BOSTICK be excused from his fine for not attending at this present court.

Ordered that a road be laid of from Hendley SNEEDs bridge the nearest and best way to Betties Bridge on Drowning and that the following person be a jury to lay of the same (vizt) James SMILEY, Donold McKOY, Dugal BLUE, John RAY, Malcom BLUE, Moses HODGE, Archabald McMILLON, Ed. McFERSHON, Thos. TURNER, Roger McNEAR, John DUNBARR, Alexander WATSON, Hendley SNEED, Solomon SNEED, and make report to the next court &c.

Mesaniah WILSON alias)
(EVERITT) and John BOUNDS)
Executors of Geor. WILSON)
    vs.) Debt
Jonathon WISE & John James)
HAIGE, Thos. BOOK & Henry)
Wm. HARRINGTON Esqr.)
Exers. of Majr. WISE decd.) In which suit the ~~following~~ aforegoing jury was sworn and upon their oaths do say that they find for the defendant and so they say all &c.

A deed from Jesse NEWBERRY & wife to Richd. PEMBERTON and proved in open court by the oath of John PEMBERTON ordered to be registred.

September 1785 — Page 219

A deed from John PARNAL to John COLE and proved in open court by the oath of Derby HANAGAN ordered to be registred.

~~F~~ Silas HALEY discharged from his attendance at this court.

Court adjourned untill tomorrow 9 o'clock.

Fryday court met according to adjournment.

Present   Charles MEDLOCK)
                John BOUNDS   ) Esqrs.
                Joseph HAYNS   )

Thomas HATHCOK) No. 23
    vs.   ) Case
Wm. HUNTER   ) The following jury impannelled & sworn viz William MIMS, William THOMAS Jr., Wm. WATKINS, Thos. SLAY, Daniel SMITH, Sterling WILLIAMSON, James BOUNDS, Thos. GIBSON, Alexr. WATSON, Wm. TERRY, James BOSTICK, Nicholas ~~GREEN~~ STONE who upon their oaths do say they find for the defendent & so you say all.

Admr. of Thos.   )
Gwillium? SCOTT decd.) No. 30
    vs.   )
Nicholas GREEN   ) The same jury impanneld and sworn as above who say that they find for the defendent.

September 1785 — Page 220

A deed from Daniel McNEIL \& wife/ to Neil SMITH & proved in open court by the oath of James GIBSON Jr. ordered to be registred.

Ord. that Thomas MOORMAN be appointed overseer of the road in the rome & stead of Robert WILSON.

William THOMAS Senr. came into court & submitted on a capias as overseer of the road & fined one penny.

Miles KING)
    vs.   ) Debt
Walter LEAK) In which cause the aforegoing jury was sworn who on thear oaths do find for the plaintiff fourteen pound ten & six pence cost & so you say all.

At the resignation of Zachariah McDANIEL as Coroner the court perceeded & chose Mr. [*blot*] Nicholas STONE his stead.

Court adjourned untill tomorrow nine o'clock. ~~Present Charles~~

Court meet according to adjournment.
    Present   ~~Charles ROBERTSON~~
                    Charles MEDLOCK)
                    John BOUND   ) Esqrs.
                    Joseph HINES   )

September 1785

Luke ROBERTSON admr. of Wm. ADAMS decd. and upon oath made return of the sail of the said estate to the amount of £480-12-10 &c.

John LEVERITT)
    vs.   )
Thos. WADE   ) Trespass   Errow
John? INGRAM)
Joshua VINEN   ) Abatement pleaded & granted.

Present Colo. Charles MEDLOCK, John SPEED, John BOWNDS & Joseph HINDS.

Ordered that William HUNTER Junr. obtain letters of administration on the estate of ~~Sary~~ Sarah HURLY deceasd.

Ord. that John McCOLMON be excused from his fine as non attending as a juror in March term on paying the cost.

Ordered that Britain BRANCH be discharged from court as attending in behalf of the State as a witness.

State   )
    vs.   )
Lovick STEALEY) No. 24 The jury impanneld & sworn Wm. MIMS, Wm. THOMAS Jr., Thomas SLAY, Daniel SMITH, Sterling WILLIAMSON, James BOUNDS, Thomas GIBSON, Alexr. WATSON, Wm. TERRY, James BOSTICK, Nicholas STONE, Wm. HUNTER & do find the defendand not guilty in in manner & form charged.

September 1785

William WALL bail for the appearance of James LONG came & surrendered him up to the court & was dischargd. from the same.

~~Ordered that~~
State)
vs.) Regr.?
James LONG) £50 for his appearance to next court – Will HUNTER bail £25?

~~Isaiah STEELY witness against the same in the behalf of the state bound in recog. £25.~~Errow

State)
vs.) Bound in recog. £50:0
Isaiah STEELY) John STEELY bail – £25:0

State)
vs.) Recog. in £100
Andrew HENDRICKS) ~~Wm. MIMS~~ \Richd. LEVERITT?/ & Edwd. ALMOND 50 each for his appearance at the next court.

~~A~~ \Two/ deed\s/ from Richard PEMBERTON Senr. to John PANKEY provd. by the oath of William LOVE & ordered to be registred.

Ord. that Burrill STRICKLAIN be allowed the sum of two pounds sixteen shillings for his attendance at June & September 1785.

John James BAKER came into court of lawful age & chose for his guardian Colo. Edward WILLI[AMS] who gave for his security Colo. Charles MEDLO[CK] and Nicholas STONE.

<u>September 1785</u>   <u>Page 223</u>

[*Several math calculations appear here that seem unrelated to the minutes.*]
Ord. that a summons issue for Rodah TURNER, Elizabeth TAYLOR, Judah WELCH, Elias JOHNSON, Winney LEWIS, William JONES son of Luraney JONES, Aron GRIFFIN son of Winney GRIFFIN to bring in thear children to shew cause if any they have why they should not be bo<u>w</u>nd out.

[*ink badly smeared*] William HUNTER admr. of ~~Anny?~~ Jonah? HURLEY deceased came into court & gave security for his faithful performance as admr. – himself bound in the sum of £100. His security Sol.? GROSS, John CROWSSON? £50? both.

Ord. that the Sheriff sell the lands of the sever<u>ill</u> delinquents of the lower district [*blot*] agreeable to the return of the collector last June term.

[*ink smeared*] Ord. that the sever<u>il</u> inventakers? still continue to receive? the inventorys as formerly, only Capt. John SPEAD in the ro<u>me</u> of Genl.

HARRINGTON and Dudley MASK Esqr. in the ro_me_ of John PEMBERTON.

Ord. that Sol. GROSS be allowd. the sum of thirty shillings specie for his repairing the gail [*jail*] door lock &c.

September 1785   Page 224

Edward WILLIAMS to divide the hands on a ___ [*cut off*] road which was appointed Charles ROBERTSON \& his hands/ Ben PA__[*cut off*] William McGUIREs hands and all the hands above grea[t?] furrow? to put the_ron_ &c.

Charles ROBERTSON acted as a Kings Magistrate in Kimborough \Tory/ Camp, upon the trial of James BOLTON for breaking his parole.

[*lighter ink*] William WALL came into court and surrendered up James LONG who was his secu_rr_ity for his appearance & was discharged for the same. [*In margin:*] Erro_ws_.

Ordered that John COLE Jr. be given or taken to custody & put into goal [*jail*] immediately & there to remain untill he compl_ys_ with an act of assembly & give security for five pound.

Ord. that Charles MEDLOCK be allowd. the sum of five pounds four shillings for his attendance as a venire_y_ [*blots*] at Salisbury Superior Court.

Ord. that a tax of two shilling on every poll & eight pence on every hundred acres of land [be?] laid as a county tax for the year 1785.

Jno. COLE professes himself indebted to the county court in the sum of five pounds & offers for security ~~Solomon GROSS~~ \Edward WILLIAMS & William? CRAWFORD/ & they have both in op[en?] court acknowledged themselves indebted as above set_t_ forth – ~~Test~~ six months after this term.

September 1785   Page 225

The following persons appointed as a jury to attend at next court Viz - Edwd. WILLIAMS, Thomas CRAWFORD, Isaac YEATES, James YEATES, John JAMES Senr., Laurance AVERITT, Jesse BOUNDS, Zachariah MOORMAN, John PANKEY, William WATKINS Jnr., Randol HALEY, Stephen COLE, George MEDLOCK, William WEBB, John WALL, Thomas BLEWITT, John COLMAN, Owin SLAUGHTER Senr., Jonathan NEWBERRY, Daniel HICKS, Dun RYE, Thomas MOORMAN, Lott STRICKLIN, Nathaniel CHEERS, William McDANIEL, Thos. CURTIS, Samuel CURTIS, William JERNAGAN, James PATTERSON, James

SMITH, John MASK, Solomon DEEREMAN, Edwd. McFARSION?, David SNEAD Jnr. Israil SNEAD Jnr., Thoroughgood PATE & Alan McKASKILL.

Ord. that Sol. GROSS be allowd. the sum of three pounds exeficious services for finding of candles table & the like. Court adjourned untill court in course.
    Charles MEDLOCK
    Jos. HINES
    John BOUNDS [*these appear to be original signatures*]

December 1785   *Page 226 blank; Page 227*

State of North Carolina)
Richmond County   )

At a County Court of Pleas and Quarter Sessions began and held for the County of Richmond at the Court House therein on the last Monday in December Anno Dom. 1785 and in the tenth year of American independence.
  Present Charles MEDLOCK)
       John BOWND)Esqrs.
       Walter LEAK   )

Grand jury sworn, John PANKEY foreman, Isaac YATES, James YATES, Jesse BOUNDS, Zacher. MOREMON, Randolph HALEY, George MEDLOCK, Wm. WEBB, Thos. BLEWITT, Daniel HICKS, Dun RYE, Thos. MOREMAN, Thos. CURTIS, Samuel CURTIS, William JARNIGAN, Solo. DEERMAN & Edward McPHERSON.

A deed from Richd. LEVERITT to Wm. LOVE for five hundred and three acres dated twenty sixth day of December 1785 and acknowledged in open court ordered to be registred &c.

Ordered that Wm. MIMS be appointed to serve as Constable the insuing year &c. and came into court and was qualified &c. agreeable to law &c.

Court adjourned untill tomorrow 9 o'clock.

Court met according to adjournment.
  Present Charles MEDLOCK)
       Joseph HINES)Esqrs.
       Walter LEAK   )

December 1785   *Page 228*

Ordered that the Sheriff sell all the perishable property of the estate of Sarah HURLEY decd. and make return to the next court &c.

In the suit Stephen COLE vs. Dugal McMILLON the bail John McALESTER surrendered the principal in open court.

John WATKINS (Virginia))
    vs.) Def. Inqy.
Thos. DOBBINS) In which suit the following jury was sworn (vizt) David SNEED, Lott STRICKLIN, Thoroughgood PATE, Wm. McDANIEL, Thos. CRAWFORD, Stephen COLE, John WALL, John COLEMAN, Owen SLAUGHT[ER] Sr., Alan McKASKILL, James PATTERSON, Phillip SNEED who upon their oaths do say that they find for the plaintiff the sum of fifty pounds and and cost and so they say all &c.

A deed from Wm. LOVE to Daniel SHAW and acknowledged in open court, ordered to be registred &c. Tax paid. Registers fee paid.

Alexander McLEOD?)
    vs) Attch.
Wm. McQUEEN) In which suit the aforegoing jury was sworn who upon their oaths that they find for the plaintiff the sum of twenty pounds and so they say all &c. \and cost/

December 1785   *Page 229*

Comfort WILLIS)
    vs.) Attch. Def. Inqy.
Elisha PARKER) In which suit the aforegoing jury was sworn and find for the plaintiff the sum of forty pounds and six pence cost and so they say all &c.

Governor)
    vs) Case Def. Inqy.
Samuel COSTANT?) In which suit the aforegoing jury was sworn who upon their oaths do say that they find one penny and six pence cost and so they say all.

A deed from Charles HUCKABY to Wm. LOVE for eighty acres of land dated the tenth day of February 1785 ordered to be registred.

Daniel McDANIEL)
    vs.) Attch. Def. Inqy.
Wm. McQUEEN) In which suit the aforegoing jury was sworn and upon their oaths do say that they find for the plaintiff the sum of six pounds eight shilling and so they say all &c.

Court adjourned untill tomorrow 9 o'clock.

Court meet according to adjournment.

Present   Charles MEDLOCK)
           Ed. WILLIAMS   )
           James COLE   ) Esqrs.
           Joseph HEINS   )

December 1785

Zach. McDANIEL)
    vs.   ) General Issue
John LEVERIT   ) In which suit the following jury was sworn (vizt) Lott STRICKLIN, Thoroughgood PATE, Wm. McDANIEL, Thos. CRAWFORD, John ~~COLE~~ WALL, John COLEMAN, Owen SLAUGHTER, James SMITH, Alexander McKASKILL, James PATTERSON, Phillip SNEED who upon their oaths do say that they say they find for the plaintiff the sum of fifty pounds and cost and so they say all &c.

Ordered that James YATES be appointed overseer of the ~~road~~ Catfish Road from the Cherraw \old/ road, to the road, that lead, to Cole Bridge and the hands contiguous work thereon &c.

Ordered Thomas GIBSON be appointed overseer of the road of the Catfish Road, from the rockey fork of Hitch-cock-creek to the Cherraw old road and all the hands contiguous work thereon &c.

A deed from Nathaniel SANDERES to John FARLEY, for 100 acres of land proved in open court by the oath of John FARLEY Senr. ordered to be registred &c.

A deed from Wm. EASTERLING to John FARLEY Senr. dated 1784 for 150 acres of land and acknowledged in open court ordered to be registred.

James CADDLE   )
    vs.   ) Genl. Issue
Jeremiah MINNASAS)
Solo. GROSS   ) In which suit the following jury was sworn (vizt) John JAMES Jr., Wm. HUNTER Jr., Phillip JAMES, Thos. JOWERS, Robert WILSON, Wm. COLTER...

December 1785

...Daniel McDANIEL, James SMITH, John COVINGTON, Daniel SNEED, John McALESTER, John EVENS, who upon their oaths do say that they find for the plaintiff the sum of nine pound and one penny and cost and so they say all &c.

A deed from Moses SMITH to Daniel HODGES and proved in open court by the oath of Thos. HINES ordered to be registred &c.

A deed from Moses TURNER & wife to Wm. McPHERSON [*blot*] and proved in open court by the oath of Daniel CARMICAL ordered to be registred &c.

Thos. CRAWFORD)
    vs   ) Case
John SMITH   ) In which suit the following jury was sworn (vizt) David SNEED, Lott STRICKLIN, Thoroughgood PATE, Wm. McDANIEL, Stephen COLE, Owen SLAUGHTER, James SMITH, Allen McCASKILL, James PATTERSON, William HUNTER, Phillip SNEED, Nathl. CHAIRS who upon their oaths do say that they find for the plaintiff two hundred and fifty pounds and so they say all &c. An appeal granted to the defendant and reason in arrest of judgment for a new tryal.

A deed from William LOUGE to Abraham YATES and proved in open court by the oath of John McALESTEN ordered to be registred.

<u>December 1785</u>   <u>Page 232</u>

Court adjourned untill tomorrow 9 o'clock.

Court met according to adjournment.
    Present   Charles MEDLOCK)
                      Edward WILLIAMS) Esqrs.
                      Dudley MASK   )

A deed from James JAMES to Robert MILSON [*WILSON?*] for 175 acres proved in open court by the oath of Wm. MIMS ordered to registred. Tax paid.

Ordered that Robert MILSON have leave to build well? a water grist mill on Wm. MIMS Spring branch.

Ordered that John HOWARD be appointed gaurden to Sanders MERIDETH and gave bond in the sum of seven hundred pound specie &c.

Present on the bench Charles MEDLOCK, Edward WILLIAMS, William EASTERLING, Dudley MASK, James COLE, Walter LEAK.

A deed from Wm. LOVE to Edmund LILLY acknowledged in open court ordered to be registred.

Ordered that Wm. LOVE Esqr. have leave to build a water grist mill, on Naked Creek, near to the mouth thereof &c.

Ordered that Edmund LILLEY be appointed to serve as surveyor for the County of Richmond.

Ordered that Duncan McFARLAND be appointed overseer of the road in room of Arther DEES. from

On motion of Martha MARTIN tis ordered by the court, that the sheriff summon a jury of twelve free holders unconnected neither by consanguinity no[r] affinity who shall go on a certain...

<u>December 1785</u>   <u>Page 233</u>

...tract of land above Blewitt Falls on Pee Dee River now in possession <u>or</u> of John JAMES Senr. or Solomon GROSS and upon oath (which oath the sheriff is hereby impowered to administer) shall allot one third part of that said tract of land containing one hundred and fifty acres, waved? untill court.

A deed from John THOMAS to John SPEED Esqr. and proved in open court by the oath of Zacherias RATLIFF, ordered to be registred &c.

Court adjourned untill tomorrow 9 o'clock.

Court met according to adjourned.
  Present Charles MEDLOCK)
        Edward WILLIAMS) Esqrs.
        Dudley MASK)

Henry EVERITT)
 vs.   )
Thos. POYTHRESS) In which suit the following jury was sworn (vizt) David SNEED, Lott STRICKLIN, Thoroughgood PATE, Wm. McDANIEL, Thomas CRAWFORD, Stephen COLE, John WALL, <u>John WALL</u>, John COLEMAN, Owen SLAUGHTER, Allen McKASKILL, James PATTERSON, Laurance EVERITT, who upon their oaths do say, that they find for the plaintiff the sum of seven pounds one shilling and so they say all.

Robert THOMAS)
 vs.   ) Atth.
Wm. BRIGMAN) In which suit the aforegoing jury was sworn and [*blot*] upon their oaths do say that they find for the plaintiff the sum of twenty one pound, and so they say all and interest untill paid.

Charles MEDLOCK)
    vs.) Att. Def. Inq.
Peter PERKINS) In which suit the fol aforegoing jury was sworn and upon their oaths do say that they find the sum of twenty two pounds and so they say all &c.

December 1785   Page 234

Ann POPE)
    vs.) Indt. F____?
Richd. POPE) In which suit the aforegoing jury was sworn, who upon their oaths do say that they find for the plaintiff, the sum of one penny and so they say all.

Solomon GROSS)
    vs.) D_?
Thos. PICKETT?) In which suit the aforegoing jury was sworn who upon oath do say that they find for the plaintiff the sum of eighteen pounds eighteen shillings and so they say all.

Edmund LILLEY ea Esqr. came into court and gave bond and security &c and was qualified agreeable to law &c.

Abner VAUGHN)
    vs.) Genl. Issue
Samuel LANE) In which suit the aforegoing jury was sworn who upon their oaths do say that they find for the plaintiff the sum of sixteen pound and so they say all.

Ordered that, the Sheriff summons Thos. GIBSON, Nelson GIBSON, Laurance OBRIYAN, James? McKATHA, John McEACHEY?, Archabald FINLAW?, John COVINGTON, Henry COVINGTON, John COVINGTON Jr., John DAWKINS, Samuel DAWKINS, Gilbert McNEAR, Wm. TERRY, Benjn. INGRAM, John SNEED, David SNEED Senr., Isreal SNEED, Joseph HALL, John HALL, Solomon DEARMAN, Jonathon NEWBERRY, Richd. ADAMS, Luke ROBERTSON, Ezra BOSTICK, Nath. HARRINGTON, George SATERFIELD, Benj. DUMAS Senr., John MASK Senr., John JAMES Jr., Wm. WATKINS Sr., Samuel CURTIS, Thomas CURTIS, \Samuel COVINGTON, Jacob MANGRUM,/ John CROWSSON, George BOUND, Jesse BOUND, Wm. SMITH, and make return to the next court as juriors and make return &c.

December 1785 — Page 235

Wm. HUNTER Jr.)
vs.) Genl. Issue
John BOUND Esqr.) In which suit the aforegoing jury was sworn who upon their oaths do say that they find for the plaintiff the sum of five pound and so they say all &c.

Ordered that the Sheriff summons Charles MEDLOCK, Edward WILLIAMS and Matthew COVINGTON to attend as a venire at the next Salisbury Superior Court on the fifteenth of March next &c.

Ordered that the following persons be appointed to receive the list of the inhabitants of all denomination in this county as followeth &c Henry Wm. HARRINGTON in Capt. SPEEDs company, Capt. EASTERLING in his own company, Capt. WALL in his own company, Capt. MASK in his own company, Capt. CARMICAL in his own company, James SMITH in Capt. McDANIELs company, and make return to the next court agreeable to law &c.

Ordered that the road, all ready laid out from Sneed Bridge over Gum Swamp to Drowning Creek at or near Farley Bridge and that the hands have leave to build a bridge over said creek.

On motion of Wm. LOVE Esqr. for an insult of John SMITH (Hogfoot) to the Clerk of the Court that he be fined forty shilling &c.

Ordered that, John BOUNDS, Benjn. COVINGTON, John WALL Esqr. be appointed as assessors of the town lotts in this county and make return to the next court.

Court adjourned untill tomorrow 9 o'clock.

Meet according to adjournment.

December 1785 — Page 236

Present   James COLE)
          John BOUND) Esqrs.
          Benjn. COVINGTON)

Wm. McDANIEL)
vs.) Def. Inqy.
Benjn. VAUGHN)
John KIMBROUGH) In which suit the following jury was sworn (vizt) David SNEED, Thos. CRAWFORD, Stephen COLE, John WALL, John COLEMAN, Owen SLAUGHTER, Samuel CHAIRS, Alen McKASKILL,

James PATERSON, Laurance EVERITT, Phillip SNEED, Wm. HUNTER who upon their oaths do say that they find for the plaintiff the sum of eighty pound and cost and so they say all.

A deed Wm. GULLEDGE? to James SMILEY and proved in open court by the oath of Daniel McCOY ordered to be registred &c.

Hutchen GROSS admr. of Aldred GROSS decd. came into court and qualified and to give bond in the sum of three hundred pounds.

State)
vs.) Indt.
Andrew HENDRICKSON) In which suit the following jury was sworn (vizt) David SNEED, Thomas CRAWFORD, Stephen COLE, John WALL, John COLEMAN, Owen SLAUGHTER, ~~Samuel?~~ \Nathl./ CHAIRS, Alen McKASKILL, Laurance EVERITT, Phillip SNEED, William HUNTER, Daniel SNEED who upon their oaths do say that they find the defendant guilty in manner & form as charged in the bill of indictment the court sat in judgt. & were of opinion that the defendant should receive fifteen stripes on his bare back.

December 1785   *Page 237*

Thomas BLEWITT comes into court and was allowed the sum of £6-6-8- on his venire tickitt.

Ordered that Benjamin NIGHT, Joseph NIGHT be bound unto Josiah FREEMAN till they come of lawfull age.

Ordered that a jury be summoned to lay off and ~~off and~~ divided ~~the~~ a certain tract of land, the property of John HICKS deceased, equally divided between the widow and the two orphans, and make return to the next court.

John CROWSSON came into court and was qualified as admr. in the estate of Comfort WILLIS bound in the sum of one hundred pounds.

Ordered that the Sheriff sell all the perishable estate of Comfort WILLIS and make return to the next court.

Ordered that, the Sheriff sell all the perishable estate of Aldred GROSS and make return to the next court.

Ordered that the Sheriff summon Hendley SNEED, Solomon SNEED, Roger McNEER, Malcom McCASKILL, Daniel McCASKILL \Jr./, Neil McNEAR, Archabald McMILLON, Edward McFERSON, John DOVE, Malcom McCASKILL, Anguish McGILL, John McBRIDE, Malcom BLUE,

Dugal BLUE, Dugal McFARLAND, and Duncan McFARLAND to be a jury to lay off a road from Sneed Bridge on Gum Swamp to Drowning Creek near Farleys and make report to the next court &c.

December 1785   *Page 238*

Ordered that John COLE Jr. be appointed Collector for this county to collect the tax for the year 1785. upon g

Court adjourned till court in course.

                            Chas. MEDLOCK
   Test. Wm. LOVE Clk.   John BOUND
                            James COLE

April 1786   *Page 239*

At a County Court of Pleas and Quarter Sessions began and held for the County of Richmond at the Court House therein on the second Monday in April in the tenth year of American independance Anno Dom 1786.
    Present   James) Esqr. [*sic*]

Court adjourned untill tomorrow 9 o'clock.

Meet according to adjournment.
    Present   Charles MEDLOCK   )
                    Henry Wm. HARRINGTON)
                    Robert WEBB   )
                    John SPEED   )

After the last will and testament of John CHILES was exhibited in open court and admitted to probate by being approved of by the said court Thomas CHILES Esqr. one of the executors therein named came into court and was duly qualified thereto as executor agreeable to law.

A bill of sale from Edward ALMOND to Solomon GROSS for fifty pound dated eleventh day of March 1786 proved in open court \by the oath of John McALESTER/ ordered to be registred.

A bill of sale from Wm. MIMS to Solomon [GROSS] for one hundred pounds dated sixteenth of February 1786 proved in open court by the oath of John McALESTER ordered to be registred &c.

Ordered that James McKATHEY be excuse from serving as a jurior this court he being sick.

April 1786

Grand jury sworn: Ezra BOSTICK, Wm. SMITH, John JAMES, Henry COVINGTON, Thos. GIBSON, John COVINGTON, Nelson GIBSON, John COVINGTON Jr., John McKATHEY, Samuel DAWKINS, John DAWKINS, Benjn. INGRAM, Nathl. HARRINGTON, Gilbert McNEAR, Joseph HALL Jr.

Ordered that Katherine CURRY have leave to admr. upon Laughlin CURRY's estate upon giving bond in the sum of one hundred & fifty \pound specie/ with Anguish JOHNSON, John McALESTER for security and came into court and qualified as administratrix.

A deed from River JORDON to Murdock SHAW for one hundred acres dated 28 day of 1785 [sic] and proved in open court by the oath of Duncan McFARLAND ordered to be registered. [in margin:] Tax fee paid 3/? __? for register.

John STOKES Esqr. came into court and upon producing a license was qualified as a practising attorney in this court &c.

Court adjourned untill tomorrow 10 o'clock.

Court met according to adjournment.
    Present   Charles MEDLOCK   )
                   Henry Wm. HARRINGTON) Esqrs.
                   John SPEED   )

April 1786

A deed from David LOVE to Daniel McCAIRN for two hundred acres dated the 20th November 1785 proved in open court by the oath of Wm. LOVE ordered to be registred.

Solo GROSS   )
    vs.   ) Att't.
George CARTER) In which suit the following jury was sworn (vizt) Isreal SNEED, Laurance O'BRYAN, John SNEED, Wm. WATKINS, Samuel COVINGTON, Laurance EVERITT, John MATTHEW, Stephen THOMAS, John COLE Jr., Robert WILSON, Wm. WALL, Wm. HUNTER Sr. upon their oaths do say that they find for the plaintiff the sum of ~~thirtee~~ thirteen pound six shilling and six pence and so they say all.

A deed from William LOVE to Dugal McBRIDGE for 183 acres of land dated 26 Decr. 1785 acknowledged in open court by Wm. LOVE ordered to be registred &c. [in margin:] Tax fee paid.

Ordered that there be a road keept open from the Grassy Islands Ford on Mountain Creek at the old bridge place on said creek &c \and that John PANKEY and William LOVE Esqr. open the same./

State)
vs.) Indt. Misdemeanor
Thos. BROWN) In which suit the aforegoing jury was sworn (Wm. WALL excepted) and Richd. ADAMS was in his room) and upon their oaths do say that the defendant is not guilty and so they say all &c.

On motion of John STOKES Esqr. in the above suit tis ordered by the court that the Prosecutor pay cost it being the opinion of the court that the prosecution in...

April 1786   *Page 242*

...was groundless present on the bench Henry Wm. HARRINGTON, John WALL, Walter LEAK, Benjn. COVINGTON.

On motion of Wm. CRAWFORD Esqr. in the suit John JOWERS vs. Wm. HUNTER Jr. the matter being altercated it was the opinion of Charles MEDLOCK, Henry Wm. HARRINGTON, John WALL, Thos. CRAWFORD & Thos. DOCKERY \that/ the suit stands as it appears on the docket \in status quo/ and Benjn. COVINGTON, Walter LEAK & Darby HANAGAN was of the opinion that the suit should be altered as it stood originally.

Court adjourned untill tomorrow 9 o'clock.

[*large blank space*]

Court met according to adjournment.

Present   Charles MEDLOCK)
            John WALL   ) Esqrs.
            Thos. DOCKERY   )

A deed from John COLEMAN to John SPURLING for one hundred acres of land dated the 6th day of February 1786 also one other from John COLEMAN to John SPURLING for two hundred acres bearing the same date as above, also one other for 180 acres bearing the same date which deeds was acknowledged in open court...

April 1786   *Page 243*

...by John COLEMAN ordered to be registered.

Ordered that Stephen THOMAS be appointed to serve as Constable the insuing year.

Ordered that John COLE (Mariland) be appointed to serve as Constable the insuing year &c.

Ordered that Hendley SNEED and the hands that work on the road under him extend the road crossing Gum Swamp near his house into the road that leads by the Green ponds above Darby HANAGANs, and make a bridge over Joes Creek near Pates mill &c.

Ordered that Edward ALMOND be discontinued from serving as a Constable &c.

Ordered that Wm. THOMAS Senr. to serve overseer of the road from Wm. BLEWITTs Ferry to to the Lick Branch and that Wm. BLEWITT, Thomas BLEWITT, Wm. THOMAS Senr., Daniel THOMAS, Simon THOMAS's, Benjn. EVERIT, Wm. THOMAS Jr., Laurance EVERIT, James HUNTER, John COVINGTON & John CLEMONS work thereon &c.

Ordered that Stephen COLE be appointed overseer of the road from the Lick Branch to the Rockey Fork and that Nathl. HARRINGTON, George SATERFIELD, James GADDY, Thos. ADCOCK, Stephen COLE, [blank] SMITH, Moses BOWMAN, Daniel McDANIEL, and the man that lives on Henry ADCOCKs plantation work thereon &c.

April 1786 Page 244

Ordered that Archelus MOREMAN be appointed to make a bridge over the Rockey Fork whereon Wm. LEGATEs bridge formerly was, and that four hands on the lower side \and four on the uper side/ build the said bridge and that they be exempted from working on the road in consequence thereof &c.

On motion of Wm. THOMAS Jr. praying to remove the road a small distance from his plantation the court taking the same into consideration and granted to Mr. THOMAS the purport of his motion agreeable to the prayer of his petition.

Ordered that a road be laid out the nearest and best way from Hillins Ford on Pee Dee to Wm. McGUIREs and that the following persons be a jury to lay off and make report to the next court (vizt) James PATTERSON, John HOWARD, Joseph GADD, Wm. JOWERS, John CROUCH, Joseph TARBUTTON, Peter USSERY, Wm. HENDLEY, Charles ROBERTSON, James BOSTICK, Thomas JOWERS, Daniel McDANIEL, Samuel USHER, Benjn. POWEL, Ezra BOSTICK, Thos. PHILLIPS, John PANKEY, Owen SLAUGHTER &c.

Solo. GROSS)
    vs.   ) Att't. Deft. Inqy.
Samuel LANE) In which suit the following jury was sworn (vizt) Richd. ADAMS, Isreal SNEED, Laurance ~~EVERITT~~ O'BRYAN, John SNEED, Wm. WATKINS, Samuel COVINGTON, Laurance EVERITT, Jesse BOUNDS, Wm. WALL, George MEDLOCK, Robert WILSON, Joseph WHITE, William THOS., &c Jury withdrawn.

Richard LEVERITT Sheriff made return of the amount of the sale of Aldred GROSS's estate which was two hundred and sixty three pounds seventeen shillings £263-17 &c.

April 1786   Page 245

A deed from George CARTER & wife to Richard ADAM dated 18 day of April 1785 for three hundred acres also one other for one hundred the same date and proved in open court by the oath of Jonathon NEWBERY ordered to be registred.

On motion of Edward WILLIAMS Esqr. ordered by the court that he be allowed the sum of £4-10-8 upon his vinire tickitt &c.

On motion of Charles MEDLOCK Esqr. ordered that he be allowed the sum of £7-13-4 upon his vinire tickitt.

A deed from Robert THOMAS to Daniel McCLENDON for one hundred acres dated 26 day of January 1786 and proved in open court by the oath of Wm. EASTERLING Esqr. ordered to be registred.

Ordered that Thomas GIBSON be appointed overseer of the road from the Rockey Fork to the widow McKATHEY's on Drowning Creek and all the hands from said creek to Drowning Creek above Cole's road, work thereon &c and build a bridge over Drowning Creek with the assistance of the hands of More County.

Court adjourned untill tomorrow 10 o'clock.

Court met according to adjournment.

A deed from Charles MEDLOCK to George MEDLOCK for two hundred acres of land dated 26 day of October 1782 acknowledged in open court ordered to be registred.

Sheriff Richd. LEVERITT made a return of the sale of Comfort WILLIS estate decd. to the amount of thirty seven pound, twelve shillings and a penny &c. £37-12-1.

April 1786 — Page 246

On motion of Hanah COULTER relict of Wm. COLTERS deceased prayed an administration upon the estate of her deceased husbands, the administration granted, and upon giving William HUNTER and Edward WILLIAMS bail in the sum of two hundred pounds which was accordingly complied with and the administratrix qualified.

On motion of John McNARY Esqr. Dugal McMILLON came into court and after performing the requisites necessary and taking the oath as an insolvent debtor is for ever requited and discharged from the execution now against &c.

Ordered that Archabald DOVE be appointed to serve as Constable the insuing year &c.

A deed from Henry ADCOCK & wife to Nicholas CLARK for 116 acres of land dated 6th day of June 1785 acknowledged in open court ordered to be registred. [*in margin:*] Tax fees paid.

Ordered that the following persons be appointed to lay of a road from Leaks Ferry the nearest and best way into the Cross Creek Road, leading by Edward INGRAMs, vizt James BOSTICK, Ezra BOSTICK, Richd. POWEL, Benjn. POWEL, Silvester CHUN, Wm. McDANIEL, Daniel McDANIEL, Samuel USHER, Peter USSERY, George JOWERS, Thos. JOWERS, John CROUCH, James SMITHs Esqr., Thos. PHILLIPS, Charles ROBERTSON and John CHAMBERS and make return to the next court &c.

On motion of Nicholas STONE Coroner came into this court and protested against the jail \for it's/ being's insufficient &c.

Ordered that James PATTERSON be appointed overseer of the road in room of Duncan McFARLAND where Arther DEES was formerly overseer &c.

April 1786 — Page 247

Ordered that William WALL Esqr. be appointed to serve as Sheriff the insuing year &c.

Wm. WALL came into court ~~and~~ qualified ~~and~~ as Sheriff and entred into bound with Wm. LOVE, Thos. CRAWFORD and John WALL securities.

Ordered that Burrel STRICKLIN be allowed the [*blot*] usial allowance as Constable for serving as Constable this court four days (see former allowance).

Ordered that Peter USSERY be appointed a gaurdin for Mary HUTCHEN daughter of James HUTCHEN deceased in consequence of the deposition of

Robert LEVERITT who says that the said Mary is an idiot and give & security agreeable to law.

Ordered that Edward ALMOND be allowed the usial allowance as Constable for serving as Constable this court three days (videe former allowance)

State)
   vs.) Ind't.
Benjn. VAUGHN) Submitted and fined pd.

~~Ordered that~~

~~On motion Nicholas STONE came into court and prayed an administration upon the estate of Nicholas STONE deceased granted upon his giving bond with Henry Wm. HARRINGTON & Edward WILLIAMS security in the sum of two thousand pounds &c.~~

On motion of Wm. WALL pleading in mitagating of two fines the one was reduced to five shillings and the other to six pence &c.

Richd. LEVERITT Sheriff made a return of the sale of Sarah HURLEYs deceased estate amounting to thirty three pounds five shillings and three pence &c. £33-5-3.

April 1786   Page 248

On motion ~~of~~ Nicholas STONE & Christopher CLARK came into this court and prayed an administration de bonis non upon the estate of Nicholas STONE deceased granted upon giving bond with ~~Nicholas~~ Henry Wm. HARRINGTON and Edward WILLIAMS security in the sum of two thousand pound and qualified agreeable to law &c.

Ordered that Wm. WEBB be appointed to serve as Constable the insuing your.

A deed from Mathew TERRY to Wm. TERRY proved in open court by Benjn. INGRAM ordered to be registred. [*in margin:*] Tax fees paid.

Ordered that the Sheriff summons the following persons to attend as juriors at the next court (viz) Danl. THOMAS, Danl. SMITH, Moses HURLEY, Henry ADCOCK, Randol HAILEY, John EZEL, Thos. BLEWIT, Mathew COVINGTON, Wm. HUNTER Senr., Zach. MOORMAN, Laurance EVERITT, Wm. THOMAS Senr., John COLE Bridge [?], John COLEMAN, Simon THOMAS, Thos. JOWERS, Wm. HUNTER Jr., Benjamin POWEL, Drury COLLIER, John PANKEY, Joseph GAD, James BOSTICK, John HOWARD, James PATTERSON, Thom. CURTIS, Saml.

CURTIS, Danl. HICKS, Wm. NEWBERRY Senr., Barnaby SKIPPER, Charles ROBERSON, Danl. McDANIEL, James BAGGET Senr., Benja. DUMAS Junr., Silas HAILEY, Thomas STANBACK, Thomas WALKER.

On motion of Edward WILLIAMS Esqr. in behalf of Nicholas STONE Coroner of Richmond County offering a resignation in behalf of the said Coroner it was accordingly accepted of by the said court &c.

April 1786   *Page 249*

Ordered that Edward WILLIAMS late Sheriff be allowed the sum of ten pounds for transporting the publick arms from Salisbury to this county.

Ordered that the Clerk be allowed the sum of four pound for furnishing of three books for the use of the county records.

Ordered that a \writ of/ duces tecum issue to the Clerk of Anson Court to send the proceeding and the resignation of James MERIDETH Sr. Execr. of James MERIDETH deceased to our next County Court of Pleas and Quarter Sessions to be held for our said County of Richmond on the second Monday in July next together with the date of his resignation Test &c.

Court adjourned untill court in course.
            Jas. COLE
            Dudley MASK
            Benjn. COVINGTON

July 1786   *Page 250*

At a County Court of Pleas and Quarter Sessions began held for the County of Richmond on the second Monday ~~of~~ in July in the eleventh \year of/ ~~day of said July in the eleventh~~ American independence Anno Dom 1786.

    Present   Charles MEDLOCK)
                     Thos. DOCKERY   ) Esqrs.
                     James COLE   )

Sarah HALL prays Letters of Admn. upon the estate of Joseph HALL Senr. decd. and gave bond in the sum of two hundred pound and, Joseph HALL security for the sum of one hundred & fifty pounds.

Grand Jury sworn John COLE Sr. foreman, James BOSTICK, Daniel HICKS, Wm. HUNTER Jr., Thos. CURTIS, Wm. NEWBERY Senr., James BAGGETT, John EZEL, Charles ROBERTSON, Henry ADCOCK, Benjn. DUMAS, \Zachs. MOREMAN,/ Wm. HUNTER Senr., John COLEMAN, Laurance EV\RE/IT, Daniel ~~HICKS~~ SMITH.

Richmond County NC Court Minutes, 1779-1786

Ordered that Joseph SIMKINS be appointed to serve as Constable the insuing year &c.

Court adjourned untill tomorrow 9 o'clock.

Court met according to adjournment.

 Present Charles MEDLOCK)
       Benjn. COVINGTON) Esqrs.
       Walter LEAK   )

July 1786   _Page 251_

On motion ~~of~~ Wm. TATUM Esqr. came into this court and qualified as an attorney of law agreeable to his license &c.

John LONG Jr.)
 vs.   ) Genl. Issue &c.
Wm. MIMS) In which suit the following jury was sworn (vizt) Joseph GADD, Randolph HALEY, Daniel McDANIEL, Daniel THOMAS, Samuel CURTIS, Moses HURLY, Wm. THOMAS, ~~B~~ Barniby SKIPPER, Silas HALEY, Simon THOMAS, Samuel USHER and John TURNAGE who upon their oaths do say that they find for the defendant and so they say all &c.

River JORDON assignee)
of John PUKITT   ) Deft. Inqy.
 vs.   )
Thos. COCKRAHAM) In which suit the aforegoing jury was sworn and upon their oaths do say that they find for the plaintiff the sum of eight pounds & cost and so they say all &c.

Richd. LEVERITT)
 vs.   ) Genl. Issue
Benjn. VAUGHN) In which suit the aforegoing jury was sworn \only John EVANS in room of Wm. THOMAS/ and upon their oaths do say that they find for the plaintiff the sum of seven pounds eight shilling and so they say all &c.

Ordered that Wm. THOMAS be fined the sum of twenty shilling agreeable to act of assembly &c.

On motion Wm. THOMAS came into court and made his excuse &c.

~~Sifias ROBERTSON)~~
~~ vs   ) Genl. Issue &c~~
~~Wm. HUNTER Jr.) In which suit the aforegoing jury was sworn who upon their oaths do say that they find for the~~

July 1786

Burrel LENAIR assignee &c)
    vs.   ) Genl. Issue &c.
Solo. GROSS   ) In which suit the aforegoing jury was sworn and upon their oaths do say that they find for the plaintiff the sum of seven pound fourteen shilling and six pence and so they say all &c.

Edward MORE)
    vs.   ) Genl. Issue
Solo. GROSS   ) In which suit the aforegoing jury was sworn and upon their oaths do say that they find for the plaintiff the sum of eight pounds two shilling and five pence and so they say all &c.

A deed from Zachs. MARTIN & wife to Solomon RYE ~~and~~ for one hundred & fifty acres of land and proved in open court by the oath of Charles MEDLOCK Esqr. ordered to be registered. [*In margin:*] Tax fees paid.

John CAIN   )
    vs.   ) Deft. Inqy.
Nathan POWEL) In which suit the following jury was sworn (vizt) Wm. SMITH, James CAMPBLE, Archelous MOREMAN, Nicholas CLARK, John COVINGTON, Richd. CAMPBLE, Benjn. DEES, Thos. TURNER, Matthew TERRY, Peter COLE, Wm. THOMAS, Joshua LONG, who being sworn and upon their oaths do say that they find for the plaintiff the sum of eighteen pounds four shilling and three pence and so they say all &c.

July 1786

Ordered that Silas HALEY have leave to build a water grist mill on Solomon Creek on his own land &c.

Wm. HUNTER Jr.   )
    vs.   ) Genl. Issue
Duncan McFARLAND) In which suit the following jury was sworn (vizt) Joseph GADD, Randolph HALEY, Daniel McDANIEL, Daniel THOMAS, Samuel CURTIS, Moses HURLEY, Wm. THOMAS, Barnaby SKIPPER, Silas HALEY, Simon THOMAS, Samuel USHER, John TURNAGE who upon their oaths do say that they find for the plaintiff the sum of eight shillings and so they say all &c.

Simon COOPER by)
his next friend) Deft. Inqy.
vs.)
Samuel LANE?) In which suit the \same/ jury was sworn that was sworn in the cause that was tried in number 98 and upon their oaths do say that they find for the plaintiff the sum of one penny and so they say all &c.

Jethro MORE)
vs) Genl. Issue & sett. off.
Wm. HUNTER Jr.) In which suit the same jury was sworn as was sworn in the suit Wm. HUNTER Jr. vs. Duncan McFARLAND, and on their oaths do say that they find for the plaintiff the sum of fifty one pounds four shilling and eight pence and so they say all.

July 1786   Page 254

Alexr. BIGHAM)
vs) Genl. Issue &c
Wm. JERMAN) In which suit the aforegoing jury was sworn, who upon their oaths do say that they find for the plaintiff the sum of thirty one pounds and so they say all, &c.

Samuel LANE)
vs) Genl. Issue with Leave
Benj. VAUGHN) In which suit the aforegoing jury was sworn who upon their oaths do say that they find for the plaintiff the sum of twenty six pounds five shillings and so they say all.

John CAIN wife)
vs.) I. A. B.
Moses CHAMBERS) In which suit the aforegoing jury was sworn, who upon their oaths do say that they find for the plaintiff the sum of twenty shillings and so they say all.

Ordered that James CAMPBLE be fined the sum of twenty shillings agreeable to act of assembly &c.

John PEMBERTON)
vs.) Deft. Inqy.
Moses PETTUS) In which suit the same jury was sworn that was sworn in the suit no. 98 except Ezra BOSTICK in lieu of James CAMPBLE who upon their oaths do say that they find for the plaintiff the sum of ten? pounds and eight pence and so they say all &c.

July 1786 *Page 255*

Court adjourned untill tomorrow 9 o'clock.

Court meet according to adjournment.
    Present   Charles MEDLOCK)
                  James COLE)
                  Benj. COVINGTON)
                  Walter LEAK) Esqrs.
                  Thos. CRAWFORD)
                  Thos. DOCKERY)

Andrew HENDRICK)
    vs.   ) Deft. Inqy.
River JORDON   ) In which suit the following jury was sworn (vizt) Randolph HALEY, Daniel McDANIEL, Daniel THOMAS, Samuel CURTIS, Wm. THOMAS, Barnaby SKIPPER, Silas HALEY, Jesse BOUNDS, Alexr. \Allen/ McKASKILL, David SNEED, Robert WILSON, Wm. DAWKINS who upon their oaths do say that they find for the plaintiff the sum of twenty two pounds ten shillings & cost & so they say all &c.

Ordered that Alexr. GORDON \Archabald SMITH/ be appointed to serve as Constable in the room of Angush McNEIL in the insuing year.

Ordered that George COLE be appointed to serve in room of Benj. ARNOLD, the insuing year as Constable.

John CHAMBERS)
    vs   ) Genl. &c
Solo. GROSS Admr.) In which suit the aforegoing jury was sworn who upon their oaths do say that they find for the plaintiff the sum of one hundred and twenty nine pounds eight shilling and four pence three farthings and so they say all, & cost.

July 1786 *Page 256*

Nathan FAULKNER)
    vs.   ) I. V. A.
Robert LEVERITT   ) In which suit the following jury was sworn (vizt) Joseph LAS\E/TER, John McNEAR, George SATERFIELD, Richd. ADAMS, Joseph GADD, Duncan McFARLAND, Moses SPIVA, Joseph HALL, John MATTHEWS, James WATSON, Wm. TERRY and Joseph WHITE who upon their oaths do say that they find for the Plaintiff the sum of four pounds & cost and so they say all &c.

Joseph FREEMAN)
vs.) Genl. Issue & Set Off
Wm. HUNTER Jr.) In which suit the same jury was sworn that tried the cause no. 7 and upon their oaths do say that they find for the plaintiff the sum of twenty four shillings and six pence & cost and so they say all &c.

Ordered that Ducan FINLEY be appointed overseer in room of Wm. BETTY and the hands that work under BETTY work under the said FINLAY agreeable to the former order.

Ordered that John HOWARD be appointed overseer of the road, from where the road crosses the river road that lead from Hillen Ford, a direct course to Matthew ~~road~~ RAYFORDs, and that Benj. DUMAS Senr. hands, Benj. DUMAS Jr., Andrew DUMAS, James PICKETTs hands, Samuel LIPSCOMBs hands, Hardy STEPHENS, Thos. WALKER, Wm. MORE, John MASK hands, James PATTERSON hands work thereon.

July 1786   Page 257

Henry Wm. HARRINGTON Esqr.)
assignee of HEARTWELL Heirs) Genl. Issue & Sett. Off.
vs.)
Samuel LANE) In which suit the aforegoing jury was sworn and upon their oaths do say that they find *find* for the plaintiff the sum of fifty pounds seventeen shillings and cost and so they say all &c.

A deed from Wm. USSERY & wife to Charles ROBERTSON dated 18 of June 1785 for 250 acres of land acknowledged in open court by Wm. USSERY ordered to be registered. [*in margin:*] tax fee paid.

Court adjourned untill tomorrow 9 o'clock.

Court met according to adjournment.
    Present   Ed. WILLIAMS)
                   John BOUNDS)
                   Benj. COVINGTON)
                   John WALL) Esqrs.
                   Dudley MASK)
                   Thos. DOCKERY)
                   Walter LEAK)

Ordered that John COLE Senr. have leave to build ~~another~~ \water/ grist mill on his own land on Falling Creek adjoining Rockingham Twon &c.

Benj. HICKS Jr.)
    vs.   ) Ginl. Issue & Sett.
John WALTER) In which suit the following jury was sworn (vizt) Joseph GADD, Randolph HALEY, Daniel McDANIEL, Daniel THOMAS, Barnaby SKIPPER, Simon THOMAS, Samuel CURTISS, Moses HURLEY, Wm. THOMAS, Daniel CURRY, Joseph LASETER, Allen McKASKILL, and... [last line of page torn, unreadable]

July 1786   Page 258

Jury call'd and one failed to answear &c miss trial.

Benj. HICKS Jr.)
    vs   ) Genl. Issue & Sett. Off &c
John WALTERS) In which ~~jury~~ \suit/ the same jury ~~as~~ was sworn as before except Wm. JERNIGAN in room of Daniel McDANIEL and upon their oaths do say that they find for the plaintiff ~~and so they~~ the sum of fifteen and cost and so they say all &c.

A deed from Richd. LEVERITT Sheriff to Thos. TURNER and proved in open court by the oath of John WALL and ~~John WALL~~ ordered to be registred &c. [in margin:] Tax fee.

Mary HOLTOM admx.)
of John HOLTOM dec.)
    vs   ) Deft. Inqy.
Richd. GREEN   )
Luke ROBERTSON   ) In which suit the following jury was sworn (vizt) Samuel DOCKINS, Duncan McFARLAND, James SMITH, Jacob MANGRUM, Thos. ADAMS, Jonathon NEWBERRY, Joseph HALL, William DOCKINS, Matthew TERRY, Matthew COVINGTON, George BOUNDS, Silas HALEY who upon their oaths do say that they find for the the plaintiff the sum of thirteen pounds fourteen shilling and five pence and so they say all &c.

State   )
    vs.   ) Ind. Petty Larceny
John CAIN) In which suit the following jury was sworn (vizt) Duncan McFARLAND, James SMITH, Thos. ADAMS, Jonathon NEWBERY, Joseph HALL, Nicholas STONE, Thos. EVERITT, Benj. ~~EVERITT~~ INGRAM, John McINNISE, Gilbert McNEAR, Wm. THOMAS, Richd. ADAMS who upon their oaths do say that they find the defendant guilty in manner and form as charged in the bill and so they say all.

Ordered that the Sheriff summon Ed. WILLIAMS, Dudley MASK Esqr. and Matthew COVINGTON be appointed as a vinire to Salisbury Superior Court 15 Sept. 1786.

July 1786 *Page 259*

A deed from Francis CLARK ~~to~~ of Guilford County to Henry Wm. HARRINGTON Esqr. and proved in open court by the affirmation Thos. MOREMAN ordered to be registered &c.

A deed from John THOMAS, of Guilford County to Henry Wm. HARRINGTON Esqr. and proved in open court by the affirmation Thos. MOREMAN ordered to be registered.

Court adjourned untill tomorrow 9 o'clock.

Court met according to adjournment &c.
    Present   Charles MEDLOCK)
                     James COLE   ) Esqrs.
                     Walter LEAK   )

Hanah COULTER administratrix of Wm. COULTER decd. returned her inventory &c. Ordered that the Sheriff sell all the perishable property of Wm. COULTER decd. and make return to the next court.

Ordered that the Sheriff sell all the perishable property of Joseph HALL decd. and make return to the next court.

Ordered that the Sheriff sell all the perishable property of the widow CURY decd. and make return to the next court.

On motion, Benj. HICKS vs. John WALTERS reasons in arrest of judgment filed, reasons argued and the court was of opinion that the reasons be over ruled and ~~on me~~ on motion of Mr. Wm. CRAWFORD for a new trial.

Ordered that James PATTERSON be appointed overseer of the road, in room of Duncan McFARLAND agreeable the former order and that Dugal GRAHAM, Daniel CAMPBLE, Daniel McD[unreadable], Daniel Mc[unreadable], Thos. [unreadable]...

July 1786 *Page 260*

...Normon McCLOUD, Archabald DOVE work thereon &c.

A deed from Edward WILLIAMS Esqr. Sheriff to Henry Wm. HARRINGTON Esqr. acknowledged in open court ordered to be registred &c. [*in margin:*] Tax fee paid.

A deed from Stephen TOUCHSTONE & wife to John STEPHENS and proved in open court by the oath of Charles ROBERTSON ordered to be registred. [*in margin:*] Tax fee paid Clk. to pay registered.

On motion Matthew COVINGTON produced his vinire claim and was allowed the sum of six pound six and eight pence.

A power of attorney from Thos. ADCOCK to Henry ADCOCK, proved in open court by the affirmation of Thos. MOREMAN &c.

Nathaniel CHAIRS came into court and qualified as a Justice of the Peace & took his seat &c.

Court adjourned untill tomorrow 9 o'clock &c.

Court met according to adjournment.
    Charles MEDLOCK)
    Thos. CRAWFORD)
    Walter LEAK   ) Esqrs.
    Nathl CHEARS)

On motion of Wm. WALL Esquire Sheriff of Richmond County, ordered that this memorandum be entered in the minutes of this court vizt. that at April session last the said Wm. WALL Esqr. was appointed & commissioned as Sheriff who at the same time gave bond and security as county treasurer ~~the condition of which \bond, we concieve/ he cannot possibly comply with~~ & no persons in the county would take upon themselves the collection of the public taxes in said county and debts have arisen whither (under the laws for collecting taxes) the Sheriff is obliged or authorised to take upon himself said collection.

July 1786   *Page 261*

A deed from John JAMES Senr. to Richard LEVERITT and proved in open court by the oath of John McALESTER, ordered to be registred &c.

A deed from Richard LEVERITT to Patrick TRAVERS and proved ~~by the oath of~~ in open court by the oath of John McALESTER ordered to be registred &c.

A deed from Patrick TRAVERS to Walter LEAK acknowledged in open court ordered to be registred &c.

Richmond County NC Court Minutes, 1779-1786   165

Ordered that Alexander WATSON be appointed overseer of the road, in stead of Duncan McFARLAND from Gum Swamp to Drowning Creek.

Ordered that Duncan McRAE be appointed overseer of the road, in stead of Randle McDONALD from Grimes Fork to Montgomery County line.

Ordered that Duncan McFARLAND, Dugal McFARLAND and their two hands be exempted from working on any road, for their services in building a bridge over Jordons Creek at Duncan McFARLANDs plantation as long as they keep the said bridge in good repair &c.

A deed from Duncan McFARLAND to Wm. CROWSSON? Esqr. and acknowledged in open court for three hundred acres of land, ordered to be registred &c.

Ordered that Wm. HUNTER Senr. and Benj. COVINGTON be appointed to lett a bridge to the lowest bidders over Hitchcock Creek near to the middle fork or at such \other/ place that they shall think fitt &c and to enter into bond, with the workmen.

Ordered that the Sheriff summons Benj. MOORMAN, David SNEAD Jr., Daniel SNEAD, John SNEAD, Geo. MEDLOCK, Thos. MOORMAN, Wm. TERRY, Benj. INGRAM, Jesse? BOUNDS, John HALL, Henry COVINGTON, John C[unreadable], [unreadable] Jr., Nath. HARRINGTON, Thos. [unreadable]...

July 1786   *Page 262*

...Nelson GIBSON, Tillotson OBRYAN, Stephen COLE, Wm. WATKINS Jr., William COTTINGHAM, William WOODELL, George GEER?/GUS?, Samuel PATE, Isaac YATES, Samuel COVINGTON, John PANKEY, Benjamin POWEL, John HOWARD, John CROWSON, Gilbert McNEAR, John JAMES Jun., William JORNIGAN, ~~William~~ John WEBB Jun., Isam HALEY, Joseph WHITE, Thomas BLEWITT, William THOMAS Jun. as jurors to attend at next court and make return thereof &c.

A deed from Moses CHAMBERS to John SNEED duly acknowledged in open court or<u>d</u>red to be registred &c. [in margin:] Tax fee paid.

Ordered that the following rates be laid upon liquors and provisions in Richmond County (vizt)

    First table with grog or cyder three shilling   3-
    Second do. with two dishes \with grog or cyder/ two shilling six pence 2- 6
    Third do. grog or cyder two shillings   2-
    Corn or oats[?] pr. quart - one shilling   1-

Blade fodder pr. bundle/2' sheaf oats[?] four pence	-4
Good West India rum pr. half pint one shilling & four pence	1-4
New Ingland do. - eight pence	-8
Brandy pr. half pint eight pence	-8
Cyder pr. quart eight pence	-8
Whiskey and French taffey[?] each four ~~shilling~~ pence	0-4
___ with loaf sugar & West India rum pr. qt.	2-?
Good wine pr. bottle eight shillings	8-
French do. do.	[sic] 4-
Lodings with clean sheets pr. night -	6?
Pasturage or stabling for a hours 24 ours	-6

Ordered that Joseph SIMPKINS be allowed the sum of forty eight shillings for his attendance as Constable this term.

Ordered that Nathl. CHEARS, be security for Peter USSERY gaurdin to Mary HUTCHEN in the sum of two hundred pounds.

July 1786   Page 263

Ordered that all the officers having public m[torn] in their hands, to settle the next \court/, on the second day of the term &c.

Ordered that Wm. WALL Esqr. be appointed to serve as Sheriff the insuing year &c.

Ordered that George MEDLOCK be appointed to serve as Publick Register for the County of Richmond &c and gave bond & Charles MEDLOCK Esqr. security &c.

Ordered that, a road be laid out from the uper corner of the widow SNEEDs fence the nearest and best way into the road near about the corner of Silas HALEYs fence then the nearest and best way to the ferry &c agreeable to a petition filed &c.

Ordered that John McALESTER be appointed to serve as Coroner the insuing year and gave John SPEED, and James COLE as security in the sum of one thousand pounds &c.

Court adjourned untill c[torn]
    Test Wm. LOVE Clk.

no date   Page 264

[scratch page, with mathematical calculations, scribbles, and some names]

[September 1785] Page 265

State of North Carolina)
To the Sheriff \of/ Richmond County, greeting. You are hereby commanded before good & lawfull men off your county you make known to William HUSBAND to appeare at our County Court of Pleas and Quarter Sessions to be held for the County of Richmond at the Court House in the town of Rockingham on the second Monday in October next then & thare to shew cause if any you have why execution may not issue against you on a judgment recovered by William JOHNSTON assignee of William GANER vs. William HUSBAND. [case on p. 215]

September 1794 Page 265

Rockingham, Septemb. 2nd? 1794
Robert DONALDSON & gentlemen the time is out that I promised to discharge my bond in - have not made out all the money but will be down in October in order to make you full payment - pleas to send by the bairer one rhim of wrighting paper such as cost ten shillings two bushell of salt 6 lb? of sugar 4 lb? coffee & your compliance will much oblige your
　　　　　　　　　　　　　Humble servt.
　　　　　　　　　　　　　Tod ROBINSON

[end of Book 1]

INDEX

ADAM[S] Jame[s] 209
Richard 47, 51, 87, 102,
  116, 120, 137, 138, 140,
  158, 163, 168, 171, 173,
  174, 183, 186, 191, 194,
  209, 234, 241, 244, 245,
  256, 258
Richard Jr. 46
Richard Sr. 46*
Sion 89
Thomas 9, 15, 21, 47, 51,
  102, 107-109*, 111*,
  113, 163, 167, 169, 171,
  173, 174, 258*
William 7, 16, 178, 200,
  209*, 221
ADCOCK 22
Delilah 54
Henry 7, 10, 11, 28, 33, 47,
  50, 54*, 70, 72, 85*, 97,
  107, 123, 127, 130,
  134*, 147, 149, 153,
  162, 172, 173, 175, 178,
  188, 243, 246, 248, 250,
  260
Thomas 114, 243, 260
ADCOCK FERRY 8, 22
ALLEN Mark 36
ALMOND Edward 5*, 33,
  60, 95, 96*, 114, 125,
  136, 140, 157, 207, 222,
  239, 243, 247
Thomas 188
ALRED Solomon 72*, 88,
  101
ALSTON William 56
AMIT 143
ANDERSON
Fay Thomas 1
ANSON COUNTY 249
ARNOLD Benjamin 213,
  255
ASHLEY William 7, 13, 101,
  155*, 200
AULD James 10
John 54*, 169
Micheal 169
AULDS FERRY 165

AVERITT see *EVERITT*
AYERS Elisabeth 203
Hartwell 156*
Lewis 203
BAGGET[T] James 88, 127,
  132, 134*, 135*-137,
  175, 191, 250
James Jr. 151, 203, 205
James Sr. 80, 203, 205, 248
Shadrack/Shadrick 192,
  203, 205
BAKER John James 222
William 27, 28, 33, 39, 40,
  46, 51, 78, 118, 123,
  175, 188
BALDEN[S] Jesse 217
Jonathon 217
Rachel 134
BARN[E]S John 64*, 85,
  102
BARRENTINE Mary 54
BEARD Benjamin 22, 30, 34,
  41, 43, 56, 58, 71, 72,
  88, 91, 95, 97, 99, 101,
  103, 114, 122
Benjamin Batt 23
John Batt 22
BEASLEY James 142
BEAVER DAM 194
BELL Zacherias 150
BENNETT John 98
William 98
BETHIGH John 89, 124,
  186
BETTY William 154, 215,
  256
BETTY'S BRIDGE 6, 109,
  215, 218
BEVERLY Sarah 152
BIGG BEAVER DAM 150
**BIGG MOUNTAIN
  CREEK** 43*, 103*
BIGHAM Alexander 183,
  254
BLACK William 56
BLADEN COUNTY 53,
  86, 89, 90, 108, 142
BLANE 62

BLEWITT Thomas 28, 33,
  47*, 51, 71, 73, 100,
  102*, 118, 127, 130,
  136, 142, 149, 163, 166,
  188, 192, 195, 198, 225,
  227, 237, 243, 248, 262
William 9, 82, 122*, 243
BLEWITT['S] FALLS 68,
  233
BLEWITTS FERRY 190,
  243
BLUE Dugal 6, 53, 69, 90,
  93, 179, 186, 218, 237
Duncan 6, 56, 145
John 6, 22, 90*
Malcom 87, 179, 188, 218,
  237
Mary 90
BOBS FORD 194
BOGGAN Patrick 43, 84
BOLTON James 176, 198,
  224
William 80, 131
BONE John 203, 205
John Jr. 203, 205
BOOK Thomas 218
BOST[W]ICK Ezra/Izra 52,
  69, 70*, 73, 98, 100,
  234, 240, 244, 246, 254
James 7, 8, 10, 15, 66, 137,
  139, 142*, 143, 145,
  147, 149, 163, 171, 175,
  178, 187, 197, 199, 210,
  217-219, 221, 244, 246,
  248, 250
John 21, 171, 217
BOUND[S]/BOWND[S]
George 22, 63*, 68, 69, 89,
  92, 98, 100, 116, 123,
  124, 127, 128, 132, 134,
  135*-137, 143, 145, 147,
  163*, 166, 187*, 195,
  197, 200, 210, 212, 234,
  235, 258
James 65, 68, 74, 76, 100,
  119, 143, 145, 181, 183,
  186, 210, 214, 215,
  217*, 219, 221

Numbers refer to page in original book. *Name appears on page more than once.

BOUNDS cont.
Jesse 6, 11, 15, 22, 36, 39, 70, 73, 92, 93, 95, 114, 116, 119, 120, 124, 130, 134*, 137*, 139, 142, 143, 145, 147, 163, 166, 180, 192, 195, 225, 227, 234, 244, 255, 261
John 13, 36, 42, 43, 71, 72, 75, 77, 78, 86, 89, 91, 94, 99, 104, 105, 107*, 111, 121, 126, 129*, 131, 136-139, 143*, 147, 152*, 155, 159, 162, 163, 165-167, 170, 174, 177, 180, 182, 186, 192, 196, 201, 208-213*, 216, 218-221, 225, 227, 235, 236, 238, 257
Stephen 176
William 202
BOWEN? John 190
BOWMAN Moses 68, 69, 100, 243
BRANCH Brit[t]ain 207, 221
BREWER Elisabeth 124
Lenoir 68, 69
BRICE Francis 11, 12*, 16*, 18, 19
George 16
John 16, 179
Joseph 16
BRIDGE CREEK 146
BRIGMAN Isaac 6, 13, 91
William 6, 57, 76, 160, 233
BROWN Benjamin 103
Edmund 108, 109*, 112, 149
Edward 80
Morgan 38, 65, 98, 113, 117, 132, 173
Morgan Sr. 39
Thomas 47, 61, 75*, 80, 88, 100, 102, 241
William 69, 70*
BULL John 58, 90
BURN[S] Darius 191, 195
James 141
BURT Is[s]able 40, 65
William 40*, 65
CADDLE James 230
CAIN John 252, 254, 258
CAMPBLE Alexander 166
Archabald 60, 170
Daniel 259

CAMPBLE cont.
James 9, 16, 131*, 133, 188, 252, 254*
John 113, 140
John Jr. 87
Richard 167, 252
William 57
CARMICAL/KERMICAL
Capt. 86, 87, 235
Daniel 58, 87, 93, 181, 191, 231
Dugal 63, 64, 139
CARTER Charles 44, 64
George 12, 15, 21, 44, 46, 47, 76, 122, 172, 184, 194, 241, 245
George Jr. 195
Thomas 187
CARTLEDGE[S] CREEK 21, 26, 29, 30*, 35, 61, 87*, 151*, 161
CASTLEHAM Nancy 124
CATFISH ROAD 8*, 12, 19, 27, 29, 82, 190, 230*
CAUDLE David 37, 45, 119
CHAIRS/CHEARS
Charles 91
Nathaniel/Natheniel 187, 192, 195*, 217, 225, 231, 236, 260*, 262
Samuel 236*
CHALK FORK 5, 109
CHALK FORK ROAD 13
CHAMBER[S]
John 246, 255
Moses 7, 10, 29, 33, 44, 47, 51, 84, 100, 102*, 123, 124, 127, 128, 132, 137, 143, 147, 158, 159, 181, 184*, 202, 254, 262
William 141
CHAP[P]LIN Samuel 110
William 110*, 125*
CHEARS *see CHAIRS*
CHERRAW [OLD] ROAD 12*, 230, 230
CHERRAWS 6
CHEVES William 93, 104, 139
CHILES John 12, 36*, 37, 39, 44*, 62*, 112, 124, 187, 188, 217, 239
Thomas 36, 41, 159, 193, 207, 239
CHISM Murdock 155

CHRISTIAN Jesse 119
Nicholas 119
CHUN Silvanus 217
Silvester 246
CLARK Christopher 248
Francis 259
Herod 152, 179, 191
Nicholas 246, 252
CLEMONS John 243
CLERK Thomas 67
CLERKS ROAD 126
COCKRAHAM Jacob 39, 40, 79, 110, 134, 143, 154*, 155, 168
John 83, 109
Thomas 251
William 93
COLE Francis 164, 192
George 168, 209, 210, 216, 255
James 18*, 21*, 23*, 25*, 26, 29, 32-34, 38*, 39, 43, 45, 48, 50, 52, 56, 59, 65, 71, 72, 75, 78, 80*, 82, 95, 99, 101, 102, 104, 105*-107, 114, 118, 143*, 146, 153, 155, 157, 162, 174, 177, 196, 198, 201, 211, 229, 232, 236, 238, 249, 250, 255, 259, 263
John 7, 8*, 10, 15-17, 23, 26*, 27, 37, 39, 60*, 65, 67, 73, 91, 93, 100, 127, 128, 209, 212, 214, 216*, 219, 224, 230, 248
John Jr. 190, 192, 224, 238, 241
John Sr. 36, 37*, 70, 75, 100, 104, 127, 130, 138, 172, 175, 178, 194, 206, 209*, 250
John (Maryland) 8, 16, 21, 23, 210, 212, 243
Mrs. 8
Peter 164, 252
Rachel 26
Stephen 47, 53-57*, 58-60, 63*, 65, 66*-69, 71, 74, 93, 95, 112, 127*, 128, 136, 154, 183, 214, 215, 225, 228*, 231, 233, 236*, 243*, 262
COLEMAN John 8, 28, 36, 46, 68, 78*, 93, 116*, 124, 127, 134*, 135*,

*Numbers refer to page in original book. *Name appears on page more than once.*

COLEMAN John *cont.* 136*,
137, 139, 163, 175*,
183, 187, 190, 197, 225,
228, 230, 233, 236*,
242*, 243, 248, 250
  John Jr. 172
  William 41
COLEMAN'S MILL 162
COLEMAN'S ROAD 160
COLE[S] BRIDGE 5, 8,
102, 109, 150, 151, 176,
191, 230
COLES MILL CREEK 20
COLE'S ROAD 245
COLESON'S FERRY 45
COLLIER Drury 248
COLLINS Charles 128
  Elisha 135
  George 83, 99, 126, 193
  George Jr. 121
  George Sr. 122
  Jacob 141
  Thomas 121, 126
COOK John 124
COOPER Simon 253
COPLAND John 190
CORNELIUS'S POND 48, 152
COSTANT? Samuel 229
COTTENGAME Elisha 7,
22, 171, 192, 195, 196,
200-202*, 205, 206, 209
  William 15, 21, 80, 84, 139,
191, 195, 196, 200-202*,
205, 206, 209
COTTINGHAM William 262
COTTON James 74
CO[U]LTER[S] Hanah 246, 259
  Jesse 82
  William 77, 88, 109, 123,
134, 135, 146, 199, 202,
230, 246, 259
COVINGTON Benjamin 6,
15, 21, 29, 33, 39*, 49*,
65, 71, 89, 91, 94, 95,
97-99, 107, 111*, 112,
121, 125-127, 129, 131,
133, 136, 138, 139,
141*-143, 146, 151, 154,
157, 162, 166, 181, 185,
192, 235, 236, 242*,
249, 250, 255, 257, 261
  Hanah 14

COVINGTON *cont.*
  Henry 4, 15, 18, 22, 28, 33,
47, 51, 93, 95, 116, 120,
137, 138, 163, 166, 202,
212, 234, 240, 261
  Henry Sr. 210
  John 28, 33, 80, 93, 120,
166, 195, 200, 202, 231,
234, 240, 243, 252
  John Jr. 71, 74, 76, 95, 102,
107, 111-113, 137, 138,
146, 174, 183, 210, 212,
234, 240
  John Sr. 4, 15, 22, 47, 51,
95, 116, 137, 138, 163,
210, 212, 216
  Mary 14
  Mat[t]hew 71, 74, 76, 95,
96*, 102, 107-109*, 111-
113, 123*, 124, 127,
128, 132, 139, 175, 191,
235, 248, 258*, 260
  Sarah 14
  Samuel 71, 74, 76, 127-
128, 139, 140, 190, 234,
241, 244, 262
CRAIG Roger 53, 56
CRAWFORD Col. 114, 177
  John 3, 4*, 5, 7, 10*, 11*,
12, 16, 17*, 22, 23*, 30,
34, 35*, 43, 52, 58, 84,
96, 99, 101, 103*, 105,
114, 120, 121, 124, 126,
130, 137, 144, 150, 154,
159-161*, 167, 172, 206
  Thomas 6, 8, 10, 13, 18,
23, 25, 29, 43, 63, 89,
91-93, 100, 101, 104*,
107, 116, 123*, 124,
127, 128, 133, 134*,
135*-137, 139, 142, 144,
145, 147, 148, 158*,
159, 165, 168, 172-174,
176, 188, 192, 195, 216,
218, 225, 228, 230, 231,
233, 236*, 242, 247,
255, 260
  William 131, 143, 146, 149,
171, 190, 195, 200-202,
205, 211, 224, 242, 259
CRAWFORD[S] [OLD] ROAD 8, 23, 29*, 30*, 164
CROSS CREEK ROAD 246
CROSSLAND Edward 36

CROUCH James 217
  Jeremiah 217
  John 244, 246
CROWS[S]ON/CRAWS-SON Charles 65
  Jehu[el]le 7, 9, 10, 12, 14,
21, 27, 30, 35, 41, 76,
170
  John 12, 14, 15, 47, 51, 57-
60, 63*, 65-69, 88, 89,
91, 92, 102, 116, 123,
124, 127, 128, 136, 137,
139, 142, 143, 145, 147,
160, 163, 168, 183, 186,
202, 210, 212, 223, 234,
237, 262
  Sarah 27, 76, 190, 191
  William 261
CROWSSONS MILL 185
CUMBERLAND COUNTY 28, 43, 53, 89, 93, 103*
CUR[R]Y Donald 163
  Iver? 168, 170
  John 108, 134, 163
  Katherine 240
  Laughlin 240
  Widow 259
CURTIS[S] Samuel 33, 80,
107, 216, 225, 227, 234,
248, 251, 253, 255
  Thomas 36, 70, 216, 225,
227, 234, 248, 250
DAVENPORT *see DEVONPORT*
DAVIS Isaac 33, 209
  John 38, 113, 203, 205
  Mary Ann Williams 34, 54
  Samuel 34*
  Vinson 88
DAVIS'S PATH 16*
DAWKINS/DOCKINS
  George 137, 180, 210, 212, 213
  John 36, 102, 180, 181,
183*, 186, 187*, 190,
234, 240
  Samuel 102, 107-109*,
111-113, 149, 154, 156,
158, 159*-161*, 163,
175, 180, 181, 183, 186,
187*, 190, 209, 234,
240, 258
  William 111, 112, 209, 255, 258

†*Name appears on p. 145 as "same" (carried over from p. 144)*

DEARMAN/DEERMAN
Solomon 89, 91*-93, 95,
109, 149, 154, 156, 158,
159*-161*, 175, 180,
181, 183, 186, 187*,
190, 225, 227, 234
DEES Arthur/Arther 58,
122*, 149, 156, 158*,
159*-161*, 232, 246
Benjamin 149, 154, 156,
158*, 159*-161*, 252
Malichi 87
Mark 6*, 13, 48
DEGARNETT John 50*,
119, 171
DEVONPORT Joseph 123
DICKERSON John 201
DICKSON/DIXON
John 80, 85, 98
Peggy 106
Richard 80, 163
Robert 190
DOBBINS 162
Thomas 200, 201, 228
DOCKERY Micheal 199,
208
Thomas 7, 14*, 26, 31, 47,
70, 74, 242*, 250, 255
DONAL[D]SON
John 3*, 4, 9, 21, 27, 30*,
35, 52, 99, 103
Robert 265
DOVE Archabald 246, 260
John 179, 181, 237
DOWNING James 7
John 25
D[R]OWN[ING] CREEK
6*, 8, 9, 12, 13*, 21,
109, 151, 152, 179, 194,
218, 235, 237, 245, 261
**DROWNING CREEK
BRIDGE** 43
DRY CREEK 162
DUDLEY Widow 162
DUMAS Andrew 192, 256
Benjamin 15, 23, 32, 116,
136, 142, 200, 206, 209,
250
Benjamin Jr. 192, 195, 196,
201, 202*, 205, 248, 256
Benjamin Sr. 155, 192,
211, 234, 256
David 50*
DUNBAR[R] James 215
John 183, 186, 187, 207,
217, 218

DUNBAR cont.
Rollin 215
DUNHUM? John 182
DUPLIN CO. 12
DURHUM? John 182
EASTERLING Capt. 89,
194, 235
James 36, 70, 76, 107, 127,
137, 138, 143, 145, 213
William 81, 84, 107, 127,
130, 133, 140, 144, 150,
155, 157, 182, 211,
212*, 213*, 230, 232,
245
EVANS John 157, 165, 177,
231, 251
EVERIT[T]/AVERITT
218
Benjamin 165, 243, 258
Henry 233
Laurance 14*, 16, 28, 33,
47, 70, 87, 116, 120,
139, 142, 149, 153, 175,
191, 192, 195, 196, 200-
202*, 205*, 206, 209,
225, 233, 236*, 241,
243, 244, 248, 250
Thomas 71, 74, 87, 102,
107-109*, 111-113, 132,
137, 163, 166, 258
EZEL/IZZEL etc. John 70,
74, 84, 87, 95, 96*, 114,
124, 135*-137, 175, 188,
191, 248, 250
FALCONBURY Jacob 68,
69, 175
FALLING CREEK 20, 28*,
45, 104, 129, 150, 151*,
164, 185
FARLEY 237
John 58, 64*, 230
John Sr. 210, 212, 230*
FARLEY[S] BRIDGE 179,
194, 235
FARR Richard 122
FAULK Right 64*
FAULKNER Nathan 256
FINLAW? Archabald 234
FINLAY/FINLEY
Du[n]can 256
FISHER Solomon 9, 179
FRAZER Charles 69, 70
William 45
FREEMAN/FREEMAS
Abraham 213
Elisabeth 100

FREEMAN cont.
Dorcas 106
George 36, 100
Joseph 196, 256
Josiah 100, 106, 183, 237
GAD[D] Joseph 142, 154,
156, 158*, 159*-161*,
244, 248, 251, 253, 256
Joseph Jr. 45, 116, 136,
137, 149, 171
Joseph Sr. 36, 171
GADDON David 60
GADDY James 243
Thomas 186
GA[I]NER William 15, 90,
215, 264
GAR[DE]NER
Elias 120, 163
GARLAND John 11
Samuel 11, 105, 157
GARNER see GARDENER
GEER? George 262
GEORGE 162
Thomas 217
GERMAN see JERMAN
GIBSON Andrew 209
James Jr. 220
Nelson 36, 70, 73, 86, 102,
106, 149, 153, 175, 178,
210, 212, 234, 240, 262
Thomas 6, 22, 28, 29, 33,
47, 70, 73, 86, 102, 106,
127, 128, 132, 149, 175,
178*, 191, 210, 214,
215, 217*, 219, 221,
230, 234, 240, 245
GILLIS Robert 61
GORDON Alexander 89, 90,
131, 179, 215, 255
GOWERS John 20
GRAHAM Archibald 157
Daniel 157
Dugal 259
Edward 214, 216, 217
George 64*, 140
John 64*, 142, 215
GRAHAM'S FORK 193*
GRASSY ISLAND[S] 20,
192, 193
GRAVES Thomas 149
GREAT FURROW? 224
GREAT JUNIPER 5
GREEN 179, 194
Nicholas 58, 91, 171, 219*
Richard 258

*Numbers refer to page in original book. *Name appears on page more than once.*

Richmond NC Court Minutes, 1779-1786

GREEN POND[S] 161, 243
GRIFFIN Aron 223
  Winney 223
GRIMES FORK 261
GRISSOM John 162
GROSS Aldred 236, 237, 244
  Allison 141
  Hutchen 236
  Mun? 153
  Solomon 52, 54, 86, 87, 89, 93, 94, 108, 110, 136, 141*, 142, 144, 149, 153*, 154, 159, 162*, 164, 171, 173, 178, 183, 198, 201, 208*, 210, 213, 214, 216, 217, 223*, 224, 225, 230, 233, 234, 239*, 241, 244, 252*, 255
GROVES Thomas 210
GUILFORD COUNTY 259*
GULLEDGE? William 236
GULLETT George 150
GUM SWAMP 86*, 138*, 170, 179, 193, 194*, 235, 237, 243, 261
GUM SWAMP BRIDGE 13*
GUS? George 262
HADLEY John 209
HAGGAN Zacherias 197
HAIGE John James 218
HAIRS Elisabeth 205
  Lewis 205
HALCOCK Thomas 73
HALE[S] Elisabeth 51, 132, 159
  Widow 55
  William 12, 51*
HALEY/HAILEY 20, 45
  Elisabeth 174
  Is[h]em/Isam 15, 21, 42*, 52, 70, 73, 78, 97, 114, 116, 140, 163, 208*, 214, 262
  Milley 77
  Randle/Randol 153, 176, 183, 225, 248
  Randolph 53-57*, 58-60, 65, 66*, 67, 76, 80, 84, 86, 126, 127*, 130, 149, 191, 195, 227, 251, 253, 255

HALEY *cont.*
  Silas 29, 33, 42, 47, 50, 70, 73, 77, 93, 95, 116, 120, 126*-128*, 134*, 135*, 136, 140, 148, 165, 175-177, 183, 189, 206, 210, 215, 217*, 219, 248, 251, 253*, 255, 258, 263
  William 128
  William Jr. 77
  William Sr. 77*
HALEY['S] FERRY 6, 20*, 28, 109, 114, 126*, 140, 165, 173
HALL Enoch 139
  Joel 194, 209
  John 114, 116, 191, 194-196, 200, 234, 261
  Joseph 76, 116, 146, 153, 191, 195, 196, 200-202*, 205, 206, 209, 234, 250, 256, 258*, 259
  Joseph Jr. 70, 149, 240
  Joseph Sr. 250
  Lewis 139, 154
  Sarah 250
  William 146, 216
HALLS BRIDGE 133*, 135, 209
HAMILTON John 61
HANAGAN Darby/Derby 7, 10, 29, 36, 39, 70, 73, 88, 89, 98, 102, 105, 106, 127, 130, 133, 144, 150, 157, 159, 161, 162, 165, 170, 172, 186, 193, 196, 198, 201, 208, 210-212, 216, 219, 242, 243
HARBERT Charles 25, 113, 123
HARRINGTON Gen. 126, 206, 223
  George 20
  Henry William 3, 4*, 5*, 6, 72, 77, 78, 94, 98, 99, 107-109, 111-113, 119, 123-125, 135, 143-145†, 147, 151, 152, 154, 158*, 169, 170*, 173, 178, 185*, 186, 206, 209*, 210, 212*, 218, 235, 239, 240, 242*, 247, 248, 256, 257, 259*, 260
  Jean Ann 206

HARRINGTON *cont.*
  Nathaniel 15, 21, 29, 33, 70, 73, 100, 116, 120, 171, 175, 178, 184, 234, 240, 243, 261
HARRY John 197
HATHCOCK Mary 152
  Thomas 67, 73*, 219
  William 152
HAYNES *see Hines*
HEARTWELL 257
HELLEN FORD 142
HENDERSON Nicholas 100
  Rice? 100
HENDLEY William 142, 244
HENDRICK[SON]
  Andrew 135, 147, 222, 236, 255
HERRING Benjamin 107, 110
HEWS John 87
HICKS Adrey 165, 177, 187
  Benjamin 259
  Benjamin Jr. 258
  Daniel 28, 29, 33*, 43, 44, 47, 69, 70, 74, 84*, 96, 98, 100, 106, 107, 127, 130, 163, 168, 171-174, 189, 192, 195, 203, 205, 216, 225, 227, 248, 250*
  George 54, 132
  James 4*, 5, 7, 10, 93
  John 237
  Sarah 27, 30
  William 15, 21, 29, 36, 47, 51, 80, 203, 205
HILL Ann 59
  George 59, 75, 203, 205
  Richard 107, 108*, 109*, 111-113
HILLEN/HILLINS FORD 244, 256
HILYARD John 19, 32, 87, 136
HILYARD/HILLAR'S FORD 120, 136, 171
HINES/HAYNS *etc.*
  Absolum 7
  Charles 7, 8, 15
  James 31
  Joseph 23, 29, 33, 71, 73, 83, 88*, 93, 97*, 98, 127, 130, 140, 141, 144,

†Name appears on p. 145 as "same" (carried over from p. 144)

HINES Joseph *cont.* 151, 154, 157, 177, 180-182*, 185, 186, 189, 190, 192, 213, 219-221, 225, 227, 229
  Thomas 87, 231
HITCHCOCK [CREEK] 8, 12, 16, 28, 43*, 86, 87, 103*, 114, 151*, 162, 164*, 173, 185, 230, 261
HODGE[S] Daniel 231
  John 132
  Moses 179, 218
HOLTOM John 258
  Mary 258
HORRY John 88
HOWARD John 232, 244, 248, 256, 262
HUCKABY Charles 53-57, 62, 65-67, 88, 108, 109*, 145, 229
HUGHES *see HEWS*
HUNT John 69
HUNTER Elisabeth 11
  James 71, 74, 76, 102, 107-109, 111, 137, 199, 202, 211, 243
  Samuel 4, 11, 26
  William 8, 10, 15, 28, 29, 51, 80, 88*, 108, 109, 120, 156, 161, 172, 182, 183, 187*, 199, 211, 219, 221-223, 231, 236*, 246
  William Jr. 111, 128, 143, 145, 150, 161, 168, 173, 181, 186, 190, 196, 199, 201, 202*, 205, 206, 209, 210, 216*, 218, 221, 230, 235, 242, 248, 250, 251, 253*, 256
  William Sr. 11, 22, 26, 47, 98, 109, 113, 116, 132, 137, 138, 154, 158, 160, 161*, 163, 166, 171, 174, 201, 202, 210, 212, 213, 241, 248, 250, 261
HUR[L]EY Anny? 223
  Jonah? 223
  Moses 120, 124, 210, 212, 248, 251, 253
  Sarah 221, 228, 247
  Timothy 7, 10, 36, 71, 73, 102, 106, 120
HUSBAND[S] William 44, 47, 68, 69, 100, 102,

HUSBAND William *cont.* 104, 116, 121, 123, 124, 127, 128, 132, 140, 160, 161, 190, 196, 197, 215, 264*
HUTCHEN[S] Anthony 41
  Elisabeth 40, 41*, 52, 185
  James 40, 41, 52*, 78, 247
  Jesse 41
  John 119
  Mary 41, 185, 247, 262
  Samuel 41
  William 41
INGRAM Benjamin 132, 137, 142, 143, 145, 147, 234, 240, 248, 258, 261
  Edward 246
  Edwin 162
  John 221
IV[E]Y Anthony 39
  James 6
JAMES James 135, 153, 180, 232
  John 23, 24, 26, 29*, 51, 88, 93, 95, 142, 153, 168, 172, 173, 202, 240
  John Jr. 7, 22, 102, 106, 132, 149, 164, 175, 178, 210, 230, 234, 262
  John Sr. 15, 27, 29, 33*, 47, 225, 233, 261
  Philip 6, 141, 143, 214, 215*, 217*, 230
JAMES [OLD] COWPENS 13*, 109
JEFFERSON 12, 144
  Elisabeth 18
  G. 144-145†, 198
  George 3, 11, 12, 18, 105, 157
  George Sr. 9
JERMAN William 254
JERNIGAN/JARNIGAN
  David 57
  William 7, 10, 29, 33, 47, 51, 76, 93, 95, 114, 116, 120, 137, 138; 156, 163, 166, 175, 178, 192, 195, 196, 200, 202*, 205, 206, 209, 225, 227, 258, 262
JINING[S] James 190
  Thomas 174, 188
JINK[IN]S John 99, 106*
JOES CREEK 138, 194, 243
JOHNSONS CREEK 28

JOHNS[T]ON Anguish 240
  Elias 223
  James 196
  Moses 6, 112
  Thomas 5, 6, 139, 187
  William 115, 140, 214, 215, 264
  Zacherias 53, 68, 171
JONES Jesse 85, 129*
  John 30, 38*, 45, 48, 49*, 52, 56, 59, 72, 77, 116, 169, 173*
  John Sr. 171
  Lucy 97
  Luraney 223
  Nathen 147
  Philip 9
  Solomon 20
  William 223
JORDON John 206
  River 39, 75*, 156, 157, 170, 188, 214, 215, 240, 251, 255
  William 89, 113
JORDON'S CREEK 5, 179, 194, 261
JOWERS George 182, 246
  John 111, 242
  Thomas 69, 70*, 106, 142, 163, 168, 171, 173, 174, 176, 230, 244, 246, 248
  William 69, 70*, 142, 244
JUNIPER 109, 138, 194
KELLEY William 133, 183, 207
KENAN Felix 12, 19*
KENDON? Kader 80
KERMICAL *see CARMICAL*
KILLIT[T]/KELLET *etc.*
  Andrew 121, 123, 127
  John 121, 128
  Solomon 121
KIMB[O]ROUGH John 176, 236
KIMBOROUGH TORY CAMP 224
KING Miles 202, 220
KINZIE Roger 172
[K]NIGHT Aron 75, 94, 189
  Benjamin 237
  Joseph 237
LAMBDAN Bexley John 198
LAMPLEY? Jacob 114

Numbers refer to page in original book. *Name appears on page more than once.

LANE Samuel 206, 234, 244, 253, 254, 257
LASENBY/LISENBY
  John 36
  Stephen 205
LASETER Joseph 33, 135, 136, 156, 202, 256
  Kader/Kedar 80, 92
LEAK Richard 131
  Walter 87, 91-93, 95, 97, 102, 123, 124, 127, 130, 144, 145, 151, 157, 170, 171, 179, 180, 186, 193, 201, 202, 212, 213, 216, 220, 227*, 232, 242*, 250, 255, 259-61
  William 93
LEAKS FERRY 217, 246
LEATON Elisabeth 141, 153
  Hugh 80, 85, 87, 89, 91, 92, 129, 149, 197
  Mary 129
LEG[G]ATE/LEGGETT
  John 53, 56
  William 3, 4*, 14*, 16*, 17, 25, 38, 45, 48, 52, 54, 71, 73, 76*, 244
LENAIR Burwell/Burrel 189, 252
LEVERETT/LIVERIT
  John 136, 141, 169, 221, 230
  Richard 66, 178, 184, 193, 200, 213, 222, 227, 244, 245, 247, 251, 258, 261*
  Robert 214, 217, 247, 256
  Thomas 208
LEWALLEN Jonathon 76*
LEWIS Elisha 131
  Leviny 170
  Winney 223
LICK BRANCH 243*
LIGHTFOOT[T] Henry 132, 142, 143, 149, 174
LILLEY Edmund 232, 234
LIPSCOMB Samuel 256
LISENBY *see LASENBY*
LITTLE RIVER 8*, 20, 22, 27, 45, 87, 97, 151*, 160, 176, 191
LITTLETON Savage 15, 22
LIVENBY Stephen 203
LOCK Leonard 59

LONG James 199, 207, 211, 222*, 224
  John 10, 31, 36, 72, 111, 112, 186
  John Jr. 7, 22, 93, 135, 160, 196, 251
  John Sr. 116, 120, 132, 140
  Joseph 217
  Joshua 252
LOUGE? Unity 181
  William 231
LOVE David 123, 241
  William 3*, 4, 9, 10, 16, 17*, 32, 38, 40, 48, 49, 58, 68, 71, 78, 79, 82, 87, 104, 105, 118, 129*, 137, 148, 149, 152, 160, 165, 176, 177, 185, 192, 197, 222, 227-229, 232*, 235, 238, 241*, 247, 263
LYON[S] John 87
  Josiah 12, 23, 91, 189
  Josias 70, 73, 93, 102, 116
MALCOM Robert 135
MALLET 143*
MALOY *see MELOY*
MANGRUM Jacob 36, 39, 70, 74, 98, 138, 149, 153, 210, 212, 234
MANOR Benjamin 122
MARTIN Alexander 75, 215
  Allen 170
  Daniel 172
  Elisabeth 36, 59
  John 73, 75, 76, 108, 181
  Joseph 55, 56
  Martha 232
  Neil 179
  Zacherias 36*, 45, 46, 91, 162, 189, 203, 205, 252
MASK[S] Capt. 235
  Dudley 7, 23*, 24*, 25, 32-34*, 35, 38, 42, 43, 45, 49*, 82, 90, 92, 103, 111, 120, 133, 167, 172, 180, 190, 198, 201, 223, 232*, 233, 249, 257, 258
  John 22*, 24*, 28, 33, 36, 45, 46, 53-57*, 58-60, 62, 63, 65, 66*, 67, 93, 95, 120*, 136-138, 156, 161, 192, 195, 225, 256
  John Jr. 15, 25
  John Sr. 15, 24, 25, 234

MASK *cont.* Martha 22
  William 28, 36, 40*, 41, 45, 46, 54, 91, 93, 136, 142
MASK[E]S CREEK 43*, 102*103, 150, 151
MASKS FERRY 15, 130, 191
MASON John 29, 88, 98, 155, 214
  Thomas 214
MAT[T]HEW[S] John 6, 12, 15, 21, 76, 142, 143, 145, 191, 194, 195, 241, 256
MAYFIELD Mary 97
McALESTER Anguish 179
  John 164, 183, 186, 187*, 193, 213, 228, 231, 231, 239*, 240, 261*, 263
McARTHUR Peter 61
McBRIDGE Dugal 241
  Duncan 87
  John 237
McCAIRN Daniel 241
McCALMON
  see McCAULMON
Mc[C]ARTER Neil 59, 61
McCASKILL *see McKASKILL*
McCAUL Daniel 98
  David 98
  Duncan 119, 158, 201
  Duncan Sr. 167
  John 97, 158, 201
  John Jr. 122
  Mary 167
McCA[U]LMON/ McCOLMON
  John 88, 175, 191, 210, 221
McCAULEY Owen 168
  Peggy 168
McCLENDON Daniel 245
McCLOUD *see McLEOUD*
McCOLLERT Hugh 75
McCOY/McKOY
  Alexander 61, 180, 186, 200
  Archabald 61, 182
  Daniel 58, 236
  Donald 178, 182, 218
  Duncan 179
  John 100, 125*, 209
  Mary 125
  Spence? 65

†*Name appears on p. 145 as "same" (carried over from p. 144)*

McCRANEY
John 89, 110, 143
McCRAY/McRAE
  Alexander 155*, 160, 167, 185
  Christian 172
  Christopher 98
  Duncan 167, 261
  Farquar 111
  Farquard Jr. 180
  Farquard Sr. 180
  John 57
McD___? Daniel 259
McDANIEL 258
  Alexander 108, 124
  Anguish 180
  Capt. 235
  Daniel 40, 54, 62, 66, 80, 83, 91-93, 95, 123, 124, 139*, 142, 146, 166, 171, 191, 195, 217, 229, 231, 243, 244, 246, 248, 251, 253, 255
  Issable 41
  Margeratt 41
  Murdock 90, 108
  Randolph 65, 68, 193
  William 34, 63*, 68-70, 73, 80, 87, 106*, 116, 120, 137, 149, 153, 155, 162, 214, 225, 228, 230, 231, 233, 236, 246
  Zacherias/Zachariah 24, 117, 139, 220, 230
McDONALD/ McDANOLD
  Daniel 163, 167
  John 168, 198, 199
  Randle 261
  Randolph 169
  William 54, 169, 175
McDUFFEE Daniel 106*, 162
McEACHEY John 234
McFARLAND Dugal 138, 179, 180, 193, 215, 237, 261
  Duncan 68, 86, 87, 93, 95, 97, 112, 131, 157, 178, 179, 194, 201, 215, 232, 237, 240, 246, 253*, 256, 258*, 259, 261*
  John 131, 178, 181, 215
McGILL Anguish 237
McGUIRE John 53, 56, 78

McGUIRE cont.
  William 36, 39, 53, 89, 109, 116, 136, 142, 171, 174, 176, 224, 244
McINNISE Alexander 215
  Daniel 57, 87, 88
  John 75, 87, 186, 209, 258
  Nancy 171, 173, 211, 216
McINTOSH Irvine 86, 126, 150, 206
McKASKILL/McCASKILL
  Alexander 126, 230, 255
  Allen/Alan 44, 206, 225, 228, 231, 233, 236*, 255
  Allen Jr. 150
  Allen Sr. 150
  Daniel 126, 171
  Daniel Jr. 237
  Findley 206
  Keneth/Kennith 126, 150, 206
  Malcom 186, 237*
  Mary 88
McKATHA/McKATHEY
  James 234, 239
  John 240
  Widow 82, 105, 245
McKAY Daniel 63, 64, 93
  John 63, 64
  John (Miller) 63, 64
McKELLER Peter 61
McKETCHAM Daniel 59
McKINSEY Sarah 64
McLEO[U]D/McCLOUD
  Alexander 74, 196, 209, 228
  Daniel 121*
  Nancy 121
  Norman 89, 260
McMILLAN/McMILLON
  Anguish 108
  Archabald/Archibold 95, 136, 179, 218, 237
  Dugal 196, 215, 228, 246
  Duncan 6, 60
  Malcom 64, 67
  Sarah 108
McNAIR/McNEAR
  Daniel 76
  Gilbert/Gelbert 133, 149, 150, 154, 156, 158*, 159*-161*, 183, 202, 205, 206, 210, 212, 234, 240, 258, 262
  John 61, 256
  Neil 170, 237

McNAIR cont. Robert 179
  Roger 168, 170, 183, 194*, 218, 237
McNARY John 131, 182, 189, 196, 197, 210, 246
McNEAR see McNAIR
McNEIL/McNEEL
  Alexander 133
  Anguish 193, 255
  Daniel 134, 168, 220
  Lacklin 215
McPHERSON/ McFERSHON etc.
  Alexand[er] 79, 149, 154
  Daniel 59, 79
  Edward 37, 39, 218, 225, 227, 237
  John 87
  Malcom 130
  Preseelar [Priscilla?] 149, 154
  William 231
McQUEEN James 41
  John 41
  William 180*, 228, 229
McRAE see McCRAY
MEDLOCK Charles 3*-5*, 7, 9*, 10, 12, 16, 17*-19*, 21, 23, 25, 26, 29, 32, 33, 38*, 39, 45, 48, 49*, 50, 52, 53, 59, 65, 71*, 72, 75, 77, 80*, 82*, 84, 85, 89, 91, 94*, 95, 97, 99, 103, 105*, 106, 111-115, 118*, 119*, 121*, 122, 126*, 129*-131, 133*, 137-139, 141*-143*, 146, 147, 150, 152-154, 157, 159, 165, 166*, 167, 172, 174, 177*, 179, 180, 185, 189, 190, 192*, 193, 196, 198, 199, 206, 208, 209*, 211*, 212*, 213, 216, 219-222, 224, 225, 227*, 229, 232*, 233*, 235, 238-240, 242*, 245*, 250*, 252, 255, 259, 260, 263
  Col. 7, 8, 20*, 28, 45, 126, 165
  George 164, 169*, 170*, 199, 200, 225, 227, 244, 245, 261, 263
  Isreal 20, 24, 71*, 73

*Numbers refer to page in original book. *Name appears on page more than once.*

PLEDGER Joseph 107
POLLEY BRIDGE 48, 86*, 129, 138, 194
PONDER John 172
POPE Ann 234
　Richard 234
POSTON Anthony 41
　Elisabeth 97
　James 21, 33, 88, 97, 98, 110, 111, 113*, 201
　Robert 31, 37, 97
　Sarah 31, 141
　William 141
POTTS Ephrain 190
POWEL Benjamin 46, 66, 89, 142, 171, 175, 183, 191*, 201, 244, 246, 248, 262
　Nathan 252
　Richard 68, 69, 174, 198, 199, 217, 246
POWERS James 203, 205
　John 15, 21, 36, 39, 71, 74, 113, 156*, 214, 215
POYTHRESS Thomas 233
PRESBYTERIAN MTG. HOUSE 3, 9
PRICE James 7, 73, 74
PU[C]KITT James 98, 187
　James Jr. 213
　John 251
　Micajah 98
　William 98, 172
QUAKERS 28
QUICK Solomon 135
RACE PATH 8, 16, 23, 29
RANDOLPH Nihemiah 85
RANDOLPH COUNTY 53
RATLIFF Zacherias 233
RAY John 5, 6, 131, 179, 218
　Marran 131
RAYFORD Matthew 15, 22, 45, 256
RAYFORDS FORD 191
RAYS MILL 194
RENFROW George 208
REYNOLDS Christopher 25, 87
　Richard 87
ROAN COUNTY 190
ROBERTS William 36, 138
ROBE[RT]SON Charles 42, 55, 70, 74, 76, 89*, 124, 132, 134, 136-138, 142,

ROBERTSON Charles cont. 154*, 171, 220, 224*, 244, 246, 248, 250, 257, 260
　Charles Jr. 39, 40
　John 83, 129, 175, 187, 191
　Luke 83*, 85, 129, 175, 178*, 181, 189, 221, 234, 258
　Luke Jr. 83
　Obedience 178
　Sifias 251
　Thomas 154
ROBINSON Tod 265
ROCHEL[S] James 182, 190*
ROCK[E]Y FORD 13, 152, 179
ROCK[E]Y FORK 12, 13*, 162, 190, 191, 243-245
ROCK[E]Y FORK BRIDGE 9*, 12, 13
ROCKINGHAM 166, 173, 206*, 209
ROE John 3, 83
　Rachel 110
　Susanna 83, 110
ROGERS James 120
ROLLINS Mark 10*, 11*
ROSE Samuel 6
RYE Absolum 203, 205
　Arther 154
　Dun 116, 120, 149, 154, 156, 158*, 159*-161*, 203, 205, 225, 227
　John 31
　Joseph 32, 36, 39, 56, 57*, 58, 60*, 63*, 65-67, 80, 123, 124, 169*
　Solomon 47, 53-57*, 58-60, 63*, 65, 66*, 67-69, 80, 91-93, 95, 132, 170, 203, 205, 252
SALISBURY SUPERIOR COURT 5, 23, 32, 46, 55, 80, 91, 102, 127, 148, 176, 211, 224, 235, 258
SANDERS James 106
　Nathaniel 178, 230
SATERFIELD George 71, 77, 102, 234, 243, 256
SAVAGE John 18
　Robert 18
SCOTCHMEN 28

SCOTT Thomas Gwillium? 219
SEAGO William 140, 188
SEALS William 108
SEAMONS William 55, 87
SELLERS Sampson 155*, 199, 200
SHAW Daniel 228
　Murdock 240
SHEPHERD Aquila 25
　Bird 119, 139
　Jacob 119
SHEW HEEL 13, 86, 152, 179, 194
SIM[P]KINS Joseph 34, 110, 111, 141, 150, 162, 176, 177, 250, 262
SKIPPER Barnaby 36, 39, 69, 70*, 75, 80, 137, 138, 203, 205, 248, 251, 253, 255
　Benjamin 149, 154, 156, 158*, 159*-161*, 203, 205
SLAUGHTER Elisabeth 55
　George 99
　Owen 7, 10, 41, 69, 70, 136, 142, 230, 231, 233, 236*, 244
　Owen Jr. 106*, 135
　Owen Sr. 108, 131, 135, 160, 192, 195, 225, 228
　Walter 167, 214, 216
SLAVES
　York 142, 147
SLAWSON Ezedick? 56
　John 53, 56
SLAY Thomas 210, 213-215, 217*, 219, 221
SMILEY James 6, 108, 179, 218, 236
SMITH 243
　Allen 157
　Archabald 60, 255
　Benjamin 5*
　Daniel 7, 8, 10, 28, 33, 47, 51, 84, 98, 102, 106, 127, 130, 139, 163, 166, 174, 210, 214*, 215, 217*, 219, 221, 248, 250
　Edward 31, 122, 188
　Edward Jr. 20
　James 154*, 171, 175, 181, 182, 192, 193*, 217, 225, 230, 231*, 235, 246, 258*

*Numbers refer to page in original book. *Name appears on page more than once.*

SMITH cont.
  John 47, 53-55, 66, 67, 98, 100, 133, 139, 156, 168, 175, 178, 217, 231
  John (Hogfoot) 235
  Moses 231
  Neal/Neil 157, 220
  Thomas 180
  William 6, 73, 74, 88, 104, 116, 169, 182, 187*, 190, 234, 240, 252
  Zacherias 78*, 140
SMITHHEART Derby 142
SNEED Daniel 7, 32, 53-57*, 58, 65, 66*, 67, 81, 83, 84, 86, 102, 106, 150, 181, 183, 203, 206, 231, 236, 261
  David 21, 80, 228, 231, 233, 236*, 255
  David Jr. 7, 29, 33, 84, 98, 102, 106, 123, 134*, 135*, 136, 149, 150, 174, 178, 206, 225, 261
  David Sr. 15, 29, 33, 47, 73, 81, 84*, 85, 102, 116, 127, 130, 147, 150, 175, 192, 206, 210, 234
  Davis 84
  Hendley 7, 10, 20, 29, 33, 47, 51, 73*, 80, 84, 102, 106, 127, 149, 152, 153, 171, 192, 195, 218*, 237, 243
  Isreal 20, 28, 33, 38, 45, 47, 74, 102, 106, 129, 130, 149, 150, 153, 181, 234, 241, 244
  Isreal Jr. 8, 29, 127, 171, 175, 180, 206, 225
  John 36, 39, 53-57*, 58, 65, 66*, 80, 84, 86, 102, 106, 121, 124, 127, 128, 130, 147, 149, 153, 175, 178, 190, 210, 212, 234, 241, 244, 261, 262
  Philip 150, 228, 230, 231, 236*
  Solomon 15, 21, 73, 74, 80, 84, 171-173, 218, 237
  Temperance 150
  Widow 206, 263
SNEED BRIDGE 235, 237
SOLOMON['S] CREEK 20, 28*, 45, 79, 86, 150, 165, 203, 205, 206*, 253

SOUTHERLAND Daniel 61
SPEED Capt. 203, 235
  John 20, 24, 26*, 28-32, 35, 38, 39, 43-45*, 48*, 49*, 56, 59, 71, 78, 80-82*, 94, 95, 97, 99, 103*, 104*, 107, 111, 114, 115, 118, 125*, 128-130, 133, 137, 138, 146, 147, 152, 156, 157*, 172, 179, 187, 189, 194, 205, 221, 223, 233, 239, 240, 263
  Robert 59, 75*, 189
  William 15, 36, 37*, 41
SPEND John 105
SPIVA Moses 256
SPRAWLS Solomon 86, 89, 98, 175, 191, 214
SPURLING John 242*
SQUARES? Andrew 217
STANDBACK
  Thomas 130, 248
STEELY/STEALY Isaiah 36, 51, 65*, 211, 222*
  John 18, 202, 222
  Lovick 199, 211, 221
STEPHENS 260
  Hardy 171, 192, 256
  Thomas 132, 142*, 146
STOE? Abraham 217
STOKES John 240, 241
STONE Benjamin 198
  Nicholas 21, 22, 27, 29, 31, 33, 47, 52-57*, 58-60*, 63*, 65, 66*-69, 88, 96, 100, 118, 127, 130, 149, 153, 171, 192, 195, 198, 219-222, 246-248*, 258
  Nicholas Sr. 35, 47
  Rebeckah 198
  Uriah 198
  Willliam 198
STRICKL[A]IN
  Burrell/Burwell 44, 45, 96*, 126, 191, 222, 247
  Joseph 99, 191
  Lott 47, 53-57*, 58-60, 63*, 65, 66*, 67-69, 89, 95, 96*, 102, 107, 111-114, 126, 139, 145-147, 149, 163, 175, 178, 214, 225, 228, 230, 231, 233
SUMMERAL Thomas 15, 22, 29, 36, 95, 127, 137, 149, 153, 191

SUMMERALS MILL 179, 194
SUMMERLAND Thomas 93
SWAY? John 72
TARBUTTON Joseph 163, 171-174, 192, 195, 196, 200-202*, 205, 206, 209, 217, 244
TATUM William 251
TAYLOR Elizabeth 223
TERRY James 78*, 138
  Mat[t]hew 76, 90, 248, 252, 258
  William 7, 10, 36, 39, 59, 60, 63*, 67, 93, 95, 116, 120, 137, 138, 150, 175, 178, 210, 214, 217*, 219, 221, 234, 248, 256, 261
TERRY'S PATH 8*
THOMAS Benjamin 77*, 127, 128*
  Daniel 7, 10, 12, 28, 31, 33, 47, 51, 80, 84, 102, 106, 122*-124, 127, 130, 163, 166, 169, 210, 212, 243, 248, 251, 253, 255
  John 15, 22, 32, 173, 233, 259
  Philemon 194
  Robert 78, 133, 233, 245
  Simon 12, 36, 39, 70, 76, 93, 102, 106, 127, 134*, 135*-137, 166, 169, 210, 212, 243, 248, 251, 253
  Simon Jr. 31
  Simon Sr. 31
  Stephen 241, 243
  Tristam 132, 142, 146
  William 111, 123, 139, 142-145†*, 147, 190, 244, 251*-253, 255, 258
  William (Green Pond) 161
  William Jr. 59, 71, 73, 137, 138, 210, 214, 215, 217*, 219, 221, 243, 244, 262
  William Sr. 137, 210, 212, 220, 243*, 248
THOM[P]SON John 208
  Richard 34
THORNTON John 67, 70
TOUCHSTONE Stephen 15, 22, 260

†Name appears on p. 145 as "same" (carried over from p. 144)

TRAVERS[E] Patrick 61, 261*
TUCKER John 26
　Matthew 11
TURNAGE John 47, 53-57*, 58-60, 63*, 65, 66*, 67-69, 80, 137, 138, 191, 195, 251, 253
TURNER John 15, 120
　Moses 6, 179, 231
　Rodah 223
　Thomas 6, 130, 142, 170, 179, 218, 252, 258
UNDER MINE BRANCH 5
UNDER MINE ROAD 6
US[S]HER James 185
　Samuel 69, 70*, 99, 140, 217, 244, 246, 251, 253
　Thomas 99
USSERY John 110
　Peter 163, 168, 175, 178, 214, 217, 244, 246, 247, 262
　Sarah 214
　William 198, 214, 257*
VAUGHN Abner 234
　Benjamin 236, 247, 251, 254
VINEN Joshua 221
WADE 114
　Holden 43
　Thomas 47, 62, 221
WALKER Thomas 248, 256
WALL Capt. 235
　John 3-5, 9, 10, 22*, 23*-25, 29, 30, 33, 34, 43, 46, 80, 82, 84*, 85, 94, 96*, 97, 101, 103, 111, 114, 117, 122, 137*, 146, 149, 156, 158*, 159*-161*, 165, 172, 175, 191, 192, 195, 216, 218, 225, 228, 230, 233*, 235, 236*, 242*, 247, 257, 258
　William 30, 31, 43, 44, 48, 63, 64, 81, 89, 91-94, 159, 168, 202, 205, 207*, 209, 217, 222, 224, 241*, 244, 247*, 260, 263
WALSH John 60
　William 58, 62, 72, 78

WALTER[S] George 4, 22, 28, 36, 52, 199
　John 119, 146, 198, 199, 258, 259
WATKINS Isreal 33*, 62
　John 7, 33, 83*, 187, 190, 209, 210
　John (Virginia) 228
　Thomas 29, 36, 127, 164
　William 15, 21, 33, 39, 64, 70, 72, 74, 76, 89, 91, 92, 102, 107-109*, 113, 123, 127, 134*-136, 164, 168, 183, 187, 190, 199, 202, 207, 210, 214, 215, 217*, 219, 241, 244
　William Jr. 36, 85, 127, 132, 199, 202, 205, 225, 262
　William Sr. 36, 80, 83, 84, 129, 164, 234
WATSON Alexander 6, 37, 39, 53, 157, 179, 186, 210, 214, 215*, 217*-219, 221, 261
　Alexander Jr. 6
　James 65, 86, 156, 168, 256
　John 40, 58, 76, 117, 168, 215
　Matthew 76
WEBB George 11, 14, 85, 168, 170
　George Sr. 6, 8
　John 64, 155
　John Jr. 262
　Margeratt 14
　Robert 3-5, 9, 10, 12, 15-17, 25, 26*, 29, 32*-35, 38, 49*, 50, 65, 72, 74*, 76*, 77*, 82, 84, 85, 90, 95, 96, 104, 114*, 119*, 122-124*, 126, 129, 130*, 133, 134*, 141*, 143, 145, 151, 153, 162, 165-167, 170, 173, 174, 177*, 182, 185, 209*, 213, 239
　William 6, 7, 33, 36, 39, 44, 70, 73, 77*, 89, 100, 113, 116, 120, 124, 134, 135*-137, 142, 145, 163, 164, 166, 183, 186, 191, 195, 225, 227, 248
WELCH Judah 223
WEST? John 206

WHITE John 190
　Joseph 243, 256, 262
WILLIAM[S] Abner 47, 55, 62
　Edward 7, 10, 11, 18*, 19, 21, 23*-25*, 26, 31, 36, 40, 41*, 46, 50, 53, 55, 56, 87, 93, 98, 112-115, 122*, 125, 132, 139, 141, 144*, 145†*, 149, 150, 157, 163, 164, 167, 174, 197, 200, 213, 216, 222, 224*, 225, 229, 232*, 233, 235, 245-248*, 249, 257, 258, 260
　Luke 180
　Mary Ann 34, 54
　Nathaniel 15, 22, 86, 127, 132, 134*, 135*-137
　Sampson 44, 117, 122, 169
　Samuel 68
　Shadrack 70
　Susanna 9*
　Thomas Plum[mb]er 34, 51, 159, 183, 184
　William 139
　Winney 9
WILLIAMSON
　Isaac 102, 152, 171
　Shadrack/Shadrick 69, 70, 89
　Sterling 93*, 95, 137, 138, 210, 214, 215, 217*, 219, 221
WILLIS Comfort 229, 237*, 245
WILSON George 218
　James 108
　James P. 201
　John 10*, 11*, 25, 56
　Mesaniah 218
　Robert 20, 47, 53-57*, 58-60, 63*, 65, 66*, 67-69, 80, 90, 109, 114, 128, 172-174, 180, 181, 192, 195, 196, 200-202*, 205*, 206, 209, 220, 230, 232, 241, 244, 255
WISE Jonathon 218
　Maj. 218
　Samuel 147
WOODLE Matthew 171
　William 15, 80, 84, 137, 138, 171, 192, 195, 196, 200-202*, 205, 206, 209, 262

*Numbers refer to page in original book. *Name appears on page more than once.*

WOODS William 22
Y[E]ATES Abraham 231
  Isaac 7, 47, 51, 91, 92, 102,
    107, 149, 154, 156, 158,
    159*-161*, 163, 167,
    175, 178, 201, 202*,
    205*, 206, 209, 225,
    227, 262
  James 8, 28, 102, 107,
    108*, 109*, 111-113,
    225, 227, 230

†*Name appears on p. 145 as "same" (carried over from p. 144)*

ABOUT THE AUTHOR

Lee G. Barrow is a music professor and long-time genealogist specializing in the eastern Carolinas and southern Georgia. He has written over a dozen articles and three books on both professional and genealogical subjects, including articles in *Pioneers of Wiregrass Georgia* and the book, *Early Court Records of Pulaski County, Georgia, 1809-1825*.

www.ingramcontent.com/pod-product-compliance
Lightning Source LLC
Chambersburg PA
CBHW071425160426
43195CB00013B/1809